WILLIAM SHAKESPEARE

Literary Lives
General Editor: Richard Dutton, Senior Lecturer in English,
University of Lancaster

This series offers stimulating accounts of the literary careers of the most widely read British and Irish authors. Volumes follow the outline of writers' working lives, not in the spirit of traditional biography, but aiming to trace the professional, publishing and social contexts which shaped their writing. The role and status of 'the author' as the creator of literary texts is a vexed issue in current critical theory, where a variety of social, linguistic and psychological approaches have challenged the old concentration on writers as specially-gifted individuals. Yet reports of 'the death of the author' in literary studies are (as Mark Twain said of a premature obituary) an exaggeration. This series aims to demonstrate how an understanding of writers' careers can promote, for students and general readers alike, a more informed historical reading of their works.

William Shakespeare

A Literary Life

Richard Dutton

Senior Lecturer in English
University of Lancaster

St. Martin's Press   New York

First published in the United States of America in 1989

Printed in Hong Kong

ISBN 0–312–03091–6

Library of Congress Cataloging-in-Publication Data
Dutton, Richard, 1948–
William Shakespeare: a literary life.
(Literary lives)
Includes index.
1. Shakespeare, William, 1564–1616.
2. Dramatists, English—Early modern, 1500–1700—
Biography. I. Title. II. Series: Literary lives
(New York, N.Y.)
PR2894.D88 1989   822.3'3 [B]   88–35561
ISBN 0–312–03091–6

For My Father
and to
the Memory of My Mother

Contents

Preface, with Suggestions for Further Reading

> Life is as tedious as a twice-told tale,
> Vexing the dull ear of a drowsy man.
> (*King John*, III.iv.108–9)

This is an account of Shakespeare's career as a dramatist and poet. Although it follows the contours of his life, it does not aim to be a biography in the conventional sense. There is nothing here about Shakespeare's antecedents and very little about his immediate family; nor do I have much to say, for instance, about his education, his property transactions and other legal dealings, or his relations with the Mountjoy family, with whom we know he lodged in Cripplegate in 1604. Anyone looking for a life of Shakespeare which incorporates such issues should go to S. Schoenbaum's masterly *William Shakespeare: A Documentary Life* (Oxford, 1975) or the abridged version, *William Shakespeare: A Compact Documentary Life* (Oxford, 1977, revised 1987). This must be regarded as our standard life of Shakespeare, though the popular biographies by J. Q. Adams (London and Cambridge, Massachusetts, 1923) and A. L. Rowse (London, 1963) are also worth consulting. Professor Schoenbaum's *Shakespeare's Lives* (Oxford, 1970) is a fascinating (and, to any biographer, daunting) account of the transmission of myths and facts about Shakespeare through the ages. Indispensable for scholars is Sir E. K. Chambers' two-volume *William Shakespeare: A Study of Facts and Problems* (Oxford, 1930), a synthesis of all the materials relating to Shakespeare's life and career. Also useful is G. E. Bentley's *Shakespeare: A Biographical Handbook* (New Haven, 1961). Among more specialised studies are Mark Eccles, *Shakespeare in Warwickshire* (Madison, Wisconsin, 1961) and E. A. J. Honigmann, *Shakespeare: The 'Lost Years'* (Manchester, 1985). The latter questions the orthodox view, represented by Chambers and Schoenbaum, of when and how Shakespeare's career began.

Sir E. K. Chambers' four-volume *The Elizabethan Stage* (Oxford, 1923) is the starting-point for all modern study of Elizabethan (and early Jacobean) theatres and theatrical practices. Andrew Gurr's

The Shakespearean Stage 1574–1642 (Cambridge, 1970; revised 1980) is a readable summation of Chambers' material and of scholarship relating to later Jacobean and Caroline theatre. R. A. Foakes and R. T. Rickert edited *Henslowe's Diary* (Cambridge, 1961), the most informative documents about the Elizabethan commercial theatre to have survived. J. L. Barroll, A. Leggatt, R. Hosley and A. Kernan, *The Revels History of Drama in English, III: 1576–1613* (London, 1975) is an authoritatively informed introduction to the theatrical period, G. E. Bentley's *The Profession of Dramatist in Shakespeare's Time, 1590–1642* (Princeton, 1971) and M. C. Bradbrook's *The Rise of the Common Player* (London, 1962) examine two major facets of the Elizabethan theatrical profession. John Orrell's *The Quest for Shakespeare's Globe* (Cambridge, 1983) is the most authoritative study of the theatre with which Shakespeare was most associated. Three volumes in Routledge and Kegan Paul's Theatre Production Studies series are illuminating about the staging of Shakespeare's plays at different phases in his career: Michael Hattaway's *Elizabethan Popular Theatre* (London, 1982); Peter Thomson's *Shakespeare's Theatre* (London, 1983) and Keith Sturgess's *Jacobean Private Theatre* (London, 1987).

Accounts of Shakespeare's life-in-his-time include E. I. Fripp's *Shakespeare: Man and Artist*, 2 vols (Oxford, 1938, 1964), which is particularly strong on local Stratford detail; M. M. Reese, *Shakespeare: His World and His Work* (London, 1953; revised 1980); and M. C. Bradbrook, *Shakespeare: the Poet in His World* (London, 1978). T. W. Baldwin exhaustively described the education he is likely to have received in *William Shakespeare's 'Small Latine & Lesse Greeke'*, 2 vols (Urbana, Illinois, 1944). The sources and analogues of Shakespeare's works have been collected in Geoffrey Bullough's *Narrative and Dramatic Sources of Shakespeare*, 8 vols (London, 1957–75), and further analysed in Kenneth Muir's *Shakespeare's Sources* (revised, London, 1977).

Many other works relating to Shakespeare's life and times are cited in my text and in the notes at the end of this book, but it is impossible to do justice to the sheer volume of material. Anyone wanting to pursue a particular topic relating to Shakespeare might usefully start with Stanley Wells (ed.) *Shakespeare: Select Bibliographical Guides* (Oxford, 1973, currently being revised), coming up to date with the annual bibliographies included in *Shakespeare Survey* (Cambridge) and *Shakespeare Quarterly* (Washington, DC). Other helpful starting-points would be Stanley Wells (ed.) *The Cambridge Companion to Shakespeare Studies* (Cambridge, 1986) or John F. Andrews (ed.) *William Shakespeare: His World, His Work, His Influence*, 3 vols (New York, 1985), both of which contain up-to-date bibliographical details on a topical basis.

I wish to record my own debt to all the works I have mentioned, particularly those by Chambers and Schoenbaum. Anyone writing about Shakespeare, of all subjects, has to be intensely aware of standing on so many other people's shoulders, some whose sturdiness it would be churlish not to acknowledge. My own small qualification for adding myself to the human pyramid, not to mention another volume to the immense pile of books, is that of having spent most of my academic career thinking and writing about Ben Jonson, the most challenging of Shakespeare's contemporary rivals but also the one who has suffered most from standing in his shadow. The history of Jonson criticism is littered with complaints (often backed by spurious accusations of envy and ingratitude) to the effect that he neither wrote like Shakespeare nor, which is worse, even tried to; it is still common enough, particularly in the classroom, to have to explain that this was not a crime or self-evidently a disqualification from genius. Nevertheless, this *can* open up fruitful ways of focusing on what is significant in Jonson's own achievement. So in this book I have tried to return the compliment. The silent question to which I keep returning is: why did Shakespeare not write, or try to write, like Jonson? Posed like this, it is a nonsense. Shakespeare led and Jonson followed, with the example of the older man to emulate or react against. But they were both professional dramatists, operating broadly within the same market-place. Why did Shakespeare work in modes and styles so different from those adopted by his younger rival? In asking the question I hope to isolate some of the qualities unique to his achievement and to offer new perspectives on a tale somewhat more than twice-told.

Quotations from Shakespeare's works refer to *William Shakespeare: The Complete Works*, general editor Alfred Harbage (revised, Baltimore, 1969). As with most editions of Shakespeare, the text has been modernised to meet the needs of students and general readers. I have followed suit with all other quotations, modernising even where my sources (notably Chambers in *The Elizabethan Stage* and *William Shakespeare: A Study of Facts and Problems* – respectively *ES* and *WS* in the notes) have preserved the original. So too, I have given all dates in New Style, treating the year as starting on 1 January, though for the Elizabethans (at least in Court and legal circles) it began on 25 March. We lose the poignancy of Elizabeth dying on New Year's Eve 1602, as they would see it. Quotations from Jonson's poems, his *Conversations with William Drummond* and his common-place book, *Timber, or Discoveries*, all refer to the versions in George Parfitt (ed.) *Ben Jonson: The Complete Poems* (Harmondsworth, 1975). To keep the notes within some kind of bounds I have not cited chapter-and-verse on all quotations from Shakespeare's contemporaries. Most of these come from prefaces, epistles and such-like items, brief and easily found in any modern edition, should the reader wish to follow them up.

I wish to thank Julia Steward for her initial enthusiasm in taking the Macmillan Literary Lives series on board, and Frances Arnold for steering the series, and this volume within it, to publication. Parts of what I say about *King Lear* in Chapter 8 appeared, in very different form, in *Literature and History* and I am grateful to the editors for permission to use the material again. Thanks finally to Maura, Katie and Claire, who must often have felt that they had lost me to a word-processor over the last few months.

Richard Dutton
1988

1
Myths, Legends and Anonymity

We do not know when William Shakespeare was born. We know that he was christened on 26 April 1564, in Holy Trinity Church, Stratford-upon-Avon in Warwickshire; there is an entry in the parish register to that effect. Given that three days was not an unusual interval, in a time of high infant mortality, between birth and christening; that 23 April 1616 was to be the day on which Shakespeare died; and that 23 April is dedicated to St George, patron saint of England, it has become usual to commemorate Shakespeare's birthday (as the national poet) on that day too. This mixture of fact, guesswork, legend and sentiment is all too typical of our knowledge of Shakespeare's life and career.

The facts are there: quite sufficient to demonstrate that the man lived, married, had children, prospered and, beyond all reasonable doubt, wrote the plays and poems for which he is famous. An industry of scholars has been busy establishing these facts for over two hundred years and sifting their implications with a scrupulosity that was once reserved for Holy Writ. As a result we know far more about Shakespeare than we do about most Elizabethans of his status. But what we know falls a long way short of what we would like to know and, only too often, the facts that have come down to us are not quite the ones we would elect to have if we had any choice in the matter. Time and again, so to speak, we have the date of the christening rather than that of the birth. We look for the story behind Shakespeare's marriage and discover only details of Hathaway family land-holdings; we look for the Dark Lady and the Rival Poet of the sonnets and find only Shakespeare involved in a succession of rather tedious legal disputes.

Some of Shakespeare's literary contemporaries contrived to leave more colourful accounts of themselves. Christopher Marlowe, Ben Jonson and John Donne, for example, all acquired a fame or notoriety in their lifetimes that ensured quite extensive documen-

tation of their activities. One detail of Donne's life ironically
underlines how colourless and indirect is so much of what we
know about Shakespeare. Donne's daughter married Edward
Alleyn, the great tragic actor who had been a leading figure in the
Lord Admiral's Men, principal rivals in the 1590s to Shakespeare's
own acting company, the Lord Chamberlain's Men. Alleyn had
previously been married to the step-daughter of Philip Henslowe,
the business manager of the Admiral's Men; when he married
Constance Donne, in his rich and pious old age, Alleyn had already
founded the College of God's Gift at Dulwich, and it was to that
college that he bequeathed his papers and those of his first father-
in-law. The Henslowe Papers are by far the most informative
documents about the Elizabethan theatre to have survived, and
much of our understanding of Shakespeare's professional activity
is based on them, even though they relate to other companies,
dramatists and theatres, never directly to Shakespeare himself.[1] It
is typical of our luck in this respect that when Henslowe and
Alleyn attempted to emulate the success of Shakespeare's company
with the Globe by building a rival, the Fortune, they insisted in
the contract (which survives at Dulwich) that it should resemble
the Globe in most particulars, and they provided a drawing of it
to guide their builders. Frustratingly, the drawing (of incalculable
potential value for our understanding of Shakespeare's theatrical
practices) has not survived. And the Globe itself burned down in
1613, very possibly destroying at source any equivalent that
Shakespeare's company had to Henslowe's papers. At every turn,
it is as if we see through a glass, darkly. Feeling the lack of direct
access to Shakespeare the man, later ages have filled in the picture
with guesswork, legend and sentiment. If we are to write a
reasonably detailed narrative of his career, there is no avoiding a
considerable amount of guesswork – inferring, for example, what
he is likely to have done from what we know that other, better-
documented, contemporaries did. We can only aim to make the
guesswork as judicious and well-informed as possible. But we
must be far more circumspect about the legend and the sentiment.

Most of the sentiment relates to Shakespeare's modern status as
the greatest writer in the English language, a status which was
only established in the second half of the eighteenth century. Dr
Johnson's edition of the *Plays*, first published in 1765, with its
inimitable Preface and notes, or David Garrick's shambolic Stratford
Jubilee of 1769 (notable for its neglect of Shakespeare's own

writings) may serve as appropriate markers. Since then, Shakespeare has been a national monument and it has become increasingly difficult to assess either the man or his writings with any objectivity; with only minor exceptions, generations of criticism have been dedicated to celebrating a genius which no one seriously questions. And this has rubbed off in assessments of the man and his career, particularly in the Victorian propensity to assume that poetic genius of this order must be matched by a high nobility of character; so popular accounts of such matters as Shakespeare's marriage or relations with Ben Jonson are bedevilled by the need always to show Shakespeare in the best possible light. More recently, as in Anthony Burgess's novel, *Nothing Like the Sun* (London, 1964), and even more so in Edward Bond's play, *Bingo* (London, 1974), it has become fashionable to insist on a Shakespeare as human and fallible as the rest of us. But these are reactions against the stereotype rather than attempts at a true objectivity, which would tell us that we know nothing for certain about any of these matters. We must, therefore, be on our guard against sentiment, particularly when it takes the form of berating Shakespeare's contemporaries for failing to appreciate what they could not know – that they had a national monument in their midst.

The Shakespeare legends pose a slightly different problem. Most of them were first recorded in the years between his death and the time he became a national monument; they are thus too late to be really trustworthy, but too early to be dismissed out of hand – they may have some basis in fact, though this is no longer verifiable. Most of them relate to the period of Shakespeare's adolescence and early manhood, and sceptics dismiss virtually all of them as attempts to put flesh on a skeleton that is embarrassingly bare. Between birth and the age of twenty-eight (by which time more than half his life was over) we *know* virtually nothing about Shakespeare beyond the fact that he was christened, was married and had three children who were christened. We assume that, as the son of a prominent citizen, he would have been educated at the Free Grammar School in Stratford. But his early employments, the circumstances of his marriage, the reason and timing of his leaving Stratford, and his first connections with the acting profession are all matters about which we know nothing. And in the absence of facts, legend flourishes.

The circumstances of Shakespeare's marriage are certainly intriguing. We do not know the date of the ceremony itself, but we

do know that a special church licence had to be obtained, late in
1582, to permit the groom to marry – at eighteen he was still a
minor; the bride, Anne Hathaway was twenty-six, if the dates on
her gravestone are correct. Their first child, Susanna, was certainly
christened within six months of the granting of the licence (26 May
1583). Explanations have ranged from a perfectly respectable hand-
fast marriage well before the church ceremony, to seduction of the
young man by (in Elizabethan terms) the ageing spinster. That
Anne Shakespeare never seems to have joined him in London,
where he spent most of his working life, and that he notoriously
bequeathed her his 'second-best bed'[2] has only fuelled the argument. But in reality we know nothing about their domestic
arrangements or their compatibility. Less than two years after
Susanna, twins, Hamnet and Judith, were also christened (2 February 1585), completing – so far as we know – William Shakespeare's
family. I should add, lest the name Hamnet evokes that of his
father's most famous creation, that the twins were almost certainly
named after Stratford neighbours, Hamnet and Judith Sadler. This
is not to say that Shakespeare might not have had his son (then
four or five years dead) in mind when he created his version of
Hamlet the Dane, but it makes it far less likely that he named his
son after the legendary character – with the implication that the
Prince of Denmark haunted him throughout his life. There are
enough myths and legends as it is, without allowing others to
germinate for lack of all the evidence.

Two of the most popular legends are among the least trustworthy:
that Shakespeare had to leave Stratford after being caught poaching
deer (Sir Thomas Lucy of Charlecote, a local magistrate and
landowner is usually cast as the villain of the piece) and that his
first connection with the London theatre was as someone employed
to hold the horses of wealthy playgoers. Sir Thomas Lucy did not
have a deer park at the time in question, while the horse-holding
is not mentioned by the earliest biographers of Shakespeare,
Nicholas Rowe (1709) and Alexander Pope (1725), but is later
recounted on their supposed authority. The story of how such
suppositions slowly acreted to the popular 'life' of Shakespeare is
excellently told in S. Schoenbaum's *Shakespeare's Lives*. There is no
harm in such popular mythology, or in the attempts to 'confirm'
such information about the man and his personality by reference
to his works – such as the attempts to track Sir Thomas Lucy in
the word-play on 'luces' and 'louses' during the prattle between

Shallow, Slender and Evans at the beginning of 2 *Henry IV* (surely a very belated and obscure in-joke), or to relate *some* of the poet's complex responses to female sexuality (such as the tale of the virginal boy and the rapacious goddess in *Venus and Adonis*)³ to the circumstances of his marriage. It will do no harm if we see evocations of a Warwickshire boyhood, particularly in the comedies, wherever Shakespeare writes about wild flowers and the countryside, or about pedantic schoolmasters, like Holofernes in *Love's Labour's Lost*. The Forest of Arden in *As You Like It* may notionally be the Ardennes in Belgium/France, not the Warwickshire Arden evoked in Shakespeare's mother's name (Mary Arden), but some of us will doubtless persist in knowing better. It must be stressed, however, that such fancies do less than justice both to Shakespeare's imagination and to his reading (which was prodigious, if not necessarily systematic). There is, moreover, nothing that we know, suspect or have made up about Shakespeare's early years that really helps us to explain the achievement of the plays and the poems. There is no biographical point of entry to his works comparable to that which we have with Marlowe, Jonson or Donne. He remains in this respect anonymous, for all the efforts of the mythographers. Oddly enough, this remains true even if we accept the most persistent piece of speculation about his early years: the possibility that he was brought up a Roman Catholic.⁴

To understand the implications of such a suggestion, it will be necessary to sketch in some background. The English Reformation was barely thirty-five years old when Shakespeare was born, and indeed had been reversed during the five-year reign of Queen Mary. Under Elizabeth, who came to the throne in 1558, England was once more formally a Protestant country;⁵ conformity to the Church of England, of which the Queen was Supreme Governor, was required by law. Religious and political allegiances were generally deemed to be indivisible, and it was a punishable offence to miss church on Sunday without good reason. The strictness of these measures should perhaps be seen as an indication of the insecurity of the regime which, not without cause, felt itself to be threatened both from without and within. A large proportion of the population (some would say a third of them, and more in remote rural areas) remained Roman Catholic at heart even if not in practice, and the authorities in London constantly feared an uprising in favour of one of the Roman Catholic claimants to the

English throne, notably Mary, Queen of Scots (who, from 1568 to 1587, was a prisoner in England and a focus of possible discontent) and Philip II of Spain.[6] The northern rebellion of 1569 and the Throckmorton Plot of 1583 demonstrated that these fears were not ungrounded, and tension increased after 1570 when a Papal Bull was published, excommunicating Elizabeth and calling upon English Catholics to regard Mary, Queen of Scots as their lawful sovereign. The Spanish Armada of 1588 and the Gunpowder Plot of 1605 were the two most traumatic national events of Shakespeare's lifetime and reflected between them (at least in the eyes of the authorities) the Roman Catholic threat from without and within.[7] With hindsight, we tend to assume that the Spanish threat evaporated after 1588, but that was not how contemporaries saw it. A second Armada almost sailed in 1595; Spanish ships actually put to sea against England in 1597, but were dispersed by the wind. Throughout the 1590s (a background to Shakespeare's English history plays) there was a succession of English expeditions against Spain – notably the Cadiz raid of 1596 and the Islands Voyage of 1597 – and of English interventions on behalf of the Dutch Protestants fighting against their Spanish overlords.

In such a context it was no small thing to be Roman Catholic, however covertly. But it is not inherently improbable that John Shakespeare, though an alderman of Stratford and (in 1568–9) holder of its highest office, that of bailiff, should have had Catholic sympathies: many of his countrymen lived such double lives. He may well even have put his mark (not, apparently, being able to write)[8] to a Spiritual Testament affirming his Catholic faith.[9] If so, it means he almost certainly came into contact with one or other of the two Jesuit priests, Robert Persons (or Parsons) and Edmund Campion, who slipped secretly into England in 1580, on a mission to support the faithful – or, as the authorities saw it, to incite rebellion. If John Shakespeare did subscribe to one of the Testaments that they carried to bind their secret flock to the faith, he was taking a considerable risk: Campion was arrested and executed for treason in 1581 and Sir William Catesby, who hid him for a time in his house at Lapworth (only twelve miles from Stratford), was imprisoned in the Fleet. A further piece of evidence which may connect John Shakespeare with Catholicism is that his attendance at church became quite infrequent in the 1580s, as did his attendance at meetings of the town council. But it is just as likely that he stayed at home for fear of being arrested in connection with the debts we know he had run up by this time.

There is no concrete evidence in William Shakespeare's own lifetime to connect him with Catholicism, though there is the terse and unsubstantiated assertion made late in the seventeenth century by a clergyman, Richard Davies, that 'he died a papist'.[10] There is, moreover, a persistent legend, recently given a new lease of life and more substantiation (if something short of proof) by E. A. J. Honigmann's *Shakespeare: The 'Lost Years'*: that as a young man he was the 'William Shakeshafte' employed in Lancashire Catholic circles, specifically by Alexander Hoghton of Lea Hall, near Preston, and later by his brother-in-law, Sir Thomas Hesketh, who were both known Catholics.[11] The Lancashire associations of John Cottom, the schoolmaster at Stratford from 1579 to 1581/2, help to make plausible the otherwise unlikely translation of the young man from the Midlands to the North. And if he was employed there as a family tutor, this would tie in with another tradition recorded by the seventeenth century antiquary, John Aubrey: 'Though as Ben Jonson says of him, that he had but little Latin and less Greek, he understood Latin pretty well; for he had been in his younger years a schoolmaster in the country'.[12] This is one of the best-founded of such anecdotes, since Aubrey had it from William Beeston, an actor himself and son of Christopher Beeston, who had been a member of Shakespeare's company.[13] If, moreover, this 'schoolmaster' in the rural obscurity of Lancashire had also been employed in theatricals (it was not unusual for country gentlemen to keep entertainers in their households) then Shakespeare might have made himself known to the local magnate, the Earl of Derby, who was a friend of Sir Thomas Hesketh, or more particularly to his charismatic son, Ferdinando, Lord Strange, who was patron to one of the leading acting companies of the 1580s. This *could* explain how Shakespeare entered the world of professional theatre. On the other hand, it is equally plausible that he contrived to join one of the troupes that visited Stratford around 1586/7, including such notable ones as the Earl of Leicester's and the Queen's Men.[14]

Fascinating as such possibilities are, they remain a tottering edifice of speculations. Perhaps Shakespeare *was* born Roman Catholic and perhaps secretly he adhered to the old faith. But if he did, nothing of the struggle it presumably entailed registers in a discernible way in the poems and plays that he wrote – another notable contrast with so many of his literary contemporaries. Ben

Jonson's conversion to Roman Catholicism while in prison and his reconversion to the Anglican communion twelve years later were obviously significant moments in his life and career.[15] John Donne's conversion to the Church of England from a family with deep Roman Catholic roots – his own brother died in prison for the faith – was obviously deeply traumatic and there are echoes of it in much of his writing. As John Carey bluntly puts it: 'The first thing to remember about Donne is that he was a Catholic; the second, that he betrayed his Faith'.[16] Even if we could now establish for certain that Shakespeare was born Roman Catholic and adhered, at heart, to that faith, we could hardly make such a statement about him.

There are obvious contexts among his works in which we might look for the pressure of his personal convictions. *King John,* for example, deals with a dispute between the English king and the Pope over the limits of their respective authorities. Bishop John Bale's much earlier play of *King Johan* and the anonymous *Troublesome Reign of King John,* which Shakespeare knew and drew on, were both virulently nationalistic and anti-Catholic. Shakespeare is more muted in his tone. His treatment of King John, for example, is ambivalent; in the first half of the play, though clearly a usurper, he is strong and purposeful, a man the nation can follow, not least in his defiance of Cardinal Pandulph, the Papal legate; but latterly he becomes weak and vacillating, and nationalistic sympathies are focused on the wit and gallantry of the fictitious Bastard of Faulconbridge rather than the unlovable king; and most of the sentiment of the play is channelled towards the tragic figures of Prince Arthur and his mother, Constance. However, it remains an odd subject for a supposed Catholic to have chosen (Cardinal Pandulph is hardly an endearing or an inspiring apologist for Rome) even if the play eschews the zealous Protestant propaganda that others had made of it.[17] There are similar ambiguities, which we shall examine in due course, about Shakespeare's writing of *Macbeth* in the wake of the Gunpowder Plot.

The religious tensions of his day do sometimes surface openly in his plays, but always parenthetically. It is hardly accident that Hamlet attends Luther's own university at Wittenberg, while Laertes goes to (Catholic) Paris, but it is not a major issue in the play. In *Measure for Measure,* the would-be (Catholic) nun, Isabella, confronts the puritan, Angelo, though – and this is one of the perplexities of that 'problem play' – it would be hard to say which of them comes off morally best. I describe Angelo as a 'puritan', but Shakespeare's implications here are difficult to construe precisely. 'Puritanism' is a term that recent scholarship has taught us to use with some caution; in the past it has been very broadly used of zealous Protestant movements in the Elizabethan period, both within and without the Church of England, or of any tendency towards sabbatarianism or stricter sexual and moral codes. In a play set in Vienna, Angelo is not, of course, a member of any English puritan movement or sect. But the Duke does describe him as 'precise' (morally strict, I.iii.50), a term often used of sectarian puritans. Angelo is also a hypocrite, which was a common charge against extreme sectaries. Where exactly should we place Angelo within these theological distinctions? A similar problem arises with Malvolio in *Twelfth Night*, who is broadly depicted as puritan ('sometimes he is a kind of Puritan', says Maria; II.iii.128) though the full doctrinal implications are never explored. Either of these characters might profitably be contrasted with the puritans in *The Alchemist* and *Bartholomew Fair*, where Jonson anatomises the theology and the hypocrisy in detail, making his own views on these subjects abundantly clear.

Wherever we look in Shakespeare's writings, however, he is self-effacing to the point of anonymity on matters of faith. Whatever secret family influences may have been at work, he would have been exposed, like everyone else, to the state machinery of orthodoxy in his weekly visits to the Anglican Church. He would have been thoroughly familiar with large parts of the Bible (probably the Bishops' Bible of 1568 or the Genevan Bible) and the Anglican Book of Common Prayer, which were required to be read in proper sequence. And, whatever the oratorical skills of the preachers in Holy Trinity Church, the congregation would have been subjected to officially-sanctioned sermons, mainly from the 1547 and 1563 Books of Homilies. These homilies spelled out Anglican doctrine in relation to every aspect of faith and the Church year, many of them stressing the authority of the Queen and the necessity for civil obedience. They are echoed frequently in Shakespeare's plays, to the extent that some have concluded that all the suggestions of Roman Catholicism are red herrings and that Shakespeare was a convinced Anglican.[18] In the end, Shakespeare achieves an anonymous orthodoxy, which stands out among the more strident doubts and certainties of contemporaries as diverse as Spenser and Marlowe, Jonson and Donne.

We may take the question of Shakespeare's personal faith as, in the end, typical of all our enquiries into the man and his character; the scanty facts are bedevilled with myth, legend and conjecture, and his written works offer us nothing that a dispassionate reader could latch on to with confidence. His works are so broad and varied as to ensure that any emphasis or intensity we try to abstract from one context can be countered from another. The result is a canon of works which is both unquestionably Elizabethan/Jacobean in its parameters and uniquely timeless in its lack of overt polemical edge.[19] It has to be said that Shakespeare's choice of subject-matter, and its ambivalent relationship to his own life and times, furthers that effect. There is no work that explicitly confronts the life and times of contemporary England, such as we find, say, in the comedies of Jonson and Middleton. Shakespeare's comedies are all (bar one) set abroad, in some never-never place that is called Syracuse, or Illyria, or ancient Athens, but could be anywhere that the sober laws of normality do not operate. The one native English comedy is *The Merry Wives of Windsor*, which is all too Elizabethan in its comic obsessions with cuckoldry and sexual deception, but it is distanced in time by the presence of Falstaff, Nym and Pistol, whom earlier plays have located in the reigns of Henry IV and V. This ambivalence, of course, exists in reverse in the other comedies. *A Midsummer Night's Dream* may nominally exist in the mythological Greece of Theseus and Hippolyta, but the English have always taken a perverse pride in claiming Quince's 'rude mechanicals' as unmistakably their own. Similarly, Shakespeare's histories are remote in time, but their application to contemporary situations is often not hard to find. Jack Cade's rebellion in *2 Henry VI* certainly draws on the riots of the feltmakers' apprentices of June 1592.[20] In *Henry V*, Shakespeare draws attention to the Earl of Essex's expedition to Ireland,[21] while Queen Elizabeth herself drew the parallel between *Richard II* and her own reign.[22] So, when Shakespeare commits a real anachronism, like having the crowds in *Julius Caesar* fling their greasy nightcaps in the air,[23] he only reinforces – perhaps in this instance inadvertently – a dualism his original audiences would be well aware of, though modern ones often miss: these plays are timeless history, but they are also very specifically Elizabethan history.[24] The same is true of the great tragedies: *Hamlet*, *King Lear* and *Macbeth* are all based on remote legends or pseudo-history, but infused with an energy of Renaissance aspiration and political awareness – some of it drawn from very particular sources, such as the accession of King James (*King Lear*) and the Gunpowder Plot (*Macbeth;* see Chapter 8). Conversely, *Othello* is the only play Shakespeare wrote which is explicitly set (give or take a decade) in his own lifetime, against the background of the Turkish threat to the Christian Mediterranean, which was not removed until the sea-battle of Lepanto, in 1571; here – almost as if to redress the balance of coming too close to home – the story is *totally* fictitious and the hero, a coloured man, would have been a rare sight for Elizabethan audiences (as would his fellow alien in sixteenth century Venice, the Jew Shylock).

In these ways, Shakespeare constantly rides the line between a timeless generality and a most particular picture of his own age. This is well exemplified in *The Tempest,* where Prospero's island is at one and the same time a perfect never-never land of theatrical illusion, something different to each person who sees it (cf.II.i.35–55), but also a real place, located in the Mediterranean, somewhere between Tunis and Milan, yet also having qualities associated with the Americas. The play thus evokes both the broad history of the European Old World exemplified by one of its key books, the *Aeneid* ('widow Dido' etc., II.i.73–97) and the immediate sensation of the exploration and exploitation of the New World (Ariel mentions 'the still vexed Bermoothes', and Shakespeare drew on very recent pamphlets describing both the Bermudas and the Bahamas);[25] and yet ultimately it is defined by neither of these issues. It is in this capacity to be both of his age and yet for all time that Shakespeare acquires a distinctive anonymity and the capacity to reward succeeding generations with convincing images of themselves.

This book cannot concern itself with what later generations have made of Shakespeare. It is concerned rather with Shakespeare in his own time – not with the figure of myth and legend, or with the uncertain personality that speaks through his works, but with the one aspect of the man of which we can speak with reasonable factual confidence: his literary career. Even here, however, as I pointed out earlier, our knowledge is often less direct or unequivocal than we would like it to be. This is not surprising. During Shakespeare's lifetime the theatrical profession was on the borderlines of respectability and little formal notice was taken of it, except when the players became a nuisance or were called upon to entertain their betters. So we often find ourselves having to track the development of the theatres through confrontations with the law (where the issues were usually marginal to our own concerns) or through records of performances at Court (which have only survived patchily and then, generally, in the form of accounts of payments for services rendered, with precise dates and titles of works performed often missing). Few people at the time kept journals or wrote gossipy, informational letters, and few of those said much, if anything, about the actors. Among the exceptions relating to Shakespeare were a law student, John Manningham, and the astrologer, Dr Simon Forman, and several foreign visitors who were mainly impressed by the theatrical buildings (the English wrote little about these, except for puritan preachers who denounced them as the works of the devil), all of whom we shall meet in due course. But we could wish there were more of them.

In the absence of more general information, we are obliged to deduce as much as we can from the printed texts of plays themselves. But, even here, the quest is fraught with difficulties. In the 1590s, plays written for commercial theatres were not generally thought to have any literary value. They were, moreover, the property of the acting company which commissioned them, rather than of their authors, and it was not generally in the actors' interests to allow them to be printed. Once a play was in print it lost its novelty value and might be taken over by a rival company. When an acting company was in severe straits, they might sell their play-texts to a printer; sometimes unscrupulous printers might put out an edition without permission, perhaps reconstructed memorially by actors who had left the troupe. The standard of such pirated texts (such as the 1603 text of *Hamlet*) was generally dire, but even when a text was authorised little thought was apparently given to adapting the copy used in production to make it more intelligible for readers. Such plays as were printed were usually in quarto format, relatively cheap, small (c. 5½ ins × 8 ins) and flimsy volumes of between 60 and 100 pages; these have not survived as well as the more substantial and prestigious volumes of the day, which were generally in the larger, folio format. Often, whole editions have disappeared completely and we only know about them from the entry in the register of the Stationers' Company, where a printer was required to lodge details of a work prior to publication in order to establish copyright. This information can be misleading, because entries were sometimes made simply to preclude a rival publication, but it does establish dates by which certain plays must have been in existence (though it does not tell us how long they had been in existence before that).

In this general context it is not surprising that, to the best of our knowledge, Shakespeare never published any of his own plays nor, on the occasions when his company apparently did authorise publication (as with *1 & 2 Henry IV* and the 1604/5 *Hamlet*), did either he or they adapt his work for the press. As a result of this casualness (compounded sometimes by the incompetence of the printers) the texts we have often leave a lot to be desired, notably in respect of stage directions. One or two of Shakespeare's later plays (e.g. *Coriolanus* and *The Tempest*) have come down to us with quite full and instructive stage directions, but most texts are far less helpful. Towards the end of Shakespeare's career the general status of plays had grown markedly, prompted in part by younger dramatists like Ben Jonson, who saw his own plays as works of literature, supervised the printing of many of them and, in the year of Shakespeare's death, published those he wished to preserve in a folio volume of his *Works*. By then an aristocrat like Lord Mountjoy could admit to reading play-books for recreation, while Sir John Harington in 1610 reckoned to have 129 of them in his library. It was in this rather different cultural climate that, in 1623, Shakespeare's fellow-actors, John Heminge[26] and Henry Condell, produced the first folio of his plays, preserving thirty-six of them (including eighteen hitherto unpublished) in respectable versions from their company's own copies.[27]

Despite the inadequacy and often equivocal nature of our information, it remains quite possible to discern the main outlines of Shakespeare's professional career, not least since it was bound up for so long with the progress of the most successful theatrical company of the age (the Lord Chamberlain's/King's Men). One thing that emerges quite clearly is that he was a consummate professional, a man who wrote a steady stream of popular plays, developing styles and subject-matter to meet new conditions, the challenge of new competition or changes in fashion. And he did so with what others saw as ease. 'His mind and hand went together', recorded Heminge and Condell in some awe; 'and what he thought, he uttered with that easiness, that we have scarce received from him a blot in his papers'.[28] What remains perhaps most difficult to speak about with certainty is the social and cultural context within which that professional career developed. Specifically, what was the nature of Shakespeare's audience? To whom were his plays addressed?

Opinions on this, as on virtually everything else, have differed widely. For many years, Alfred Harbage's book, *Shakespeare's Audience* (1941), was regarded as the standard work on the question:

'We should distinguish among three Elizabethan audiences, recognizing that various occasions and various theatres would obscure our distinction: there was the genteel audience of the private theatres; there was the plebeian audience of such theatres as the Red Bull and perhaps the Fortune after the private houses had filched the gentry away; and then there was that audience both genteel and plebeian, or neither, of the nineties and, because of its peculiar prestige, of the Globe in the early decades of the seventeenth century. It was the audience for which nearly all the great Elizabethan plays were written. It was Shakespeare's audience . . . Although the more leisured classes would have been better represented than by their pro rata of the population, it was predominantly a working-class audience because of the great numerical superiority of the working classes in the London area and because theatrical tariffs had been designed largely for them.[29]

This has recently been challenged in Ann Jennalie Cook's *The Privileged Playgoers of Shakespeare's London, 1576–1642* (Princeton, 1981), in which she argues that 'the more leisured classes' (whom she defines more closely as the 'privileged' minority, who had the wealth and social position to behave independently) comprised the overwhelming majority of the audience, not only at the 'private theatres' or hall playhouses (like the Blackfriars, for which Shakespeare partly wrote after 1609) but also at 'public' ones, like the Globe. This writer inclines more to Harbage's view than to Cook's, though he undoubtedly idealised the working classes, and the broad, quasi-democratic cross-section of society which he envisaged them underpinning. Most recently of all, in *Playgoing in Shakespeare's London*, Andrew Gurr has challenged the generalised demographic approach of both Harbage and Cook, insisting that we need to look more closely at the specific evidence of named individuals known to have attended theatres, at the repertoires staged at particular theatres (and so, by deduction the tastes they catered for) and at the contemporary reputations of those theatres. On the Globe, for example, he concludes: 'As always . . . its offerings and playgoers stood midway between the familiar extremes of amphitheatre reputation and hall playhouse snobbery which first began to show themselves in the year the Globe was built'.[30]

But the problem of 'placing' a particular play is even more complex than that. Shakespeare was involved with the theatre, certainly for twenty years and possibly for a good deal longer. It was a period in which, as I have already suggested, the cultural status of (at least some) play-texts changed and there is some reason for supposing that the status of actors and theatres – and consequently the complexion of their audiences – changed too. In Elizabethan legislation, actors are invariably categorised with vagabonds and 'masterless men', in need of close supervision. Yet Edward Alleyn died a rich and pious benefactor of the community, while the Earl of Pembroke – reputedly the richest man in the kingdom – was deeply moved by the death of Richard Burbage, 'my old acquaintance'.[31] Queen Elizabeth enjoyed theatricals of all kinds, but she never set foot in a commercial playhouse. In 1634, King Charles's queen, Henrietta Maria, went to the Blackfriars to see a play by Massinger. It is very difficult to determine the extent to which Shakespeare's working life, and specific texts within it, would have been affected by the kind of social development these facts (apparently) reflect.

A different, if parallel, problem is posed by the question of the relationship between actors and the Court. At least in theory, the professional acting companies around London were only allowed to ply their trade because they were deemed to be rehearsing against a possible demand for their services at Court. Certainly, Shakespeare's own company performed regularly at Court after 1594 and was taken under direct royal patronage in 1603. To what extent were any or all of Shakespeare's plays written with potential Court, rather than public, performance primarily in mind? Were any written as special commissions for the Court (or indeed for individual noblemen, or other potential patrons, such as the Inns of Court) to celebrate particular events? More subtly, were any specially *revised* to suit such occasions and, if so, is it the revised version of the play which has survived in print? The Elizabethan theatre enjoyed a considerable degree of commercial freedom, but most literary men of the day, and virtually all other forms of artistic endeavour, depended directly upon aristocratic patronage;[32] given their undoubted close involvement with the Court, it is difficult to be sure that Shakespeare and his company were, or attempted to

be, as free of its influence as some people suppose. There is
virtually no verifiable evidence on any of these questions. In most
instances, we have to infer what we can from ambiguous evidence
within the plays themselves.

As I have suggested, therefore, the broad outline – the skeleton –
of Shakespeare's professional career is documented clearly enough.
It is when we come to try to put the flesh on the bones that the
real problems arise. I therefore make no apologies for the repeated
doubts and hesitations with which this text is punctuated. To leave
them out would be false to the facts we possess and to our
understanding of them.

2

Beginnings

The earliest documented allusion to Shakespeare's career as a dramatist is a notorious passage in Robert Greene's autobiographical tract, *A Groatsworth of Wit bought with a Million of Repentance* (1592). This sorry tale of his own degradation was no doubt fictionalised, but had a strain of desperate truth about it, since Greene was living in debt and squalour when he wrote it, and death was imminent. The tract ends with an address to three of Greene's 'fellow scholars about this city' – Marlowe and (probably) Thomas Nashe and George Peele:

> Base minded men all three of you, if by my misery you be not warned: for unto none of you (like me) sought those burrs to cleave: those puppets (I mean) that spake from our mouths, those antics garnished in our colours. Is it not strange, that I, to whom they all have been beholding; is it not like that you, to whom they all have been beholding, shall (were ye in that case as I am now) be both at once of them forsaken? Yes, trust them not: for there is an upstart crow, beautified with our feathers, that with his *Tiger's heart wrapped in a player's hide*, supposes he is as well able to bombast out a blank verse as the best of you; and, being an absolute *Johannes fac totum*, is in his own conceit the only Shake-scene in a country.[1]

The passage is such a good example of the pitfalls involved in trying to write about the career of *any* Elizabethan author, that it is worth examining in detail. I have introduced it as being about Shakespeare and by Greene; but neither assertion is beyond dispute. It is written in an indirect and allusive manner, typical of Elizabethan polemical literature: long on righteous indignation but short on hard substance. So the butt of the scorn apparent towards the end of the passage is never named, and we are left to infer his identity from two details: the possible pun in 'Shake-scene' and, more conclusively, the phrase about 'his *Tiger's heart wrapped in a player's hide*'. This is a pointed mis-quotation from Shakespeare's

17

3 Henry VI, in which the Duke of York reproaches his captor, Queen Margaret: 'O tiger's heart wrapped in a woman's hide' (I.iv.137).[2] Taking the pun and the quotation together, it is reasonable to conclude that Shakespeare is the target here; such reasonable conclusions often have to carry the force of fact. But if Shakespeare *is* the target, what is he accused of? York's charge against Queen Margaret is one of unnatural cruelty coupled with deceitful appearance. The tiger was proverbially cruel (lacking the innate nobility of the lion) while women, equally proverbially, were tenderhearted. To be one in the guise of the other was to be doubly vicious. The misquotation substitutes the 'player' (actor) for the woman and this presumably reinforces the charge of deceit or false-seeming. The passage as a whole appears to be an attack upon the actors ('those puppets . . . that spake from our mouths') for their ingratitude in deserting Greene ('to whom they all have been beholding') in his hour of need – an ingratitude of which he warns his fellow authors. In particular, they should beware of one of the actors, Shakespeare, an 'upstart crow', whose pretensions are such that he has taken to writing plays, believing himself to be 'an absolute' jack-of-all-trades.

The force of these charges will be more apparent if we consider the status of actors at this time. To the Elizabethan authorities (and most particularly the Lord Mayor and Common Council of London) players were no better than vagabonds, unruly in themselves and a focus for all manner of disreputable activity by others. Most of them only escaped the harsh legal penalties prescribed for dealing with 'rogues, vagabonds and sturdy beggars' by attaching themselves to the service of an aristocrat, whose livery they would wear.[3] Despite the protection this afforded them, the city authorities made repeated attempts to prevent them from performing in and around London, and it was for this reason that, when the first permanent theatres were erected, they were sited outside the city's jurisdiction.[4] Greene, Marlowe, Nashe and Peele might well consider themselves superior to a profession on the margins of society. Together with a few others, such as Thomas Lodge and John Lyly, they were known as 'the University Wits', erstwhile students of Oxford and Cambridge who tried to make a living in London with their pens. In an age when social distinctions were carefully marked and jealously guarded, and even if (like Greene) they died in a lice-ridden bed, they would not forget their status as gentlemen scholars. Hence, surely, the bitterness in the passage. University wits like Greene had been the chief suppliers of play-scripts for the major acting companies in the 1570s and 80s, who were thus 'garnished in our colours'. Now, not only have they forsaken him, but one of their number has had the temerity to set himself up as a playwright ('beautified with our feathers'), with an education no better than that afforded by a rural grammar school.

So Shakespeare is accused of aping his betters and sharing in the general ingratitude of the players towards the writer. The implied cruelty may thus be intended as a comment on the acting profession as a whole. On the other hand, 'beautified with our feathers' might mean not only that he was imitating his betters but also *borrowing* from them, perhaps in the sense of reworking their plays and so stealing some of their glory. Partly on the strength of this *possible* insinuation, it has often been held that Shakespeare's earliest efforts as a dramatist were reworkings of successes by writers like Greene. It should be said that there would be nothing illicit or discreditable about such a practice. In as much as the Elizabethans recognised any concept of copyright in respect of a play, it resided with the acting company that commissioned and performed it rather than with its author. The demand of the audiences was always for *new* plays, as Shakespeare's company protested when they were asked, in 1601, for a special performance of a play on Richard II: 'holding [it] to be so old and so long out of use that they should have small or no company at it'.[5] Occasionally, however, a company would judge it worth their while reviving an old favourite and advertising it as having new scenes or sensations; so, for example, Ben Jonson was paid by Henslowe for new scenes to Thomas Kyd's phenomenally popular revenge melodrama, *The Spanish Tragedy*.[6]

Shakespeare *could* have been employed like this in the *Henry VI* plays, though there is no external corroboration that he was. And even if he was, there was no call for Greene to take umbrage, beyond the sour grapes of a disappointed and dying man, who resented the success of a younger dramatist less well educated than himself. But did Greene actually write this attack? For convenience, I shall assume that he did, but there are grounds for doubting as much. We can rarely be *certain* who wrote the sensationalist popular tracts, of which *A Groatsworth of Wit* is not untypical; many are anonymous or written under pen-names as befits their teasing, allusive knowingness; and unscrupulous

printers were not above miscrediting real authors if they saw a
profit in it.[7] A cynic might say that the death-bed testament of a
popular author – Greene was dead before it was published – is too
timely to be true; certainly, there were Elizabethan cynics who
thought so, and Thomas Nashe publicly denied having written it.[8]
So did Henry Chettle, a master printer who was later a prolific,
if undistinguished, dramatist. Chettle had actually prepared *A
Groatsworth of Wit* for the press. When a number of people took
exception to what the pamphlet said about them, he felt it politic
to offer a famous apology, in a pamphlet called *Kind Heart's Dream*,
which appeared early in 1593:

> About three months since died M. Robert Greene, leaving
> many papers in sundry booksellers hands, among other his
> *Groatsworth of Wit*, in which a letter written to divers play-
> makers, is offensively by one or two of them taken; and because
> on the dead they cannot be avenged, they wilfully forge in their
> conceits a living author: and after tossing it to and fro, no
> remedy, but it must light on me . . . With neither of them that
> take offence was I acquainted, and with one of them I care not
> if I never be: the other, whom at that time I did not so much
> spare, as since I wish I had, for that as I have moderated the
> heat of living writers, and might have used my own discretion
> (especially in such a case) the author being dead; that I did not,
> I am as sorry as if the original fault had been my fault, because
> my self have seen his demeanour, no less civil than he excellent
> in the quality he professes: besides, divers of worship have
> reported his uprightness of dealing, which argues his honesty,
> and his facetious grace in writing, that approves his art.[9]

Chettle's point is that he only edited Greene's manuscript, not
adding anything of his own, and he regrets not taking out the
offensive remarks about one author he now knows to be 'no less
civil than . . . excellent in the quality he professes'. He distances
himself, however, from the other author who took offence: 'with
one of them I care not if I never be [acquainted]'. On other evidence
in the apology, this must be the intemperate and homosexual
Marlowe. There is every reason to suppose that the 'civil'
playwright, of whom reputable people speak well, is Shakespeare.
This is the first of a number of tributes to him for being what we
should today call a gentleman, though for the Elizabethans that

was more a social rank than a matter of personality and behaviour. 'Gentle' Shakespeare, as several contemporaries referred to him, had to work hard to shake off the stigma of the 'upstart crow', to gain the standing which finally entitled him to style himself a 'gentleman'.

Chettle's tribute, however, calls attention to an aspect of Shakespeare's effect on other people which must have had a bearing on his career as a whole. After *A Groatsworth of Wit*, he attracted little abuse from fellow-authors; in an age noted for its satire, invective and back-biting he seems to have been respected on all sides. His friend and rival, Ben Jonson, might criticise aspects of his plays, but not the man himself: 'for I loved the man, and do honour his memory – on this side idolatry – as much as any. He was (indeed) honest, and of an open, and free nature: had an excellent fancy; brave notions, and gentle expressions . . .'.[10] This parallels the notable fact that Shakespeare's career and life-style never seem to have incurred the disapproval or suspicion of the Privy Council (effectively the government of the day, under the monarch); on a few occasions the company to which he belonged incurred their displeasure, but that is very different from the track-records of Marlowe, Kyd, Nashe, Jonson, Chapman, Marston, Middleton and Massinger, all of whom personally incurred official wrath on one occasion or another. At a time of political and religious insecurity, it was something of an achievement in itself to have avoided such attention and not to have caused offence.

When all the possible inferences of *A Groatsworth of Wit* and *Kind Heart's Dream* are sifted, little of substance is left beyond the bare information that, by 1592, Shakespeare was an actor and dramatist who had made sufficient of a mark to be worth attacking in print, and who also had some reputable friends. Neither passage helps us, in particular, with the question of how long he had been involved with the theatre before this. When did his career begin? Broadly speaking, there are two opinions on the matter. Sir Edmund Chambers, the most influential Shakespearean scholar of this century, saw no reason to suppose that either the acting or the writing career began before 1590; there is no documentation before 1592, and Greene's attack seems to be aimed at a relative newcomer.[11] This is, broadly speaking, the position of most subsequent scholars including, notably, Sam Schoenbaum. E. A. J. Honigmann is the most forceful proponent of an alternative view: that Shakespeare started writing for the theatre some time before this, perhaps as early as 1586.[12] The critical issue here is the dating of many of the earliest plays. Honigmann argues, for example, that *Titus Andronicus, Two Gentlemen of Verona, The Taming of the Shrew, King John* and *Romeo and Juliet* are all *significantly* (perhaps five or eight years) earlier than most of the standard, post-Chambers accounts suggest.[13] The Chambers position is easier to defend in terms of the (absence of) evidence but we should never make too much of the fact that the documentary record is so thin. Professor Honigmann's case does carry with it the point that 26/28 was relatively late in life to start out in such a profession. Marlowe (Shakespeare's exact contemporary) probably wrote for the theatre by 1588 (*Tamburlaine*), at the age of 24. Jonson was to be involved by the same age. I have no resolution to this knotty problem, though if any of Shakespeare's earliest (that is, pre-1590) compositions had been for companies mainly touring outside London, this might explain why he did not incur Greene's wrath until 1592. For the purposes of this book I assume that all of Shakespeare's dramatic works were composed for London-based companies, broadly after 1590, but I shall not speculate on the precise dating of early plays and trust that readers will appreciate that this is only a working hypothesis.

Although Greene's attack does not help us on this matter, it does deserve our closest attention because it contains one item of information which, in many ways, is the key to Shakespeare's career and to his success (and which is presumably valid even if everything else was a fiction). In 1592, Shakespeare was an actor *and* a playwright. This may seem unexceptionable but, as the sarcasm of *A Groatsworth of Wit* makes clear, it was a matter of note in the early 1590s. It was not unknown for actors to write plays; Robert Wilson, for example, had been a playwright and leading comic actor with, successively, Leicester's and the Queen's Men. But it had not been a common arrangement. Moreover, Wilson had written comedies, whereas Shakespeare 'supposes he is as well able to bombast out a blank verse as the best of you' – bombastic blank verse being (since Marlowe's example) the staple medium for serious works of history and tragedy. Possibly, in Shakespeare, Greene saw a threatening straw in the wind.

James Burbage's Theatre, erected in 1576 north of London, was the first purpose-built structure for the peformance of plays in England since Roman times; it was immediately successful and within months inspired a rival, the Curtain, in the same Shoreditch area. Before their construction acting had been essentially an itinerant profession; even the leading companies like the Earl of Leicester's Men, to whom Burbage at this time belonged, performed in inn-yards or the halls of great houses, wherever a paying audience was assured, and this meant being more or less continually on the move, which contributed to the official view of them as little better than vagrants. The protection of a man as powerful as Robert Dudley, Earl of Leicester and a favourite of the Queen, saved them from arbitrary harassment by local magistrates and civic authorities.[14] Aristocrats felt it befitted their dignity as men of Renaissance culture to patronise the players and this alliance, to some extent against the civic authorities, was an important element in the development of the theatrical profession in Shakespeare's lifetime. Occasionally the noble patron might pay his servants for special performances, as when Leicester magnificently entertained the Queen at his Warwickshire castle of Kenilworth in the summer of 1575, and theatricals were much to the fore. But normally they had to earn a living commercially. (William Shakespeare, incidentally, was eleven years old and lived twelve miles down the road from Kenilworth; it is not at all impossible that, as the son of a Stratford alderman, he should have seen something of these legendary entertainments, as he must certainly have seen Leicester's Men and other troupes on their visits to Stratford.) Such direct patronage was only intermittent and the constant travelling in search of audiences must have been a fraught business. As early as the 1560s we hear of troupes seeking a more permanent base in London, the booming commerical centre of England and now one of the great cities of Europe, with a population beginning to be big enough to sustain regular theatregoing. At the start of Elizabeth's reign its population is estimated to have been c.100 000; by the end, in 1603, it was perhaps 220 000.[15] In the first instance the players converted inn-yards like the Bull in Bishopsgate Street and the Red Lion in Whitechapel for their performances; as late as 1594 it is recorded that Shakespeare's own company played 'this winter time within the city at the Cross Keyes in Gracious Street'.

Burbage's Theatre, financially a considerable gamble, was a statement of faith in the viability of a more settled profession. We get the best impression of what it was like in such a theatre (probably the Curtain) from an account by a Swiss tourist, Thomas Platter:

> On another occasion, I also saw after dinner a comedy, not far from our inn, in the suburb; if I remember right, in Bishopsgate . . . At the end they danced very elegantly both in English and in Irish fashion. And thus every day at two o'clock in the afternoon in the city of London two and sometimes three comedies are performed, at separate places, wherewith folk make merry together, and whichever does best gets the best audience. The places are so built, that they play on a raised platform, and every one can well see it all. There are, however, separate galleries and there one stands more comfortably and moreover can sit, but one pays more for it. Thus anyone who remains on the level standing pays only one English penny: but if he wants to sit, he is let in at a further door, and there he gives another penny. If he desires to sit on a cushion in the most comfortable place of all, where he not only sees everything well, but can also be seen, then he gives yet another English penny at another door. And in the pauses of the comedy food and drink are carried round amongst the people, and one can thus refresh himself at his own cost.
>
> The comedians are most expensively and elgantly apparelled, since it is customary in England, when distinguished gentlemen or knights die, for nearly the finest of their clothes to be made over and given to their servants, and as it is not proper for them to wear such clothes but only to imitate them, they give them to the comedians to purchase for a small sum.
>
> What they can thus produce daily by way of mirth in the comedies, every one knows well, who has happened to see them acting or playing.[16]

This is a classic example of what I described as seeing through a glass darkly. Platter is far more concerned about the facilities for the audience – how they stand or sit, how much it costs them to see or be seen, the availability of food and drink – than he is about what might really interest us: the precise nature of the acting and the staging. One telling detail, however, is the dancing, with which *all* performances seem to have ended. We might expect it of a romantic comedy, but Platter also mentions having seen *Julius Caesar* (of all plays!) at the Globe and there too, at the end 'they danced according to their custom with extreme elegance'. The main thing that emerges clearly, however, is the shrewd commercialism of the whole enterprise, wresting ever more pennies from those willing and able to pay; it is reminiscent more of modern sports stadia than of theatres – an analogy which is even more apt when we take into account that the capacity of such theatres was in the region of 2500 bodies.[17] The average attendance (based on Henslowe's receipts) half-filled the theatre, with more when a new play was performed or on a public holiday. Even so, it is no wonder that Platter was struck to find two or three such performances a day – the companies normally performed six times a week (excluding Sundays), so that perhaps 15 000 people were visiting the theatre weekly. Even if the same persons went more than once (and the repertoire usually changed almost daily to encourage this) it was still a very high proportion of the 200 000 or so in the city. No wonder, either, that the whole phenomenon made the authorities very nervous, with the possibility of riots or the plague probably causing more concern than the lewd or satirical nature of actual performances.

One obvious inference to be drawn from the commercialism and the large audiences is that the theatres were, at least potentially, very profitable. Presumably someone told Platter this tale of how the 'comedians' acquired their magnificent costumes, which may have some truth in it. But Henslowe's accounts reveal that he also spent a great deal on costumes that were clearly not second-hand; he itemises, for example, a 'black velvet cloak with sleeves embroidered all with silver and gold' costing £20 10s 6d – at a time when the annual salary of the schoolmaster in Stratford was £20.[18] Such expenditure on 'apparel' was clearly an investment in the kind of spectacle which drew the audiences. Not surprisingly, he had a rule against the actors leaving the theatre in these costumes, which at one point he carefully inventoried, with constant references to velvet, satin, silk, with lace, buttons and embroidery in gold and silver.[19] The sheer magnificence of the costumes was clearly an attraction to audiences in itself. Describing the play on stage when the Globe burned down, Sir Henry Wotton records: 'The King's players had a new play . . . which was set forth with many extraordinary circumstances of pomp and majesty, even to the matting of the stage; the Knights of the Order with their Georges and garters, the Guards with their embroidered coats, and the like: sufficient in truth within a while to make greatness very familiar, if not ridiculous'.[20]

From their foundation, preachers fulminated against the *sumptuousness* of the Theatre and the Curtain, bemoaning as a sign of the times that the players could afford such costly edifices. Conspicuous capitalist investments of this nature clearly cut across the orthodox hierarchical thinking of the day and were the subject of much envy and misunderstanding. It would be a mistake, of course, to assume that everyone involved in the theatrical business made a fortune: the real money, as ever, went to the shrewdest investors and those who were careful with what they earned – men like Henslowe and Alleyn, and Shakespeare. And there were severe risks in such an enterprise: fire, plague or the authorities could wipe it out overnight. But it would equally be wrong to perpetuate the popular notion that most people working in the Elizabethan theatre, and particularly those who wrote for it, were constantly on the breadline – archetypal poets starving in their garrets. The fact that a man like Robert Greene actually came to such a squalid end obviously needs some explanation.

The short answer seems to be that Greene was so prodigal and unruly by nature that no amount of money from his writing would have suited his needs. It is difficult to be categorical in this judgement since it is, of necessity, based on partial evidence – satirical attacks, pious defences and his own lurid and sentimental 'confessions'. But the picture adds up. He wrote at a prodigious rate – popular romances, 'coney-catching' pamphlets (descriptions of how his underworld fellows robbed and cheated gullible 'coneys') and plays, including *Alphonsus, King of Aragon, The Scottish History of James IV* and the one best known today, *Friar Bacon and Friar Bungay*. He was writing to stay out of debt – we hear at one stage that he had to pawn his sword and cloak – but it does not follow that he was badly paid for what he wrote, at least for his plays. An anecdote by one of his 'coney-catching' rivals is revealing, if it can be trusted: 'Ask the Queen's players if you sold them not *Orlando Furioso* for twenty nobles, and when they were in the country sold the same play to the Lord Admiral's Men for as many more . . .'.[21] Twenty nobles would translate to £6 13s 4d, which is very similar to the sums known to have been paid for plays in the late 1590s and so quite plausible; in addition (assuming the tradition dated back to Greene's time) he could expect to receive at least a portion of the profits from the second or third performance of his play. It was not uncommon for a dramatist to produce three or four plays a year, or to collaborate in the writing of twice that many. Thomas Heywood claimed in the Epistle to *The English Traveller* (1633) that the play was 'one reserved amongst two hundred and twenty, in which I have either an entire hand, or at least a main finger';[22] since he started writing around 1596, this meant about six plays a year. So this offered a decent if unspectacular income, better than that available, say, to most schoolmasters and parsons and certainly better than that to be gained from any other kind of writing, unless it led to sustained patronage.[23]

The fact is that the permanent theatres needed a steady stream of new plays to keep customers coming in. Plays were performed in a sort of repertory system. Henslowe's records, for example, suggest that in 1594/5 the Lord Admiral's Men performed thirty-eight plays in all, of which twenty-one were new and introduced into the repertory at fortnightly intervals; in the next season, thirty-seven plays were performed, of which nineteen were new.[24] The demands on the actors – to keep so many parts at their finger-tips – must have been phenomenal. They needed to be flexible, to be able to respond to the popular verdict as, for example, when Ben Jonson's *Catiline* was hissed off the stage at its first performance in 1611; they had to have alternatives in reserve to cover such contingencies. Francis Beaumont's, *The Knight of the Burning Pestle* (c.1607) makes great comic play of their willingness and ability to adapt to the audience's demands, almost scene by scene. In such circumstances, dependable playwrights must always have been in steady demand, and have received a *reasonable* return for their labour. Of course, it was a matter of business rather than art; virtually all the playwrights, including Shakespeare, collaborated on plays on occasions and some of them, including John Webster and William Rowley, seem to have devoted most of their careers to such collaborative enterprises, in ways that do not altogether square with modern notions of artistic integrity.[25] Doubtless much of this was hack-work, commissioned and completed with little regard to the dignity of the written word. Few people, after all, thought of plays as *literature* until Jonson blazed a trail, scorning the title of 'playwright' and demanding to be known as a 'poet'. In the main, Elizabethan dramatic writing was efficient stuff that caught the taste of its day; its patrons did not ask for more, and paid accordingly. Perhaps the 'writing factories' attached to the

Hollywood movie studios in the 1930s and 40s offer a reasonable analogy.

It is a matter of sobering chance that Shakespeare, and a few others, were in a position to offer much more than mere competence. In his case, as we shall see, the critical factor was that, from quite early on, Shakespeare had the relative luxury of three incomes – as an actor, a playwright, and a shareholder in the company for which he wrote and acted. Latterly, he enjoyed additional incomes as a shareholder in the two theatres where his company was based. Shakespeare took the opportunity provided by relative financial stability to reduce the rate of his writing to about two plays a year, apparently alternating with some regularity between comedy and serious drama. The thirty-seven or so plays that he wrote in a little over twenty years may seem prodigious by modern standards; but it was a modest output by the standards of the day, as Heywood's testimony suggests. Of his serious professional rivals, perhaps only Jonson – once he had secured the lucrative Court masque commissions – wrote less.

So men like Greene were in a position to make a decent living out of writing steadily for the acting companies; men with arguably lesser talents, like Henry Chettle and Anthony Munday, appear to have done just that. But Greene himself seems to have been constitutionally incapable of such steadiness. If it is true that he sold the same play to two companies, they would both have been chary of employing him again. It seems reasonable to conclude that his squalid end, begging a penny-pot of malmsey wine on his lice-ridden bed, was of his own making, not a product of the 'system' for which he worked and perhaps sometimes cheated. The problem was that he was not strictly a professional, in the sense that he had no dedication to his craft; he was a gifted amateur, who exploited the growing market as it suited him, admirably catering to a demand for spectacle and fantasy, but with no real commitment to those who employed him. Much the same might be said of Marlowe, a much more talented University Wit, whom Greene disparaged along with Shakespeare in *A Groatsworth of Wit*. The following year Marlowe came to an equally sordid end, stabbed through the eye in a pub brawl in Deptford. Whether it really was a quarrel over the bill, as the official version had it, or whether (as has been claimed)[26] Marlowe was done away with as a political embarrassment, it was in every way a great reckoning in a little room. Taken in conjunction with Greene's death, it marks the end of the University Wits as the dominant voices in the Elizabethan theatre, and reveals the true force of Greene's dying gibes against Shakespeare. An actor who was also a playwright had all the makings of a true professional, being able to supply his own troupe with what they needed on a regular basis; the incentive to deal fairly and on time was obvious; and no one knew better than an actor the practical requirements of the trade, whatever he might lack in the way of education.

By 1592, therefore, Shakespeare was in a position to lead the Elizabethan theatre into a new and more professional phase – though it is a measure of how little we know that we cannot be sure which company stood to benefit from his talents. Professor Honigmann has argued vigorously for his connections with Lord Strange's Men,[27] which seems plausible. When *Titus Andronicus* was published in 1594, its title page proclaimed that it 'was played by the Right Honourable the Earl of Derby, Earl of Pembroke and Earl of Sussex their Servants' – that is, successively by three different companies. By then Lord Strange had succeeded to his father's title as Earl of Derby, so the first reference is very likely to his players.[28] But it seems that, by 1590 if not earlier, this troupe was ailing, since it amalgamated (at least on occasions) with the Lord Admiral's Men. Perhaps this is why they sold some of their play-texts to the Earl of Pembroke's Men, including *Titus Andronicus* and possibly one or more of the *Henry VI* plays, which they are thought to have performed. It is *possible* that Shakespeare accompanied his own plays in the transfer to Pembroke's, though he could not have been with them long, since by September 1593 they were reported to be in debt[29] and they, in turn, sold their play-scripts – some, at least, to the Earl of Sussex's Men. Again, Shakespeare *may* have followed his own plays, but Sussex's Men seem to have disintegrated shortly after the death of their patron, the fourth earl, in December 1593. Not until 1594 and the formation of the Lord Chamberlain's Men can we be *certain* of Shakespeare's professional associations.

Even by Elizabethan standards, troupes were disintegrating and re-forming with unusual frequency. Why this was so before 1592 has never been explained, but the explanation thereafter is incontestable. The city authorities failed in their various attempts to close the theatres, but the plague succeeded, with a vengeance. The narrow, refuse-strewn and rat-infested streets of London were always a prey to the plague. But the visitation of 1592, which lasted

almost unabated until 1594, was a particularly virulent one, killing
upwards of ten thousand people. In January 1593 the weekly bills
of mortality began to look alarming and the Privy Council closed
the theatres. Their order went not only to the London authorities,
who controlled playing in the inn-yards, but also to the justices in
Middlesex, with jurisdiction over the Theatre and the Curtain, and
in Surrey, where there was a theatre at Newington Butts and
where (more significantly) Henslowe had already set up the Rose
(c.1587), the first of the successful theatres on the Bankside, south
of the Thames:

> . . . we think it fit that all manner of concourse and public
> meetings of the people at plays, bear-baitings, bowlings and
> other like assemblies for sports be forbidden, and therefore do
> hereby require you and in Her Majesty's name straightly charge
> and command you forthwith to inhibit within your jurisdiction
> all plays, baiting of bears, bulls, bowling and any other like
> occasions to assemble any numbers of people together (preaching
> and divine service at churches excepted), whereby no occasions
> be offered to increase the infection within the city.[30]

The theatres reopened briefly in the winter of 1593–4 and the
spring of 1594, but on each occasion the Privy Council quickly took
fright again. It was not until the autumn/winter of 1594 that
something like regular theatrical business resumed. The closures
obviously hit the players very hard; some went touring in areas
not touched by the plague; others went abroad; in London there
were the desperate amalgamations and disintegrations we have
seen.

One intriguing possibility of how Shakespeare might have been
employed for some of this time – though the dating is extremely
problematic – is that he was amongst those who were called in to
try to 'mend' a problem play about the life of Sir Thomas More,
perhaps with a view to having it serviceable when the theatres
reopened.[31] *Sir Thomas More* is one of the few surviving manuscript
plays of the Elizabethan period, and one of even fewer which
shows in detail evidence of formal censorship. The bulk of the
manuscript is in the handwriting of Anthony Munday, though it
was not necessarily all his own work; the censor has, however,
called for substantial changes in that, and we may deduce that
several additional pieces of writing, in a variety of hands, were

commissioned to try to salvage the play. One of these, three pages in what scholars have labelled hand D, is widely, though not universally, thought to be by Shakespeare; if so, apart from signatures on various legal documents, it is the only piece of his handwriting that we possess.[32] The passage in question is an address by More to the rioting citizens on 'Ill May-Day', placating them with his bravery and humour, but arguing with intense conviction the dangers of insurrection and the need for an ordered, hierarchic structure of society, in which all citizens must know and accept their place. The theme recurs often in Shakespeare's plays, notably in *Troilus and Cressida*, where Ulysees asserts the frightening consequences of disregarding 'degree' (I.iii.83–126) and in *Coriolanus*, where Menenius Agrippa handles the fractious citizens of Rome (a scene very similar to that of 'Ill May-Day') with a parable of the members of the body rebelling against the belly (I.i.91–158). Shakespeare shows no signs of having been at heart a democrat.

Irrespective of Shakespeare's possible involvement in revising *Sir Thomas More*, the manuscript usefully focuses our attention on the activities of the official censor – a figure who must have been well to the fore of Shakespeare's mind throughout the writing of his plays. The Master of the Revels was a subordinate of the Lord Chamberlain, whose duties involved checking the suitability of plays and other 'sports' for performance at Court. Shakespeare actually offers a portrait of such an official in *A Midsummer Night's Dream*. When Theseus is anxious for entertainment to pass the time before bed, he demands:

> Where is our usual manager of mirth?
> What revels are in hand? Is there no play
> To ease the anguish of a torturing hour?
> (V.i.35–7)

Philostrate appears,[33] offering a description of what is available. When Theseus shows interest in 'Pyramus and Thisbe', he does his best to talk his master out of it: 'I have heard it over, / And it is nothing, nothing in the world' (77–8), but he is finally overruled. From this function of 'perusing' plays for Court performance grew a more general role of censoring plays for the public theatres.

It would be a mistake, however, to think of this as an entirely repressive measure, aimed at restricting free expression. In some respects it was one of the ways in which the Court protected the players from the civic officials, both in London and the provinces, who regarded them as a nuisance. This is reflected in the royal patent granted to the Earl of Leicester's Men in 1574, which stood as a model for patents granted to other major companies thereafter. It is addressed to all officers of the crown in what we should today call local government:

> we . . . have licensed and authorised, and by these presents do license and authorise, our loving subjects . . . servants to our trusty and welbeloved cousin and counsellor the Earl of Leicester, to use exercise, and occupy the art and faculty of playing comedies, tragedies, interludes, stage plays, and such other like as they have already used and studied, or hereafter shall use and study, as well for the recreation of our loving subjects, as for our solace and pleasure when we shall think good to see them . . . Willing and commanding you and every of you, as ye tender our pleasure, to permit and suffer them herein without any your lets, hindrance, or molestation during the term aforesaid, any act, statute, proclamation, or commandment heretofore made, or hereafter to be made, to the contrary notwithstanding. Provided that the said comedies, tragedies, interludes, and stage plays be by the Master of our Revels for the time being before seen and allowed, and that the same be not published or shown in the time of common prayer, or in the time of great and common plague in our said City of London.[34]

The 'allowance' of the Master of the Revels as part of the umbrella of patronage was thus a measure of protection for professional actors against the interference of local officials, who might otherwise have interpreted the regulations as it suited themselves. There were general statutes in force inhibiting certain subject-matter in public performances. A proclamation of 1559 instructed officials not to allow any 'common interludes in the English tongue . . . to be played wherein either matters of religion or of the governance of the estate of the common weal shall be handled or treated, being no meet matters to be written or treated upon, but by men of authority, learning and wisdom, nor to be handled before any audience, but of grave and discreet persons'.[35] This was carefully phrased to allow the performance of *some* plays dealing with such matters, possibly in Latin but certainly in privileged contexts – at

Court, the universities and other great houses, not in public theatres. Once the Master of the Revels asserted his authority in these matters, at least in the London area (which we might date from the confirmation of Edmund Tilney's assumption of the office in 1581),[36] we must suspect that distinctions became somewhat blurred.

This is not to suggest that Tilney or his successors were lax in their job. Surviving manuscripts on which they have left their mark, including *Sir Thomas More*, show them to have been scrupulous in demanding changes or deletions in particular contexts, often apparently when they suspected allusions to important persons or current events. But their 'allowance' of what was permissible appears to have been primarily based on what was acceptable at Court – there is no evidence that they ever distinguished between what was 'allowed' there and what was 'allowed' elsewhere – and this seems to have been somewhat broader than a strict interpretation of the statutes in force would have permitted. Consider, in particular, plays about English history, including Shakespeare's own. They frequently deal with 'matters of the governance of the estate of the common weal' and occasionally (as in *King John*) with matters of religion, and it would be naive to suppose that they were always intended or interpreted as scholarly examinations of times past, divorced from contemporary concerns. They were not necessarily seditious or disrespectful of those in power, but they do comment more freely on potentially controversial matters than we might have expected in an Elizabethan context,[37] and the 'allowance' of the Master of the Revels must have been critical in making this possible. We have no evidence of any Shakespeare play being refused this 'allowance', censored before performance or called into question after it had been performed. This perhaps reveals how little we actually know about the activities of Edmund Tilney and his successor, Sir George Buc – very few of their papers have survived. But, as we have commented before, Shakespeare figures remarkably little in what we *do* know about official disquiet over the drama and the dramatists of the period.

In this context, the censorship of *Sir Thomas Moore* itself is quite revealing. In the first place, it is remarkable that any Elizabethan dramatist should have felt able to write a play about More at all. Although he was widely respected as a great man, he had resisted the policies of the Queen's father, Henry VIII, and died – in the opinion of many – as a Roman Catholic martyr. It is apparent in the original version of the play that those responsible were sensitive to these problems. More is shown refusing to subscribe to certain 'articles' but we are never told that these are, in effect, the Act of Supremacy, denying the Pope's jurisdiction over the King of England. And there is no overt criticism of Henry VIII, though the play is quite openly sympathetic towards More. The blandly non-committal comment of the Earl of Surrey after More has bravely met his death – 'A very learned worthy gentleman / Seals error with his blood' (1983–4) – is typical of the authors' discretion throughout. Perhaps because of this, Tilney seems to have had no reservations about this aspect of the play at all.

It is, rather, the opening scenes of the play, showing the notorious 'Ill May-Day' riots against French residents in London, that disturbed him, possibly because of their topical relevance, and he wrote at the head of the manuscript: 'Leave out the insurrection wholly, and the cause thereof, and begin with Sir Thomas More at the Mayor's Sessions, with a report afterwards of his good service done, being Sheriff of London, upon a meeting against the Lombards, only a short report, and not otherwise, at your own perils.' Several other specific amendments make it plain that he was concerned about rioting in general and about anti-alien feeling in particular, being most sensitive of all over references to the French (for which he prefers to substitute 'Lombards', who were doubtless rarer in sixteenth century London). It might not be unreasonable to conclude, therefore, that these issues weighed particularly heavily when he was sent the play to 'peruse' and this is why he was so severe on it. Otherwise, it is difficult to explain why he did not similarly refuse to permit, for example, the scenes of the Jack Cade riots in *2 Henry VI,* or why he or his successor allowed through the scenes of civil unrest in *Coriolanus.* The Master of the Revels must have placed real constraints on what Shakespeare and his contemporaries felt able to write about and the ways they presented what they did write about; it is not unlikely that they enforced changes on Shakespeare's texts that we know nothing about. On the other hand, they were a good deal more liberal in the subject-matter that they allowed through than many people seem to assume who have not considered the evidence. On the whole, it seems to have been imprudent allusions to current matters of public policy or persons of note which caused them to draw the line, rather than broader issues of doctrine or philosophy. They never were concerned, I should add, with matters of sexual or personal morality, or bawdy language, such as have concerned censors in later ages; after 1606, however, Parliament made it an offence to blaspheme on stage, and the Master of the Revels enforced this.

Between 1592 and 1594 these considerations must have seemed relatively remote to Shakespeare. With the theatres closed, he presumably had to look elsewhere, in the main, for his living. We do know that he made a bid for aristocratic patronage. Prior to the establishment of the settled theatres, this had been the only realistic route to secure employment for a man of literary talents. As the careers of men like Spenser and Donne demonstrate, it was still the only *respectable* route. In Shakespeare's case, it seems to have been a route he adopted for a limited period, because his chosen one was blocked.

3

Poems and Patrons

With the theatres closed, Shakespeare only had two ways of making a living by his pen in Elizabethan England. He could have thrown himself into the popular market for ballads, satirical abuse, pious tracts and pseudo-courtly romances, which was fed by the likes of Robert Greene, Thomas Nashe and Thomas Lodge. Or he could look for the patronage of some great nobleman, who might reward the dedication of a work to him with a handsome sum; the outward show of magnificence, including patronage of the arts, was expected of a Renaissance aristocrat, a manifestation of his power as much as of his taste.[1] For many authors, like Spenser, Daniel and Donne in the early part of their careers, the ideal arrangement was to be taken into a noble household as a secretary or tutor; against such security, writing could be a stepping-stone to further advancement. It is clear that Shakespeare chose the latter option, though it is not known if he was ever formally employed in the household to which he turned, that of the young Earl of Southampton. *Venus and Adonis* was entered in the Stationers' Register on 18 April 1593 by its printer, Richard Field, who came, like Shakespeare, from Stratford. The poem bears a signed dedication which, while elaborate to modern tastes, is less florid and servile than many of its day:

> To the Right Honourable / Henry Wriothesley, / Earl of Southampton, and Baron of Titchfield.

> Right Honourable, / I know not how I shall offend in dedicating my unpolished lines to your Lordship, nor how the world will censure me for choosing so strong a prop to support so weak a burden; only, if your Honour seem but pleased, I account myself highly praised, and vow to take advantage of all idle hours, till I have honoured you with some graver labour. But if the first heir of my invention prove deformed, I shall be sorry it had so noble a god-father, and never after ear so barren a land, for fear it yield me still so bad a harvest. I leave it to your honourable survey, and your Honour to your heart's content; which I wish

may always answer your own wish and the world's hopeful expectation.

Your Honour's in all duty, / William Shakespeare[2]

There is nothing here to suggest that Shakespeare yet knew Southampton; it seems, rather, a speculative dedication to a young man (he was only nineteen, against Shakespeare's twenty-eight) who was emerging from the tutelage of his guardian, Lord Burghley. Southampton had already made his mark at Court, where he formed an attachment to the old Queen's last favourite, the Earl of Essex;[3] and he had acquired a reputation for encouraging writers, employing the Italian translator and lexicographer, John Florio.[4] But his patronage could not be taken for granted; Thomas Nashe dedicated his *Unfortunate Traveller* to him, but met with no success. Hence, perhaps, Shakespeare's diffidence: was *this* the sort of thing to take the fancy of the young lord? If not, there is the careful promise of a 'graver labour' to follow.

In many ways, *Venus and Adonis* might seem calculated to please such a reader: an erotic tale, based on Ovid's *Metamorphoses*, purveying titillation under a modest wisp of classical scholarship. Southampton had been at Cambridge and, like most Renaissance aristocrats, would make a show of intellectual interests, without necessarily wanting to make too much of them. This is consonant with one of the most sustained affectations of the literature written around Renaissance Courts: that it is the work of gentlemen amateurs, writing for relaxation and amusement, not for profit. Note Sir Philip Sidney's tone, for example, (despite his unusually intense concern for literature), when writing to his sister Mary about his *Arcadia:* 'Here now have you . . . this idle work of mine, which I fear, like the spider's web, will be thought fitter to be swept away than worn to any other purpose . . . Read it, then, at your idle times, and the follies your good judgement will find in it blame not, but laugh at.'[5] It is the *sprezzatura* tradition of courtier authorship, playing down craftsmanship and scholarship, and denying that anything was of sufficient weight to be worth revising. We can see in the dedication that Shakespeare wanted to be associated with this tradition: his lines, he claims, are 'unpolished' and his next offering is to be written in 'all idle hours'. The latter is a more poignant phrase, perhaps, for an out-of-work actor/dramatist than for a gentleman of leisure, but it is clear that Shakespeare is not referring to his stage-career: he describes *Venus*

and Adonis as 'the first heir of my invention'. This could refer to its
being his first work (of any sort) in print, which is apparently true;
but it is more likely to mean that he regards it as his first *real* work,
his first work of literature, discounting everything he had written
for the stage as unworthy of such consideration. It is a graphic
exposition of the social and critical status of play-texts at this time,
and we should bear in mind that there is no evidence that
Shakespeare himself deviated from this view.

But *Venus and Adonis* was different: its printed success mattered.
We do not know Southampton's reaction, but the popular verdict
was unequivocal; it was one of the most reprinted pieces of the
era, running to sixteen editions before 1640. It was frequently
quoted, including a reference to it in *The Return to Parnassus*, a play
staged by students at St John's College, Cambridge, around 1600.
Such a topical reference might suggest that it found favour with
undergraduates and similar types, including students at the Inns
of Court (the law schools in London, virtually a third university,
whose members must always have been a significant element in
Shakespeare's audience and readership). So we may surmise that
it was the successful reception of *Venus and Adonis*, rather than its
proving 'deformed', that prompted Shakespeare to fulfil his promise of a 'graver labour'. *The Rape of Lucrece* was entered in the
Stationers' Register on 9 May 1594, and was also dedicated to
Southampton, in rather warmer terms:

> The love I dedicate to your Lordship is without end; whereof
> this pamphlet without beginning is but a superfluous moiety.
> The warrant I have of your honourable disposition, not the
> worth of my untutored lines, makes it assured of acceptance.
> What I have done is yours; what I have to do is yours; being
> part in all I have, devoted yours. Were my worth greater, my
> duty would show greater; meantime, as it is, it is bound to your
> Lordship, to whom I wish long life still lengthened with all
> happiness.[6]

'Graver' the subject of the poem may be: the rape of the chaste
and beautiful Lucretia by Sextus, son of Tarquin, the King of Rome,
which leads to her suicide and plays a part in the banishment of
the Tarquins from Rome. But it is essentially the same mix of
ingredients as *Venus and Adonis*: violence and eroticism discreetly
handled within a classical framework. Its success was less over-

whelming than that of the earlier poem, though it elicited the first printed reference (autumn 1594) to its author as a *poet*, in verses prefacing an obscurely allusive poem, *Willobie his Avisa*, which relate how: 'Tarquin plucked his glistering grape / And Shakespeare paints poor Lucrece's rape'.[7] The two poems thereafter lodged together in the general contemporary estimate of Shakespeare, which saw him pre-eminently as a poet of love. Francis Meres, in 1598, listed him as one of 'the most passionate among us to bewail and bemoan the perplexities of love', a 'mellifluous and honey-tongued' poet of 'fine filed' phrases in the tradition of Ovid. Shortly thereafter (c.1601–2), the students of St John's staged another play, *The Second Return to Parnassus*, which compliments Shakespeare's verse:

> Who loves not Adon's love, or Lucrece's rape?
> His sweeter verse contains heart-robbing lines,
> Could but a graver subject him content,
> Without love's foolish lazy languishment.[8]

This is slightly odd, since *The Rape of Lucrece* is hardly about 'love's foolish lazy languishment', but they seem to have felt that it did not constitute the 'graver subject' promised earlier. One thing is clear, however: this estimate of his poetry takes no account of his plays, which by then included all his English histories (bar *Henry VIII*), *Julius Caesar* and possibly *Hamlet*.

This is as far as the factual record of Shakespeare's relations with the Earl of Southampton takes us. Late in 1594 the theatres reopened and Shakespeare resumed his interrupted career: there is no evidence that he sought aristocratic patronage again after this date, or that he maintained any links with Southampton (whose association with the Earl of Essex was shortly to lead to disaster). But it seems appropriate here to raise the question of the sonnets, which many commentators (including this one) believe were written for Southampton. No single topic relating to Shakespeare's life and art has provoked so much controversy or conjecture as the 154 sonnets published in 1609 by the printer Thomas Thorpe, and ascribed to William Shakespeare. We do not *know* when they were written, or for whom, or whether they were meant to be read in the sequence in which we find them in that quarto volume. Two of the poems (138 and 144) had appeared, in somewhat different versions, in a miscellany of 1599 called *The Passionate Pilgrim;* and the year before that, fleshing out his view of Shakespeare as the poet of love, Francis Meres had referred to Shakespeare's 'sugared sonnets among his private friends', suggesting that (like so much of the courtly verse of the day) they had not been intended for publication in print. There is no way of knowing, however, whether Meres's 'sugared sonnets' represented all, or even some, of those printed by Thorpe, or from how much earlier they might have dated.

In the absence of fact there has been no shortage of conjecture, with any two of the variable factors – dating, inspirer(s) and order of composition – being permutated in order to 'establish' a fancied third. There are serious proponents of datings ranging anywhere from the mid-1580s to the late 1590s, the dates having to gravitate to accommodate the age of prospective inspirers. The pursuit of objective knowledge in this area has not been helped by the indisputable fact that the stated inspirer of the majority of the sonnets is not a woman but a young man – a Fair Youth whom, in the first seventeen sonnets, Shakespeare urges to marry and have children, but with whom (in later sonnets) he seems to adopt a more intimate and passionate tone. It has caused some embarrassment that England's Poet should be open to suspicions of homoerotic tendencies. There was, however, a Renaissance tradition of strong male friendships, giving rise to strong affections but stopping well short of homosexuality, and it is reasonable to associate Shakespeare's sonnets with it. In fact, Shakespeare seems to state quite explicitly, in Sonnet 20, that for all the Fair Youth's beauty, he has no physical interest in him. He complains how nature:

> by addition me of thee defeated
> By adding one thing to my purpose nothing.
> But since she prick'd thee out for women's pleasure,
> Mine be thy love, and thy love's use their treasure.

The pun (prick = phallus) makes it abundantly clear that the 'one thing to my purpose nothing' is the Fair Youth's genitalia. Nevertheless, many commentators clearly wish that the issue had never arisen at all and turn with relief to the two other enigmas in the drama of the sonnets, the Rival Poet of Sonnets 79–86, who vies with Shakespeare for the Fair Youth's affections, and the Dark Lady of Sonnets 127–52 who (if it is the same woman referred to throughout) is married, though not to Shakespeare or the Youth, has been lover to the former and is now having an affair with the latter. Shakespeare's passion for the Dark Lady has the advantage of being 'normal', though it is adulterous and compounded with jealousy, bitterness, world-weariness, spite and heterosexual lust.

Who are these three people, and what do the sonnets tell us about Shakespeare and his relationship with them? The adamant answer is: we do not know. The most teasing of the possible clues is the dedication prefaced to the sonnets in the 1609 quarto:

TO.THE.ONLY.BEGETTER.OF.
THESE.ENSUING.SONNETS.
Mr.W.H.ALL.HAPPINESS.
AND.THAT.ETERNITY.
PROMISED.
BY.
OUR.EVER-LIVING.POET.
WISHETH.
THE.WELL-WISHING.
ADVENTURER.IN.
SETTING.
FORTH.

T.T.

The grammar of the piece is almost sufficient to quell interpretation in itself. How many sentences are hidden within the unusual punctuation (which is reproduced faithfully, as is the lay-out, in case they are essential to some cryptogram of the kind beloved by sleuths)?[9] Who exactly is the subject of 'WISHETH'? Most attention has focused on the identity of 'Mr W. H.'. Could this be an allusion to Henry Wriothesley, the initials reversed to deflect uninitiated snoopers? Or is it William Herbert, the third Earl of Pembroke, son of the patron of the acting troupe to which Shakespeare may briefly have been attached c.1591–3? He was to be one of 'the incomparable pair of brethren' to whom the Shakespeare first folio was dedicated in 1623. If it were Herbert, the sonnets would probably have to be later than *most* people assume, since he was not born until 1580 and many of the sonnets would be pretty strong meat addressed to a boy under the age of, say, sixteen. But in any case, both of these noble candidates are surely ruled out by the use of the humble 'Mr.', which is far below the dignity of earls of the realm (unless this, too, is a teaser for the uninitiated). To complicate matters further, we have to take into account that the dedication is signed by Thomas Thorpe, the printer, rather than – as would be usual – the author, which is perhaps evidence that Shakespeare did not authorise the poems' publication, and may indeed have been embarrassed to see them in print. This has led to speculation that the word 'BEGETTER' does not mean the person who *inspired* the poems at all, but the one who procured them for Thorpe's publication (conceivably, if the compositor inserted one full-stop too many, a Mr W. Hall).

The enigmas, in short, are impenetrable and in many ways would remain so even if we could with confidence put names to the Fair Youth, the Rival Poet and the Dark Lady. This is because there would still remain the enigmatic dimension of art itself, for in the Courtly genre of the Elizabethan sonnet-sequence, traditionally meant for 'private friends' rather than public print, the relationship between art and life was always teasingly an issue. In the prototype of the form in England, Sir Philip Sidney's *Astrophil and Stella* (first published posthumously in 1591) it is tantalisingly clear that 'Stella' refers to Penelope Devereux, Lady Rich, just as 'Astrophil' puns on Sidney's own name.[10] But it is far from clear what real relationship, as distinct from literary game, existed between her and the poet. Samuel Daniel's 'mistress', Delia, in the sonnet-sequence of that name published in 1592, looks suspiciously like an anagram of his own name and was probably fictitious. So other examples of the genre suggest that there *need* be no simple correlation between the narrative that slowly unfolds in a sonnet sequence and the biographical circumstances of the poet. Whatever its contact with real life, the sonnet-sequence always retained some of the Humanist aspirations of its originator, Petrarch. It embodied in concentrated form the endlessly ironic and paradoxical conflicts between human nature at its best and at its worst, when motivated by love. It always conveyed something of a teasing moral lesson, enticing the reader in to experience vicariously the impossible contradictions of virtue and passion, love and time, art and nature. And this element of a formal Renaissance poetic exercise was always likely to be very much to the fore when any question of patronage was involved. No less a love poet than John Donne testified to a friend, late in life: 'You know my uttermost when it was best, and even then I did best when I had least truth for my subjects'.[11]

So, in Shakespeare's case, if indeed the sonnets were connected with a bid for patronage, we can only begin to guess the extent to which they might reflect any real relationships between himself, the Fair Youth and the other characters. The choice of a 'master-mistress' (Sonnet 20) as the main focus of the sequence may simply have been a witty exploitation of the poet/patron relationship, which mirrors in interesting ways the frustrations of a lover's courtship of his mistress in the traditional Petrarchan sonnet-sequence. For the Petrarchan poet, the mistress is unattainable, a near-divinity, probably married to someone else; he himself is a pitiful wretch, his manliness (which, in other respects, we must not doubt) scotched by her disdainful virtue. It is an impossible situation, as Shakespeare points out in the ridiculous relationship of Silvius and Phoebe in *As You Like It*, offering only endless frustration or a short-lived adulterous affair as possible solutions. The relationship of the poet and a male patron is as impossible as that of Petrarchan lovers: their path to true union is frustrated both by the unbridgeable inferiority of one to the other and by the facts of nature. Looked at in this light, we may see Shakespeare's sonnet-sequence as a witty adaptation of the conventions, subverting expectations and exploring unusual sexual waters as a metaphor for the uncomfortable client/patron relationship. That is to say, Shakespeare may be doing in the sequence as a whole what he does specifically in his upside-down praise of the Dark Lady (Sonnet 130), who is physically the very antithesis of the conventional blonde-haired, blue-eyed, fair-skinned mistress of Petrarchan sonneteers:

> My mistress' eyes are nothing like the sun;
> Coral is far more red than her lips' red;
> If snow be white, why then her breasts are dun;
> If hairs be wires, black wires grow on her head . . .

To this extent, and however they may refractedly comment on the circumstances of his own life, Shakespeare's sonnets should always be seen first as works of the literary imagination – ones which play sophisticated games with their readers that should be readily comprehensible to a generation brought up on the works of Jorge Luis Borges, Vladimir Nabokov, John Fowles, David Lodge and others. The sincerity inheres in the achievement of the literature, not in its approximation to 'reality'. It would be odd to deny that the man who imagined so sincerely the love lives of Romeo and Juliet, Troilus and Cressida and Antony and Cleopatra could not similarly have conjured up the vicissitudes of a fictitious 'affair' in the sonnets.

If we accept that the sonnets were very probably connected with a bid for patronage, the strongest argument for their being associated with Southampton, in the period 1592–4, is that he is the only man whose patronage we know for certain that Shakespeare sought. And it can be said at least that he fits the bill. A Nicholas Hilliard miniature of Southampton, painted when he was about twenty, is in no way inconsistent with what we hear of the Fair Youth. Southampton was not only unmarried but resisting pressure from his guardian, Burghley, to marry his daughter. The possibility that Shakespeare's pen was enlisted to add pressure cannot be excluded: the first seventeen sonnets might well be read as dutiful commissions, exhorting the youth to marry and find immortality through children, though a different relationship and tone is apparent thereafter. This *could* explain how Shakespeare's attentions switched to Southampton despite his possible earlier associations (not proven, but widely suspected) with Lord Strange. Strange, incidentally, was far too old and long married ever to have been suspected as the Fair Youth, and had only daughters to succeed him, so this is one enigma in which the Stanley family has never figured.[12] Shakespeare, though approaching thirty, was not exactly old, even by Elizabethan standards, but he was long married, knew the cares of parenthood, and there was sufficient disparity between his age and that of the Youth to make the complaints of lengthening years credible in a poetic context:

> That time of year thou mayst in me behold
> When yellow leaves, or none, or few, do hang
> Upon those boughs which shake against the cold,
> Bare ruined choirs where late the sweet birds sang.
>   (Sonnet 73)

Clearly, other candidates than Southampton have plausible cases, though the age factor makes it difficult to entertain those from much earlier than 1592–4. If we look to those dates, too, there is the tantalising possibility that the Rival Poet (assuming he existed in the flesh) could have been Christopher Marlowe, whose unfinished *Hero and Leander* is in the same general mode as *Venus and Adonis* and probably belongs to the same period: it is not inconceivable that the two greatest dramatists of the era should have been chasing the same patronage while the theatres were closed, though other candidates, including George Chapman, have been proposed.[13] I fear I have no candidates, either plausible or tantalising, for the role of the Dark Lady.[14]

We cannot leave the question of patronage without asking what mark, if any, it may have left on Shakespeare's early *plays*. Numerous attempts have been made to explain the apparent peculiarities, in particular, of some of the early comedies by reference to the tastes or interests of supposed patrons. *Love's Labour's Lost* and *A Midsummer Night's Dream* are most often cited in this regard. The former is a tantalisingly enigmatic work, which has elicited a number of ingenious datings and interpretations, including the suggestions that it satirises such unorthodox thinkers as Sir Walter Ralegh, Thomas Harriot and George Chapman, associates in some shadowy 'school of night' (cf. IV.iii.250); that the Armado–Moth scenes poke fun at the pamphleteering quarrels of Thomas Nashe and Gabriel Harvey; and that it is about the Inns of Court and specifically William Hatcliff, one candidate for 'Mr W.H.'.[15] Any of the satirical interpretations might be read, moreover, as evidence for its being tailored to suit patrons with known opinions on these matters. A. L. Rowse links the play with the sonnets and so with 'Southampton and his friends', rashly identifying Rosaline with the Dark Lady, Berowne with Shakespeare himself, while 'it is probable that the fantastic Don Armado in the play owes some strokes to [John Florio]'. By contrast, Professor Honigmann finds allusions in the play to Ferdinando, Lord Strange, who may well have been one of the supposed 'school of night', (in which case we are to look on the play more as an injoke than as a satire on a rival faction).[16]

In the case of *A Midsummer Night's Dream*, the suggestion is that a play which revolves so conspicuously around a number of weddings may well have been written – or at least adapted – to celebrate a particular wedding. Although we *know*, from the title page of the play's first (1600) edition that the play was 'sundry times publicly acted by the Right Honourable the Lord Chamberlain his servants', this hypothesis of more exclusive origins has met with such remarkable agreement that the question has become not *whether* it was so, but *whose* wedding?[17] Since the play contains an elaborate compliment to Queen Elizabeth as 'a fair vestal, throned by the west' (II.i.158), it has seemed reasonable to assume that she was present at the wedding and this has conveniently narrowed the range of conjecture, with the prime candidates being: the marriage of William, sixth Earl of Derby, to Elizabeth Vere on 26 January 1595, and that of Thomas Berkeley and Elizabeth Carey on 19 February 1596. Both have plausible Shakespearean connections: the Earl of Derby was the younger brother of Ferdinando, Lord Strange, maintained a troupe of actors and was (according to one report) the author of 'comedies for the common players'; Elizabeth Carey was the granddaughter of Lord Hunsdon, the Lord Chamberlain, who was patron of Shakespeare's company after 1594. Which to choose? Harold Brooks, the New Arden editor of the play, favoured the latter connection; E. A. J. Honigmann has championed the former; William B. Hunter has ingeniously argued that the text as we have it is confusing because it reflects adaptations not for one but for *two* weddings.[18]

The sheer proliferation of theories must, of itself, give us pause. How plausible is it, by verifiable criteria, that *any* of these covert meanings or special contexts really existed? Unfortunately, it is not possible to give an unqualified answer to that question; the absence of hard facts takes us into one of those grey areas of judgement. To put it simply, we know very little about relationships between aristocratic patrons and the acting companies whose liveries they wore, particularly before 1594, after which the documentary evidence becomes somewhat more plentiful and consistent. Some assume that it was essentially a convenient business arrangement, conferring prestige on the patron and protection from official harassment on the actors.[19] In their view this patronage would have no bearing on the plays that were performed in public. There is no *evidence* that any professional playwright ever wrote a full-scale stage play during Shakespeare's career other than with public, commercial performance in mind. Those who think in these terms emphasise that the Elizabethan theatre was commercially orientated, a proto-capitalist enterprise (something which Henslowe's *Diary* very much suggests), catering for the broadest possible audience rather than exclusive coteries. Others, however, point to the fact that the public theatres did not exist in isolation. At Court and in other great houses, in the universities and the Inns of Court, Renaissance traditions of patronised and coterie drama flourished. Writers like George Gascoigne, Samuel Daniel and Ben Jonson were commissioned to write a variety of masques and other entertainments topically pointed for special audiences, and professional actors were regularly employed in them. Leceister's entertainment of Elizabeth at Kenilworth is one notable example; Jonson's Jacobean Court masques, staged with great magnificence by (usually) Inigo Jones, are another. The question is whether, or to what extent, these styles and traditions affected practice among playwrights working normally in the public theatres – making more likely the kinds of private allusions or special performances that have been hypothesised for *Love's Labour's Lost* and *A Midsummer Night's Dream*.

In these comedies Shakespeare may to an extent have been following John Lyly's lead. His plays for various children's companies in the 1580s were aimed both at the Court (a kind of coterie audience in itself) and at the paying audiences of the indoor theatres at the Blackfriars and St Paul's; some of them, and notably *Endymion* (1588), seem to have been written with the interests of his patron, the Earl of Oxford, in mind, though we should probably beware of trying to read their allegories too systematically.[20] Lyly himself was a would-be courtier, in this respect more like Spenser or Donne than Shakespeare, hoping by his writing to advance himself at Court rather than to make it his permanent career. His paying audiences probably felt that they had a privileged if oblique insight into the Court and its goings on through his mannered quasi-mythological dramas. But this first generation of 'private' theatres (private only in the sense of being smaller and charging considerably more to get in) were outgrowths of privileged choir-schools and different in many ways from their 'public' rivals: they were roofed in, candle-lit, smaller and relatively intimate, perhaps better placed in their relationship with the Court to make subtle allusions to persons of note.

Of course, those who then attended the Theatre, the Curtain and the Rose were probably also interested in the rich and famous, but it must be doubtful if they would have appreciated the kind of subtle references and in-jokes which the special circumstances of the private theatres perhaps encouraged. Could it ever have made professional sense to write plays with elements that would have been unintelligible to the majority of the audience, the regular paying customers? This kind of common-sense logic collapses, however, when we consider periods like 1592–94 in which the public theatres were shut, and Shakespeare might easily have turned to closet drama (as well as poetry) for patrons like Lord

Strange or the Earl of Southampton. Samuel Daniel, for example, wrote plays like *Cleopatra* and *Philotas*, which were apparently never intended for the commercial stage, though the latter was eventually staged in unusual circumstances.[21] We do know that, even when the theatres were open, performances were sometimes given at private houses. Sir Edward Hoby invited Sir Robert Cecil to a performance of what is usually taken to be Shakespeare's *Richard II*, in December 1595: 'I am bold to send to know whether Tuesday may be any more in your grace to visit poor Canon Row where as late as it shall please you a gate for your supper shall be open: & K. Richard present himself to your view'.[22] There is no way of knowing, however, whether such performances were tailored, much less originally written, to meet the taste of such a host or his guests. Daniel wrote *Hymen's Triumph* in 1614, the first full-length play *known* to have been commissioned for an actual wedding, that of Lord Roxborough; although it must have required professional actors for its performance, there is no evidence of its having been performed subsequently in public, so it is a dubious analogue for *A Midsummer Night's Dream*. Daniel's occasional career as a dramatist in fact underlines the differences – the social gulf – between aristocratic entertainments and commercial drama rather than their similarities.

There is a modern instinct to resist the notion of Shakespeare's plays being conditioned by anything so arcane or elitist as the tastes of particular patrons. We commonly assume that success in his own time (like his later acclaim as a universal genius) depended upon cultivating the broadest possible audience. But the most successful members of his profession (and there can be no doubting that he was one of those) were intimately connected with the Court and the patronage of courtiers during his lifetime, in a relationship that intensified in the half century prior to the Civil War. Inevitably, therefore, he had links with both the old tradition of aristocratic patronage and the modern concept of free commercial enterprise. The examples of Lyly and Daniel are tantalising; they demonstrate that a market for élitist, closet or Court-orientated drama did exist throughout Shakespeare's career. But there is no evidence (apart from the equivocal nature of the plays themselves) to associate Shakespare with either the kinds of theatre or the kinds of dramatic patronage that these writers exploited. So it remains at every point a matter of interpretation or intuition to determine which weighed the more heavily with him – the interests of wealthy patrons or those of a broad-based public audience. There is scope, then, for explaining features of some of his plays in terms of veiled allusions to patrons, or of specially commissioned performances, but it is a limited one, always to be used with discretion.

If any of the early plays was indeed written for the Southampton circle, thus belonging alongside the narrative poems and possibly the sonnets, as part of the bid for Southampton's patronage, it would help to make more plausible one anecdote first recorded by Nicholas Rowe in 1709: 'There is one instance so singular in the magnificence of this patron of Shakespeare's, that if I had not been assured that the story was handed down by Sir William D'Avenant, who was probably very well acquainted with his affairs, I should not have ventured to have inserted, that my Lord Southampton, at one time, gave him a thousand pounds, to enable him to go through with a purchase which he heard he had a mind to'.[25] Rowe credited D'Avenant (self-styled bastard son of Shakespeare) more highly as a witness than we are likely to do, and the figure of a thousand pounds is absurdly high. But the substance of the story may be true, and the purchase Shakespeare 'had a mind to' may have been a stake in what was to become the most successful theatrical company of the era. Those who prefer the myth of the self-made man would perhaps rather assume that he bought it with something as valuable in its own way: the plays that he had written to date. These probably included the three parts of *Henry VI* and *Richard III*, *Titus Andronicus*, and the comedies, *The Comedy of Errors*, *The Taming of the Shrew* and *Two Gentlemen of Verona*. Their subsequent performance and printing histories suggest that they passed into the repertoire of the new company, the Lord Chamberlain's Men. Heminge and Condell certainly had access to them, presumably among the papers of the King's Men, for the production of the 1623 first folio. Which perhaps suggests that Shakespeare contrived somehow to hold on to them through all the dissolutions and amalgamations of companies (be it Leicester's, Queen's, Strange's, Pembroke's or Sussex's) with which he or they were associated. Given the context in which the new company started – with so many of their rivals dispersed, and with Marlowe, Kyd, Greene, Peele, Lodge and Lyly either dead or no longer writing for the stage – such a collection of plays would have been ideal collateral for a founding shareholder.

4

Servant to the Lord Chamberlain

Speculation as to Shakespeare's theatrical associations ceases on 15 March 1595, when the royal household accounts detail payments to William Shakespeare, William Kempe and Richard Burbage ('servants to the Lord Chamberlain') for the performance of two plays the previous Christmas season, before the Queen at Greenwich Palace. This tells us a good deal: not only was Shakespeare a member of the newly-formed Lord Chamberlain's Men (our earliest record is of them playing a short and unremunerative season for Philip Henslowe, in conjunction with the Lord Admiral's Men, at Newington Butts in June 1594) but he was a leading member, a joint payee in this important transaction, and therefore almost certainly already a shareholder. Kempe and Burbage (son of James) were respectively the leading comic and tragic actors of the troupe, and we may infer that Shakespeare enjoyed some seniority to be numbered with them. Kempe's career can be dated back at least as far as 1586, when he went as a travelling player with the Earl of Leicester on his expedition to the Low Countries; two of his fellows then, Thomas Pope and George Bryan were also members of the new company. All three are mentioned, along with two other notable Chamberlain's Men, John Heminge and Augustine Phillips, in a special licence to travel granted by the Privy Council to Lord Strange's Men in May 1593. Richard Burbage probably began performing in the mid-1580s, but the first roles to which we can confidently assign him are leading ones in the revival of a play called *The Second Part of the Seven Deadly Sins,* staged by Strange's Men or the Admiral's Men, or a combination of the troupes, some time between 1590 and 1592. Pope, Phillips and Bryan also had parts, as did other Chamberlain's conscripts, William Sly, John Duke and John Sincler. We look in vain for concrete evidence of Shakespeare's earlier associations with these men. But he was now to remain in partnership with Burbage for the rest of his career, and was to write some of his finest roles for him. Of the others probably there at the formation of the new company, Heminge and Henry Condell were also to remain throughout. Kempe departed from the company at the height of his fame.

The Lord Chamberlain who patronised the troupe was Henry Carey, Lord Hunsdon, a first cousin of the Queen; his office was one of the most senior in the royal household, carrying responsibility, among other things, for royal entertainments, including theatricals. He was thus an ideal choice of patron for the actors. His letter to the Lord Mayor of London on 8 October 1594, when the great plague had finally remitted, doubtless carried the weight virtually of a royal command:

> After my hearty commendations. Where my now company of players have been accustomed for the better exercise of their quality, & for the service of her Majesty if need so require, to play this winter time within the City at the Cross Keys in Gracious Street. These are to require and pray your Lo[rdship] (the time being such as, thanks be to God, there is now no danger of the sickness) to permit & suffer them so to do; the which I pray you the rather to do for that they have undertaken to me that, where heretofore they began not their plays till towards four a clock, they will now begin at two, & have done between four and five, and will not use any drums or trumpets at all for the calling of the people together, and shall be contributories to the poor of the parish where they play according to their abilities. And so not doubting of your willingness to yield hereunto, upon these reasonable conditions, I commit you to the Almighty.[1]

This letter suggests that Hunsdon's servants were doing their best to appear responsible citizens – finishing performances before sunset, not causing undue commotion and contributing a portion of their profits to the upkeep of the poor. Similar arrangements are reported elsewhere in the period. Hunsdon was already an old man when he became Shakespeare's patron, and he died in 1596. The troupe passed into the protection of his son, the second Lord Hunsdon, and were briefly known as Hunsdon's Men, until he attained his father's former office, and they were known again as the Lord Chamberlain's Men until the end of the reign. We know very little about relations between either of the Lords Hunsdon and their players, though we may surmise the theatrical interests of the elder from the fact that troupes had intermittently carried his name since 1564. He had also defended the actors, in the 1580s, against efforts by the city authorities to curtail their activities. The phrase 'my now company of players' suggests, however, that this was a new arrangement. The young Hunsdon, as we shall see, may have been involved in the Falstaff saga.

It says something for the 'early start' theory of Shakespeare's career that, when he finally emerges in the written record as one of the Lord Chamberlain's Men, he was in a position of some prominence and trust. As shareholder, actor and resident dramatist in the company he held three roles in a virtually unique combination that made him a complete man of the theatre.[2] It was his profits as a shareholder, pre-eminently, that were soon to make him a solid man of property. Being a shareholder, a permanent member of the troupe, distinguished him from some of the other actors, who would be hired and paid a weekly rate. There were about eight actor/shareholders at the inception of the Lord Chamberlain's Men, rising to twelve by the time they became the King's Men. And there must regularly have been three or four boys associated with the company, mainly to play women's parts, since actresses did not appear on English stages until the Restoration. The average play, however, required something like twenty actors, even allowing for the regular doubling of parts, which was a feature of Elizabethan performances. The hire of additional actors would be only one of the calls on the shareholders; they would also invest in items such as costumes, props and play-scripts. It should be noted, moreover, that the acting company *as such* never owned the theatres in which it performed; the hire of theatres was another expense to be off-set against income. Nevertheless, the rewards for a shareholder in a successful company were considerable, and this (over and above what he earned from writing his plays) must have been the basis of Shakespeare's considerable wealth.

We know very little about Shakespeare's achievements as an actor. Heminge and Condell dutifully placed him at the head of the list of 'the principal actors in all these plays' in the first folio, but that hardly constitutes evidence of his thespian abilities or even that he necessarily acted in *all* his own plays. Two not very reliable eighteenth-century reports credit him with the roles of Adam in *As You Like It* and the Ghost in *Hamlet* – old and dignified men, if not very substantial parts. Ben Jonson includes him prominently in the lists of the actors who played in his *Every Man*

In His Humour (1598) and *Sejanus* (1603), though not in *Every Man Out of His Humour* (1599). It has been deduced that he may have played Lorenzo Senior in the former[3] and, less certainly, Tiberius in the latter. The little and unreliable information we have would thus suggest that he was a character actor who favoured old men's roles, rather than a star performer. Modern speculation – noting that he might not therefore be too heavily taxed during rehearsals and that there was no such person as a director in the Elizabethan theatre – has hypothesised that Shakespeare would be naturally placed to act as what we might call an artistic co-ordinator for the company. But there is no evidence for this.

In their early days the new company played at a number of venues, including the unpopular Newington Butts south of the river and the Cross Keys inn-yard within the city. We might presume that, with a Burbage in the company, their preferred venue would be the Theatre, but we should not assume that they played there exclusively or to the exclusion of rivals. It is very likely that they sometimes played at the Curtain. Our knowledge of these early theatres is sketchy in the extreme. The following general description owes a good deal to the snippets we know about other early purpose-built public theatres besides the Theatre itself, including the Swan (1595), of which we possess a rough sketch. It seems reasonably safe to assume that they were not very different from each other in essentials.[4] The design of the Theatre seems to have been based on that of a bull- or bear-baiting pit, a large polygonal amphitheatre, appearing circular at a distance, and three storeys high.[5] The stage, which was attached to one of the inner walls, was raised to between waist- and head-height and jutted out into the central courtyard; it was covered by a canopy or 'heavens', supported by pillars, though the yard itself, where the lowest-paying groundlings stood, was open to the weather. Some, though not all, of these yards were paved, to help the drainage. Those able to pay more stood or (for even more money) sat in the stalls and galleries within the building itself, including the 'gentlemen's rooms', probably adjacent to the stage. Behind the stage was the tiring-house, containing the business offices of the company, their costumes and properties. Two broad doorways, which might be curtained if necessary, allowed access from the tiring-house on to the stage, which was quite large, probably not less than 40 feet broad and 25 feet deep. Some way above the doors, in the façade of the tiring-house and overlooking the stage, were a number of windows; some of these probably belonged to the 'Lords' room' or 'rooms', such as we hear of in later theatres, the most prestigious and doubtless most expensive of all the accommodation for spectators. Other windows allowed a limited upper playing area, sometimes used by the actors, sometimes by their musicians. These would have been used, for example, for 'balcony' scenes such as (to restrict ourselves to plays probably of this period) the ones in *Two Gentlemen of Verona* (IV.ii and iii.) and, most famous of all, *Romeo and Juliet* (II.ii.).

The actors thus played 'in the round', without scenery in a modern sense, though props could be brought on and off as required. What these might include is indicated by an inventory that Philip Henslowe made of his stock used by the Lord Admiral's Men at the Rose in 1598:

Item, 1 rock, 1 cage, 1 tomb, 1 hell-mouth.
Item, 1 tomb of Guido, 1 tomb of Dido, 1 bedstead.
Item, 8 lances, 1 pair of stairs for Phaeton.
Item, 2 steeples, & 1 chime of bells, & 1 beacon.
Item, 1 hecfor [heifer?] for the play of Phaeton, the limes [limbs?] dead.
Item, 1 globe, & 1 golden sceptre, 3 clobes [clubs?].
Item, 2 marchpanes [cakes?], & the city of Rome.
Item, 1 golden fleece; 2 rackets; 1 bay tree.
Item, 1 wooden hatchet; 1 leather hatchet.
Item, 1 wooden canopy; old Mahomet's head.
Item, 1 lion skin; 1 bear's skin, & Phaeton's limbs, & Phaeton chariot; & Argus's head.
Item, Nep[t]une's fork & garland.
Item, 1 crosier's staff; Kent's wooden leg.
Item, Jeros's (Iris's?) head, & rainbow; 1 little altar.
Item, 8 vizards; Tamburlaine's bridle; 1 wooden mattock.
Item, Cupid's bow, & quiver; the cloth of the Sun & Moon.
Item, 1 boar's head & Cerberus's 3 heads.
Item, 1 caduceus; 2 mossy banks, & 1 snake.
Item, 2 fans of feathers; Belendon stable; 1 tree of golden apples; Tantalus's tree; 9 iron targets.
Item, 1 copper target [shield], & 17 foils.
Item, 4 wooden targets; 1 greve [heavy?] armour.
Item, 1 sign for Mother Redcap; 1 buckler.

Item, Mercury's wings; Tasso's picture; 1 helmet with a dragon; 1 shield, with 3 lions; 1 elm bowl.

Item, 1 chain of dragons; 1 gilt spear.

Item, 2 coffins; 1 bull's head; and 1 vylter [philtre?].

Item, 3 tumbrils; 1 dragon in fostes [Faustus?].

Item, 1 lion; 2 lions' heads; 1 great horse with his legs; 1 sackbut.

Item, 1 wheel and frame in the siege of London.

Item, 1 pair of wrought gloves.

Item, 1 pope's mitre.

Item, 3 imperial crowns; 1 plain crown.

Item, 1 ghost's crown; 1 crown with a sun.

Item, 1 frame for the heading in Black Joan.

Item, 1 black dog.

Item, 1 caldron for the Jew.[6]

It is a motley collection of items, reflecting a good deal of fighting, mythological and fabulous subjects, animals, royal regalia, and a fascination with death (the tombs, coffins, hell-mouth etc.) Many items can be traced back to particular plays by Greene and Marlowe (e.g. the hell-mouth for *Dr Faustus*, Tamburlaine's bridle, the cauldron for *The Jew of Malta*) though doubtless they also came in for other productions. And the Lord Chamberlain's Men must have had many similar items. All the history plays, for example, would have required the foils, lances and 'targets', most of them a variety of crowns, and several of them prelates' mitres. Jonson was probably less than just in 1616 when he mockingly recalled how the actors would 'with three rusty swords, / And help of some few foot-and-half-foot words, / Fight over York, and Lancaster's long jars'.[7] *Romeo and Juliet* required 'swords and bucklers' and 'clubs, bills and partisans' for the early street fighting, 'visors' for the masked ball, a tomb for Juliet and (according to one early text) 'a mattock, and a crow of iron' to open it with. The same prop might have been used for 'old Ninny's tomb' in the ludicrous performance of 'Pyramus and Thisby' at the end of *A Midsummer Night's Dream*, Shakespeare's own playful parody of *Romeo and Juliet*: it is the only suggested prop that the 'rude mechanicals' do not impersonate themselves! Certainly, they needed a lion's skin for Snug the joiner to perform in, and earlier an ass's head for Bottom, and possibly a 'flow'ry bed' for Titania, similar to the 'mossy banks'. Perhaps Henslowe's 'black dog' was stuffed, but Shakespeare was able to call on the services of a live one for Launce's companion in *The*

Two Gentlemen of Verona. And for *Macbeth* the company obviously had a 'cauldron'.

With little in the way of fixed scenery, plays were performed without intermissions, scene succeeding scene fluidly. Audiences thus experienced the plays as a concatenation of relatively brief sequences, often arranged for pointed effects of comparisons or contrast. Many of the quarto texts of Shakespeare's plays were printed with no indication of divisions into either acts or scenes; the first folio provides act and scene divisions for some, but by no means all of the plays (there are none, for example, for *Troilus and Cressida* or *Antony and Cleopatra*), but these are often unsatisfactory and seem to be literary and publishing conventions in imitation of the Romans, rather than a reflection of theatrical practice. Jonson and others began a deliberate emulation of classical structures in their plays, which affected general printing habits, but it is questionable whether Shakespeare ever did so. It is just possible that, in some of his latest plays, the first folio act divisions reflect pauses in the action to allow for the inter-act music which was a feature of at least some Blackfriars performances, but the evidence is far from conclusive (see Chapter 9). The modern editorial habit of printing the plays with formal acts and scenes has its conveniences, but we should beware of assuming that it indicates anything either in Shakespeare's compositional method or in his original staging.

Almost all of the items in Henslowe's inventory were portable and designed to perform specific functions, rather than being merely for display, and the list reinforces the general belief that, on the whole, the words in the Elizabethan theatre took precedence over the spectacle. There were obviously some spectacular set-pieces and moments of high visual drama: the play of *Phaeton* clearly called for some elaborate props, and heaven only knows what 'the city of Rome' amounted to. Beheadings on stage (the 'frame for the heading in Black Joan') must have required complex apparatus – one was called for in *Sir Thomas More* and the King's Men performed one in Fletcher and Massinger's *Sir John Van Olden Barnavelt* (1619). Shakespeare himself kept such executions off-stage, though probably not out of squeamishness: severed heads are called for in *2 Henry VI*, *Richard III*, *Cymbeline* and *Macbeth*, and there was apparently an attempt at realistic gore in such scenes as the assassination in *Julius Caesar*. But if Henslowe's list reflects the total resources of the company in a flourishing period, elaborate and spectacular effects were hardly the stock-in-trade of the average production. We must remember, however, that the expensive costumes, on which we commented earlier, would have added to the visual splendour; audiences would have been particularly sensitive to this, since sumptuary laws were in force, restricting the finery that ordinary citizens might wear. The social gap between an actor, whom many would consider little better than a vagabond, and some of the roles he played might be very marked, and contemporaries frequently remarked upon it.

One of the sonnets (111) suggests that Shakespeare was sensitive to the social stigma attached to his profession:

> O, for my sake do you with Fortune chide,
> The guilty goddess of my harmful deeds,
> That did not better for my life provide
> Than public means which public manners breeds.
> Thence comes it that my name receives a brand;
> And almost thence my nature is subdued
> To what it works in, like the dyer's hand.

By 1596, however, he was in a position to improve his social standing. The Garter King of Arms granted his father, John Shakespeare, a coat of arms, with his shield: 'Gold, on a bend sables, a spear of the first steeled argent, and for his crest or cognizance a falcon, his wings displayed argent, standing on a wreath of his colours, supporting a spear gold, steeled as aforesaid, set upon a helmet with mantles and tassles as hath been accustomed . . .' The helmet would have had a closed visor, denoting the rank of gentleman, which the Shakespeares were now entitled to style themselves; during his father's lifetime, William should have 'differenced' his own shield with an addition, such as a 'label'. The arms were granted to the father as the eldest in the male line, but we may suspect that William arranged matters, being on the spot in London and, moreover, having the money which such a process would have entailed, while we know his father was in debt by this time. In Ben Jonson's *Every Man Out of His Humour*, the country buffoon Sogliardo, who is determined to 'be a gentleman, whatsoever it cost me', pays out £30 for his coat of arms and then is mocked with the motto, 'Not Without Mustard'. The Shakespeares appear to have adopted the motto, 'Non Sanz

Droict' – Not Without Right – so it is not impossible that Jonson
was mocking his rival's pretensions. However, since the Lord
Chamberlain's Men staged the play, it is hard to believe that it was
maliciously meant.[8] William Shakespeare also paid out a good deal
of money the following year to buy New Place, the second most
substantial house in Stratford. We cannot be sure how much, since
the £60 mentioned in the records is probably a legal fiction, under-
stating the case. The house would have been a solid investment
of capital, an addition to the one that we know (from his tax debts)
he owned around this time in Bishopsgate, probably not too far
from the Theatre. New Place offered ample accommodation for his
family and for Shakespeare himself on his returns home (Aubrey
records that he managed this once a year) and may also have had
the attraction of no lingering associations with his son: Hamnet
had died, aged eleven, in 1596. These investments in status
and property suggest that the Lord Chamberlain's Men were
prospering, and that Shakespeare was prospering with them.

Nevertheless, it remained a precarious business. In and around
1597 members of the company faced several distinct threats – to
the Theatre and to their livelihood over-all. In January James
Burbage died, leaving his interest in the Theatre to his sons,
Cuthbert and Richard. On 13 April his lease on the land where
the Theatre stood ran out, with no renewal agreed; the landlord,
Giles Allen, was demanding not only an increase in rent but also
that the building itself should become his property in the near
future. By the end of the year, if not before, the company would
seem to have transferred to the Curtain and in 1598 we hear of
'the unfrequented Theatre'.[9] When the Burbages got wind of
Allen's intention to pull down the playhouse they took resolute
action. Under cover of darkness on 28 December 1598, with a friend
and financial backer, William Smith, a chief carpenter, Peter Street,
and some dozen workmen, they 'did' (as Allen later protested, in
indignant legalese):

> riotously assemble themselves together and then and there
> armed themselves with divers and many unlawful and offensive
> weapons, as namely swords, daggers, bills, axes, and such like,
> and so armed did then repair unto the said Theatre. And then
> and there, armed as aforesaid, in very riotous, outrageous, and
> forcible manner, and contrary to the laws of your Highness's
> realm, attempted to pull down the said Theatre, whereupon

divers of your subjects, servants and farmers, then going about
in peaceable manner to procure them to desist from that their
unlawful enterprise, they, the said riotous persons aforesaid,
notwithstanding procured then therein with great violence, not
only then and there forcibly and riotously resisting your subjects,
servants and farmers, but also then and there pulling, breaking
and throwing down the said Theatre in very outrageous, violent
and riotous sort, to the great disturbance and terrifying not only
of your subjects, said servants and farmers, but of divers others
of your Majesty's loving subjects there near inhabiting.[10]

The 'pulling, breaking and throwing down' of the building cannot
have been too violent since this riotous bunch then proceeded to
ship the timbers across the Thames, to the Bankside, where they
were to be used in the erection of the company's new playhouse,
the Globe. Nor had the enterprise been unlawful, since the courts
found against Allen, who continued to file unsuccessful suits
against those involved for some time to come. It might be nice to
imagine Shakespeare himself involved in this derring-do, armed
to the teeth in the dead of night; but the absence of his name in
the subsequent litigation makes it unlikely.

That the Theatre was still standing for the Burbages to dismantle
it in this fashion is something of a surprise in the light of a Privy
Council order of 28 July 1597:

Her Majesty being informed that there are very great disorders
committed in the common playhouses both by lewd matters that
are handled on the stages and by resort and confluence of bad
people, hath given direction that not only no plays shall be used
within London or about the city or in any public place during
this time of summer, but that also those playhouses that are
erected and built only for such purposes shall be plucked down,
namely the Curtain and the Theatre near to Shoreditch or any
other within that county. These are therefore in her Majesty's
name to charge and command you that you take present order
there be no more plays used in any public place within three
miles of the city until All-Hallowtide next, and likewise that you
do send for the owners of the Curtain, Theatre or any other
common playhouse and enjoin them by virtue hereof forthwith
to pluck down quite the stages, galleries and rooms that are
made for people to stand in, and so to deface the same as they

may not be employed again to such use, which if they shall not speedily perform you shall advertise us, that order may be taken to see the same done according to her Majesty's pleasure and commandment . . .[11]

The reason for the order is a letter of that date, from the Lord Mayor and Alderman of London to the Privy Council earnestly requesting 'the present stay and final suppressing of . . . stage plays'.[12] It is less clear why the Privy Council should have acceded to this request, and so promptly, when they had declined in the past to do anything so drastic; nor do we know why, having issued so explicit an order, they failed to enforce it, but several explanations suggests themselves. The political situation is one. The Queen was nearly sixty-four, unmarried, with no children and no acknowledged heir. It was far from foreseeable that the eventual transfer of power would be peaceful, and the playhouses, as congregating-points for large numbers of persons, were a major threat to public order. Furthermore, the following February, Parliament was to pass even more stringent legislation to deal with the problem of vagrancy, which was increasing with the growth of London, and the theatres were inevitably a focal point for vagrants and other low-life characters. The same legislation specifically restricted professional acting to those who were servants of 'any Baron of this realm, or any other honourable Personage of greater degree', whereas previously troupes had been able to perform with a licence from local Justices of the Peace.[13] We may suspect, then, that the order for the plucking down of the playhouses was a precipitate solution to what was already seen as a problem, before the Lord Mayor's petition arrived.

But someone prevented it. Back in 1584, when the Privy Council nearly agreed to their suppression, old Lord Hunsdon had argued against it.[14] Perhaps it was his son, by now Lord Chamberlain in turn, who convinced his fellow Lords to think again this time. If so, he cannot have been very pleased at the way some of the actors promptly abused their reprieve, though he might have been relieved that it was not his own company that was involved. On August 1597, the Privy Council wrote to the Justices in Surrey: 'Upon information given us of a lewd play that was played in one of the playhouses on the Bankside, containing very seditious and slanderous matter, we caused some of the players to be apprehended and committed to prison, whereof one of them was not only an actor but a maker of part of the said play'.[15] The theatre was the newly-opened Swan, and they had chosen something racy to draw the crowds. The play, a political satire, was the, now lost, *Isle of Dogs,* written by Thomas Nashe – who fled when the controversy broke out – and Ben Jonson, the actor/part-maker who was arrested. This is the first official notice of Jonson in the theatre and sets exactly the right note for what was to come in the career of Shakespeare's most gifted rival – turbulent, antagonistic, constantly confronting authority in ways we never hear of the older man. Following the threatened eradication of the theatres, the crack down on *The Isle of Dogs* is the first move in what seems to have been a more intensive effort by the Privy Council over the next decade to control the theatres and what they staged. So far as we know, Shakespeare himself was never personally under suspicion, as Jonson (several times), Daniel, Chapman, Day and Marston were, but as we shall see his company was sometimes collectively under a cloud.

In the short run the *Isle of Dogs* affair and related moves to control the actors redounded to the advantage of the Lord Chamberlain's Men. At some time before 19 February 1598 they and the Lord Admiral's Men became – on paper, at least – the only two companies licensed to perform in and around London. We know this from letters sent by the Privy Council, confirming this exclusive privilege of the two companies and ordering the suppression of an unnamed third company which had been performing without a licence.[16] The letter reiterates the old justification for allowing the actors to perform commercially, that they were rehearsing for performances at Court. Restricted to these two companies there was more substance to the claim: from the resumption of playing in 1594 until 1599, the royal chamber accounts record that these were the only two companies to perform at Court. The Lord Chamberlain's Men gave performances there *every* festive season (that is, between Christmas Day and the end of February): two in 1594/5, five in 1595/6, six in 1596/7 (when the Lord Admiral's Men did not perform there at all), four in 1597/8, three in 1598/9 and again in 1599/1600. They were paid £10 per performance, a major contribution to their total income. It is logical to conclude that the concession to the two companies of monopoly status in the London area, complementing the monopoly they already enjoyed at Court, was a less drastic alternative to the total suppression of the theatres. Abolishing professional theatre around the capital altogether would have been unpopular, difficult to police, and perhaps counter-productive. It was surely more constructive to allow outlets for the drama, but to restrict them to two companies who were closely bound up with the Court and its interests, not only financially but through their patrons (both cousins of the Queen) and the close attentions of the Master of the Revels. In fact, these monopoly conditions did not last for very long. The second generation of 'private' theatres had opened up by early 1600, possibly in direct response to the limited theatrical entertainment in the growing city: they were not subject to these restrictions because of their privileged status as choir-schools. At the end of 1601 the Privy Council complained that the monopoly was not being enforced and that other companies were being allowed to perform.[17] The Earl of Derby's Men was apparently one of these, based at the Boar's Head playhouse; they were even accorded two performances at Court. By March 1602 the Earls of Oxford and Worcester prevailed to have a joint company of their players, which had taken over the Boar's Head, formally admitted to the monopoly.[18] But by then, the Lord Chamberlain's Men had established themselves as the most successful company of the era, a status they retained (as the King's Men) until the theatres were closed in 1642.

Although Shakespeare escaped the attentions of the Privy Council, it may not follow that his plays were without a pointed topicality, as the circumstances surrounding the creation of Sir John Falstaff suggest. In *1 Henry IV*, Falstaff was originally called Sir John Oldcastle, an actual historical person (c.1378–1417) who fought valiantly in Henry V's French wars but was executed for heresy as a Lollard or follower of John Wycliffe. We know this from several clues that survived revision before the play went into print, including a pun on 'my old lad of the castle' (I.ii.39). Even in *2 Henry IV* there is a residual speech-prefix of 'Old.' for 'Fal.' (I.ii.114); it must be doubtful if the Falstaff character in that play was ever performed under the name of Oldcastle, but the slip suggests how long the identification lingered in the mind of Shakespeare or of someone who transcribed his text. By the 1590s there were two traditions about Oldcastle: that of a brave martyr for a proto-Protestant faith, and that of a lying gluttonous coward; the latter was incorporated in the old *Famous Victories of Henry the Fifth*, one of Shakespeare's main sources for the low-life scenes in the *Henry IV* plays. There is no knowing whether it was deliberate or ill-considered of him to have followed this source so closely. Both plays were performed, to great applause and comment, possibly by early 1597.[19] After *1 Henry IV* had been staged, however, it appears that someone objected to the use of Oldcastle's name for Shakespeare's character, this disreputable cross between the traditional figures of Vice and the Braggart Soldier. In the Epilogue to *2 Henry IV*, printed in 1600 (though it must earlier have been spoken on stage without the disclaimer), Shakespeare denied that he had ever meant disrespect for the historical figure; he promised to bring back 'Sir John' in his projected play about Henry V in France: 'Where, for anything I know, Falstaff shall die of a sweat, unless already 'a be killed with your hard opinions, for Oldcastle died a martyr, and this is not the man' (25–8).

What made him change his mind? Oldcastle had died with the title of Lord Cobham. In 1596 the holder of that title was Sir William Brooke, who briefly succeeded the elder Lord Hunsdon as Lord Chamberlain; he might well have objected to the traducing of his ancestor's memory – an objection which, of course, would carry considerable weight. Or the complaint might have come later, from Sir William's son, Sir Henry, who was never Lord Chamberlain, but was a man of some political weight. His great rival, the Earl of Essex, wrote to Sir Robert Cecil in February 1598 asking him to tell their mutual friend, Sir Alex Ratcliff, that 'his sister is married to Sir John Falstaff' – a joke about a rumoured relationship between Cobham and Margaret Ratcliff. This suggests that, whether or not audiences originally identified either of the Cobhams with 'Oldcastle', they certainly identified the younger one with the character under his new name. The switch from 'Oldcastle' to 'Falstaff' had clearly been made by the date of the Essex letter, a fact confirmed by the entry of *1 Henry IV* in the Stationers' Register on 25 February 1598, mentioning the 'conceited mirth of Sir John Falstaff'. In changing the name, Shakespeare adopted that of a minor character who had appeared in his *1 Henry VI* (IV.i.9–47), where the hero Talbot stripped him of the Order of the Garter for his cowardice at Poitiers. The choice of a man with such associations is interesting in relation to the third Falstaff play (in which, again, the character was probably never called Oldcastle, though the Cobham association still reverberated), *The Merry Wives of Windsor*. This play is anomalous in several ways within the Shakespeare canon: it translates Sir John Falstaff and some of his cronies from their quasi-historical roles in the *Henry IV* plays into a tale of middle-class (would-be) cuckoldry, more akin to the satiric 'citizen comedies' of Chapman and Middleton than anything else he wrote. There is a tradition (though not recorded before Dennis and Rowe in the eighteenth century) that Queen Elizabeth herself commanded Shakespeare to write the play, showing Falstaff in love, and moreover that she demanded it in the space of two weeks. The 1602 quarto of the play more soberly confirms that it was acted both 'before her Majesty, and elsewhere'. This leaves us some scope to imagine a special, royal first performance. One context that would fit the bill is the feast of the Knights of the Garter, held annually on St George's Day, 23 April. This would accord with the Windsor setting of the play, the Garter Inn, and Mistress Quickly's speech as the Fairy Queen (a common fiction for Queen Elizabeth) to her 'fairies', in which she refers at length to the Garter Knights and their installation in St George's Chapel at Windsor Castle:

> The several chairs of order look you scour
> With juice of balm and every precious flower.
> Each fair instalment, coat, and several crest,
> With loyal blazon, evermore be blest! –
> And nightly, meadow-fairies, look you sing,
> Like to the Garter's compass, in a ring . . .
> . . . And 'Honi soit qui mal y pense' write
> In emerald tufts, flowers purple, blue, and white,
> Like sapphire, pearl, and rich embroidery,
> Buckled below fair knighthood's bending knee.
>   (V.v.59–70)

It may well be significant that, in casting round for a new name for his disreputable 'Oldcastle' character, he lighted upon that of a man he had earlier shown dishonourably stripped of the Order of the Garter.

The Garter feast in 1597 would have been a special one for the younger Lord Hunsdon, since he was elected then as one of five new Knights of the Garter. He had, moreover, been made Lord Chamberlain less than a month before (following the death of the elder Lord Cobham) and in that role would be in charge of the lavish festivities for the first time. Could the tradition of the play's hasty writing relate to Hundson's sudden decision, on receiving this appointment, to have his actors perform for the occasion a new play (or, more probably, a revised version of an old one) by their resident playwright, suitably slanted for the special audience and the known tastes of their royal host? The hypothesis is an attractive one as such things go; it explains some odd features of an unusual play, and has most things in its favour apart from proof. Does *The Merry Wives of Windsor* throw any light on the Oldcastle/Falstaff wrangle and its possible associations with the contemporary Lord Cobhams? The play almost certainly contains gibes directed at the Cobhams, in their family name of Brooke, of a kind not immediately apparent in the *Henry IV* plays. The jealous husband, Ford, disguises himself as a 'Master Brook' in order to discover what is going on between Falstaff and his wife, and the name is much belaboured:

> *Bardolph:* Sir John, there's one Master Brook below would fain speak with you, and be acquainted with you; and hath sent your worship a morning's draught of sack.
> *Falstaff:* Brook is his name?
> *Bardolph:* Ay, sir.
> *Falstaff:* Call him in . . . Such Brooks are welcome to me, that o'erflows such liquor.
>
> (II.ii.132-8, and *ff*)

That this was not accidental is confirmed by the first folio text, where the name was changed to Broom, spoiling all the puns about liquids, but removing the last offensive gesture towards the Cobhams. How would this have sounded at the 1597 Garter feast – the new Lord Chamberlain's players mocking the name of the late Lord Chamberlain, then barely cold in his grave? It is likely, of course, that there were sour grapes about the award of the Chamberlain's staff to Hunsdon; the younger Lord Cobham had hoped to succeed his own father, and there was no love lost between him and Shakespeare's patron. Possibly, under the direct protection of the new Lord Chamberlain, Shakespeare felt able to chide Brooke/Cobham about the whole Oldcastle controversy.

So much of this is and has to be conjecture – the dating and so much of the evidence is too insecure to allow of anything else. But, for once, there is an element of irreducible fact here: Falstaff was at some stage known as Oldcastle; was by 1598 identified in some minds with Henry Brooke, Lord Cobham; and was by 1600 explicitly dissociated in print from the historical Oldcastle. In connection with his latter point, it seems likely that the quarto publication of both the *Henry IV* plays – in unusually good texts, which must have been furnished by the Lord Chamberlain's Men, contrary to their normal practice – was an attempt to demonstrate their good faith to those concerned. There is no explaining, however, why Shakespeare failed to live up to his promise in the Epilogue to *2 Henry IV* to bring back Falstaff in *Henry V*. (All we get is Mistress Quickly's touching account of his death, II.iii.) Possibly by then the associations with Lord Cobham had become too dangerous to pursue. Or was Shakespeare just not able to breathe new life into the old man after three incarnations?[20] There are some who find even the Falstaff in *Merry Wives* a pale shadow of his old self. Perhaps there was simply no room for the incorrigible but all-too-human rogue in *Henry V*, that ambivalent hymn to national glory; he made room for Falstaff's less amiable colleagues, Ancient Pistol, Nym and Bardolph, only to have the last of these executed for stealing from a church (III.vi.) The whole Falstaff business intriguingly runs together questions of art and influence, patronage and topical allusion, religion and politics. It is true, as Ben Jonson put it, that 'nothing can be so innocently writ or carried, but may be made obnoxious to construction' (i.e. made subject to misconstruction). 'Application', he warned (the identification of characters in plays with real people), 'is now grown a trade with many, and there are that profess to have a key for the deciphering of everything; but let wise and noble persons take heed how they be too credulous, or give leave to these invading interpreters to be over-familiar with their fames, who cunningly, and often, utter their own virulent malice under other men's simplest meanings'.[21] But he was writing in the wake of nearly having suffered savage mutilation for what had, probably quite rightly, been 'deciphered' in *Eastward Ho*. Shakespeare may not have meant anything malicious in Oldcastle/Falstaff, but equally he may have courted 'applications'; the 'Brook' allusions in *Merry Wives* can hardly be accidental and *might* have incurred official wrath. It was always *potentially* a dangerous trade he was engaged in, however respectable he may have grown in the course of it.

While expenditure on the Elizabethan theatre always involved considerable risk – plague, fire or political action could wipe it out overnight – the building of the Globe in 1599 must have seemed to the Burbages and most of the principals of the Lord Chamberlain's Men (who were to become shareholders in the *playhouse*, as well as the company) a sensible way of capitalising on their special good fortune at that juncture, an investment for the future. Apart from the Burbage brothers (of whom Cuthbert was never an actor), five members of the troupe were involved in the financing, and hence profits, of the deal: Shakespeare, Heminge, Kempe, Thomas Pope and Augustine Phillips. The actors concerned arranged the terms of the syndicate in an attempt to ensure that only active participants in the whole enterprise should be involved: if a shareholder died or withdrew, his share would be redistributed among the survivors, and not to his legal heirs, though they would be compensated financially.[22] Thus, the size of an individual's share would fluctuate depending on the number of members left in the syndicate. The Burbages held larger shares than other members, reflecting a larger investment of capital, including the materials from the Theatre. Shakespeare initially had a one-tenth stake, going up to one-eighth when Kempe left, but going down again to one-twelfth when Condell and Sly were admitted (between 1605 and 1608) and down to one-fourteenth when William Ostler joined in 1612 (by which time, however, he also had a stake in the Blackfriars theatre, which was a separate matter). There is no knowing Shakespeare's total income from all sources - the acting company, writing plays, the theatres, latterly his investments in land and property. But even conservative estimates have put it, from this time, at around £200 in a plague-free year – ten times that of the Stratford schoolmaster.

What, then, do we know of the new theatre, around which Shakespeare's fortunes, and those of his fellows were principally to revolve for the next decade? The answer, as so often, is: not as much as we would like to.[23] It was built on the Bankside in the parish of St Saviour's, about one hundred and fifty yards from the Thames and a quarter of a mile west of London Bridge (then the only bridge across the river in London, though many playgoers chose to go by ferry). Our best information about the structure of the building comes from the surviving contract for the Fortune theatre which Henslowe and Alleyn hurriedly built for the Lord Admiral's Men in response to their rivals' splendid new edifice. The Lord Chamberlain's Men were presumably attracted to the Bankside by the earlier success of the Admiral's Men at the Rose.[24] Ironically, the popularity of the Globe seems to have convinced Henslowe and Alleyn not to build again in the same vicinity, and they went for a new location, north-west of the city, in Finsbury. But it is clear from their contract with Peter Street (the master carpenter employed by the Burbages) that they had the example of the Globe very much in mind. They several times referred to the rival structure as a model:

> the frame of the said house [is] to be set square and to contain fourscore foot [80] of lawful assize every way square without and fifty-five foot of like assize square every way within, with a good, sure and strong foundation of piles, brick, lime and sand both without and within, to be wrought one foot of assize at the least above the ground; and the said frame to contain three storeys in height, the first or lower storey to contain twelve foot of lawful assize in height, the second storey eleven foot of lawful assize in height, and the third or upper storey to contain nine foot of lawful assize in height; all which storeys shall contain twelve foot and a half of lawful assize in breadth throughout, besides a jutty forwards in either of the said two upper storeys of ten inches of lawful assize, with four convenient divisions for gentlemen's rooms, and other sufficient and convenient divisions for two penny rooms, with necessary seats to be placed and set, as well in those rooms as throughout all the rest of the galleries of the said house, and with suchlike stairs, conveyances and divisions without and within, as are made and contrived in and to the late erected playhouse on the Bank and in the said parish of St Saviour's called the Globe; with a stage and tiring-house to be made, erected and set up within the said frame, with a shadow or cover over the said stage . . . which stage shall contain in length forty and three foot of lawful assize and in breadth to extend to the middle of the yard of the said house; the same stage to be paled in below with good, strong and sufficient new oaken boards, and likewise the lower storey of the said frame withinside, and the same lower storey to be also laid over and fenced with strong iron pikes; and the said stage to be to be in all other proportions contrived and fashioned like unto the stage of the said playhouse called the Globe; with convenient windows and lights glazed to the said tiring-house; and the said frame, stage and staircases to be covered with tile, and to have a sufficient gutter of lead to carry and convey the water from the covering of the said stage to fall backwards; and also the said frame and the staircases thereof to be sufficiently enclosed without with lath, lime and hair [i.e. lath and plaster], and the gentlemen's rooms and two penny rooms to be sealed with lath,

lime and hair, and all the floors of the said galleries, storeys and stage to be boarded with good and sufficient new deal boards of the whole thickness, where need shall be; and the said house and other things beforementioned to be made and done to be in all other contrivitions, conveyances, fashions, thing and things effected, finished and done according to the manner and fashion of the said house called the Globe, saving only that all the principal and main posts of the said frame and stage forward shall be square and wrought pilasterwise, with carved proportions called satyrs to be placed and set on the top of every of the same posts, and saving also that the said Peter Street shall . . . also make all the said frame in every point for scantlings [builders' regulated measure] larger and bigger in assize than the scantlings of the timber of the said new erected house called the Globe.[25]

So it was eighty feet square on the outside, fifty-five feet square on the inside, rose three storeys to thirty-two feet above a brick-and-pile foundation, was built of wood, lath and plaster, and had a stage forty-three feet wide by twenty-seven feet six inches (if we take 'to the middle of the yard' literally). The contract leaves much unsaid, particularly about the disposition and facilities of the stage and the tiring-house. The only specified divergencies from the Globe are that the timbers shall be stouter and that the main posts shall be square and decorated with satyrs. The main difference is that the Fortune was to be square (following the inn-yard theatre model) where the Globe was round or, strictly, polygonal (like the animal-baiting pits). The circular shape of the latter is confirmed in the rough drawings of London from this period, and elsewhere. The Prologue to Jonson's *Every Man Out of His Humour*, which was performed there, refers to 'this thronged round', while a verse prefaced to his *Sejanus* mentions 'the Globe's fair ring'.[26] Parts of the Fortune (the stage 'heavens', galleries and staircases) were tiled; the roof of the Globe was improvidently thatched.

We can add a few details from other sources. Just as the Fortune had staircases 'without', pictures of the Globe suggest that it had two external staircases or stair-towers, which presumably allowed access to the upper galleries; we also hear of there being two general entrances to the theatre. It is perhaps reasonable to assume that the entrances were at the foot of the stair-towers, facilitating the process of paying for entry that Thomas Platter described.[27] The pictures also suggest that, above the tiring-house, there was a hut-like structure, but whether it had some functional role in the running of the theatre, or whether it was only used by trumpeters to announce a performance we do not know. The 'sign' of the theatre (an emblem on the building or on the flag that flew when there was a performance) was the figure of Hercules carrying the globe, with the motto *Totus mundus agit historionem* – 'All the world plays the player'.[28] We can also glean a good deal about the theatre from the plays (mostly by Shakespeare himself) which were written with performance there in mind. This is possible for the Globe, unlike earlier theatres with which he was associated, because from 1599 until 1608–9 (when they also started performing at the Blackfriars) it was the *only* permanent theatre at which the Lord Chamberlain's/King's Men performed. In June 1600, still keeping a tight rein on London theatricals, the Privy Council restricted the two 'allowed' companies to the use of one 'house' each, and since 'the servants of the L. Chamberlain, that are to play there [on the Bankside] have made choice of the house called the Globe, it is ordered that the said house and none other shall be there allowed'.[29] Of course, their plays were all 'portable' enough to be performed at Court and at other great halls and houses when necessary. But such information about stage practices as the texts from this period contain may with reasonable confidence be related to the Globe. Before we embark on this, however, it is time to consider in more detail the nature of Shakespeare's theatrical writing hitherto; this will be the subject of the next two chapters.

5

English Chronicle Histories

Although Shakespeare also wrote comedies from the start (see Chapter 6), his early theatrical reputation seems to have rested mainly on his English chronicle histories, a dramatic mode he largely pioneered.[1] Greene's taunt against the 'upstart crow' quoted from *3 Henry VI*; later in 1592 Thomas Nashe paid tribute to a scene from *1 Henry VI* (IV.vii):

> How would it have joyed brave Talbot (the terror of the French) to think that after he had lain two hundred years in his tomb he should triumph again on the stage, and have his bones new embalmed with the tears of ten thousand spectators at least (at several times) who, in the tragedian that represents his person, imagine they behold him fresh bleeding.
>
> (*Pierce Penniless*)

To call chronicle histories a clearly-defined genre would be over-stating the case. Early quartos of *Richard II* and *Richard III*, for example, described them both as tragedies, while the 1608 quarto of *King Lear*, which we classify confidently as a tragedy, called it a 'true chronicle history'.[2] But the term broadly identified a class of drama whose main preoccupation was the facts of history; and Heminge and Condell found it useful in their division of the first folio. A helpful, if not absolute, distinction is to think of 'chronicle histories' as plays in which the historical record had a determining influence on the shape of the drama, whereas other factors weighed more heavily in the design of tragedies.

There is scurrilous confirmation of Shakespeare's identification with this form of drama in the diary of John Manningham, a student at the Middle Temple, who recorded this anecdote in March 1602: 'Upon a time when Burbage played Richard III there was a citizen grew so far in liking with him, that before she went from the play she appointed him to come that night unto her by the name of Richard III. Shakespeare, overhearing their conclusion, went before, was entertained and at his game ere Burbage came.

Then message being brought that Richard III was at the door, Shakespeare caused return to be made that William the Conqueror was before Richard III'.[3] He carefully added the note, 'Shakespeare's name William', to ensure that he did not miss the point of the joke for later retellings. It is a pretty improbable scenario, reminiscent of the bed-tricks in *Measure for Measure* and *All's Well that Ends Well*, where one character secretly substitutes for another; these are often castigated for their implausibility. We should probably regard it as the kind of sexually-charged tittle-tattle that often attaches itself to people in glamorous professions. Manningham and his fellows probably had Shakespeare and Burbage on their minds, since the diary also records that the Lord Chamberlain's Men – presumably including its two luminaries – performed *Twelfth Night* at the Middle Temple only the month before. But whatever its factual basis, the anecdote does suggest the linking of Burbage and Shakespeare in the public mind, and focuses it on what was undoubtedly one of their early joint successes (probably antedating the formation of the Lord Chamberlain's Men), *Richard III.*

Let us therefore take this play as the starting point for an examination of Shakespeare's dramatic practice in this form. It was probably written after 1587, the date of the second edition of Raphael Holinshed's *Chronicles of England, Scotland and Ireland*, which was a principal source for *Richard III*, as it was for twelve other plays by Shakespeare, including not only the obvious English history plays, but also works as diverse as *King Lear, Macbeth* and *Cymbeline.*[4] It seems reasonable to assume that it was written after the three *Henry VI* plays, to which it is a fitting concluding-piece: Richard himself had figured in *2 & 3 Henry VI* as Duke of Gloucester, as had his brothers, King Edward IV and the Duke of Clarence; Queen Margaret, wife and latterly widow of Henry VI, figures in all four plays. *Richard III*, as a play, resolves all the threads of history in which these characters were involved. This would be appropriate for a play written as the last part of what modern critics call the first tetralogy (to distinguish it from the second tetralogy of *Richard II, 1 & 2 Henry IV* and *Henry V* – plays dealing with anterior history, but written later). 'Tetralogy' only means a sequence of four plays, and will mislead us if we take it to imply that the individual plays were conceived as part of a larger design. There is no evidence that they were ever performed or printed as a unit until modern times.[5] It is more likely that successive plays grew out of the success of their predecessors. So, for example, we can see the seeds of the Richard III character in *2 & 3 Henry VI*, but we do not need to refer to those earlier works to make sense of the memorable monster of the play that bears his name.

Elizabethan drama drew widely on earlier forms of theatre, both native and foreign. So, in creating a tryrant like Richard, Shakespeare inevitably drew on the archetypal tyrant of the medieval 'mystery' cycles, King Herod. And, in depicting a character so devoted to evil almost for its own sake ('I am determined to prove a villain', I.i.30), he naturally drew on the Vice of the old morality plays and interludes; indeed, Richard explicitly likens himself to the character: 'Thus, like the formal Vice, Iniquity, / I moralise two meanings in one word' (III.i.82–3). Shakespeare may also have been influenced by one or more of the plays of Marlowe, though the uncertainty of the dating makes it impossible to be sure. Richard is certainly a larger-than-life figure in the manner of Tamburlaine and is a type to which Marlowe reverted constantly (Barabas in *The Jew of Malta*, the Duc de Guise in *The Massacre at Paris*, Gaveston and Young Mortimer in *Edward II*): restless, ambitious, unscrupulous, amoral. A play which incorporates the ghoulish humour of ingenious deaths (Clarence), the gory frisson of severed heads (Hastings) and the shock effect of ghosts must owe something to Senecan revenge tragedy, the so-called 'theatre of blood', which had been domesticated in Thomas Kyd's *The Spanish Tragedy* (dated between 1586 and 1592) and to which Shakespeare himself contributed *Titus Andronicus*. Some flavour of the latter, a strong brew of family honour, intrigue, mutilation, rape and cannibalism, is captured in this stage direction: '*Enter the Empress' Sons with Lavinia, her hands cut off, and her tongue cut out, and ravished*' (beginning of II.iv.). It perhaps says something for the audience appeal of *Titus Andronicus* that it is the only play from the entire period of which we possess the sketch of a performance.[6] It depicts Tamora, the Queen of the Goths, kneeling and pleading for the life of her sons to Titus, who stands erect and proud; Aaron, the evil Moor, looks on. Titus wears quasi-Roman dress and carries a staff of office to match, while two attendant soldiers have conspicuously Elizabethan uniforms and halberds, an interesting and suggestive mixture. Although it is difficult to make either *The Spanish Tragedy* or *Titus Andronicus* work for modern audiences, scholars find a good deal to admire in the crude energy, passionate rhetoric and stage sense of these 'revenge' plays;[7] both were phenomenally popular at the time and frequently revived.[8] Most people would probably agree, however, that *Richard III* is more controlled and therefore more effective than either of them in its use of Senecan horror.

Other precedents notwithstanding, it is the Machiavel in Richard which makes the part – second only to Hamlet as the longest Shakespeare wrote – such a *tour-de-force*. The stage Machiavel is a ghoul who owes as much to theatrical history as he does to the doctrines of Niccolo Machiavelli, whose frank discussion of *realpolitik* was anathema to Christian moralists and luridly distorted by the popular dramatists.[9] Richard is not only a creature of blood and evil, but one of restless energy, intelligence and deviousness, a believer in his own ability to outwit all opposition unaided, who moreover shares this self-belief with the audience in frequent soliloquies and asides. And this makes him, in a perverse and dangerous way, an attractive character, for all the wickedness writ large in his hunched back and withered arm; it is the genuine sexual potency of the man, for example, that makes credible the otherwise unbelievable scene (I.ii) in which Richard successfully woos the Lady Anne, widow and daughter-in-law of men he has slain: 'Was ever woman in this humour wooed? / Was ever woman in this humour won?' (I.ii.227–8). So he crows to us, half-amazed at his own success. It may explain why Manningham's joke attached itself to Burbage in this part.

An issue which continually bedevils modern responses to *Richard III* is its accuracy or otherwise as *history*: apologists for Richard insist that he was neither hunchbacked nor Machiavellian (at least, no more so than other politicians of his time), nor responsible for many of the crimes that Shakespeare lays at his door, even (perhaps) the killing of the Princes in the Tower. In one sense, this is a red herring; the play ultimately stands as drama rather than as a factual record, and Shakespeare marshalled his material for the best *dramatic* effects. Nevertheless, it is apparent that Shakespeare himself was sensitive to the whole question of the 'truth' of history and confronted it in his plays. The issue arises at the heart of *Richard III* itself, when Richard and Buckingham are taking Prince Edward (i.e. Edward V) to the Tower of London:

> Pr Ed: I do not like the Tower, of any place.
> Did Julius Caesar build that place, my lord?

Buck:	He did, my gracious lord, begin that place,
	Which, since, succeeding ages have re-edified.
Pr Ed:	Is it upon record, or else reported
	Successively from age to age, he built it?
Buck:	Upon record, my gracious lord.
Pr Ed:	But say, my lord, it were not regist'red,
	Methinks the truth should live from age to age,
	As 'twere retailed to all posterity,
	Even to the general all-ending day.
Richard	[*aside*]:
	So wise so young, they say, do never live long.
Pr Ed:	What say you, uncle?
Richard:	I say, without characters fame lives long.

(III.i.68–81)

The 'general all-ending day' is the Day of Judgment promised in Revelation, the end of the Christian providential pattern of history; 'characters' are written records. The Prince places a trust in written records – assuming that, if they existed, they would tell the truth – which cannot but seem ironic in the context of the systematically chronicled character assassination of Richard III which culminates in this play. Similarly, his assertion that the truth *'should'* survive to the end of time by word of mouth alone is a masterpiece of ambiguity. At the Day of Judgment all the records will be complete, truthful and known to all. There is no knowing if Shakespeare is here obliquely questioning the trustworthiness of the chronicles of Richard III he is himself following, but Richard's 'without characters fame lives long' is an onion with endless layers of irony. The spoken word is shown in all its treachery in *2 Henry IV*, which opens with Rumour, *'painted full of tongues'*, 'stuffing the ears of men with false reports' (Induction, 1.8) – in fact, spreading the news that the rebels have won the Battle of Shrewsbury, which those who know *1 Henry IV* are aware is not true.

Since the historical record, be it written or spoken, was so unreliable, Shakespeare may have felt that he need make no excuses for adjusting it himself on occasions; he seems usually to have done so for dramatic effect rather than to alter the general import of the chronicles. One obvious example is the presence of Queen Margaret in *Richard III*. In reality she was in France during the early events depicted in the play, and dead before some of the later ones, but Shakespeare finds her useful as an all-embracing reminder of Richard's bloody progress towards the crown and uses her, not altogether subtly, as a chorus to the action. In the latter half of the play he conflates a number of rebellions against Richard together and omits all mention of the Earl of Richmond's first, abortive, expedition against him. Such adjustments (similar ones can be found in all the English histories) are obviously necessary if the play is not to degenerate into a shapeless unravelling of plots, intrigues and campaigns. But they can never be *entirely* neutral in their effect. Here, for example, they stress the inevitability of its being Richmond who overthrows Richard.

And Shakespeare was not above making simple *mistakes* in transforming his sources. In one scene (II.i.53–74) Richard pretends to make his peace with all present; these include Lord Rivers, Lord Woodville and Lord Scales, each of whom he addresses individually. Had Shakespeare read his source, in Edward Hall, more closely, he would have realised that they were all the same person.[10] But it was almost certainly not a mistake that prompted him to the most famous 'adjustment' of his sources in the history plays, that of making Hotspur (Sir Harry Percy) about the same age as young Prince Hal. This begins in *Richard II*, where his father, the Earl of Northumberland, addresses him as 'boy' (II.iii.36), though he was in fact older than Hal's father, Bolingbroke, to whom he is here being introduced; and it continues through *1 Henry IV*. Shakespeare obviously disregards the fact that Hotspur was twenty-two years older than Hal, and had at one time been his guardian, because he wishes to emphasise the dramatic contrast between the two men: Hotspur is a warrior, rash and ever anxious 'To pluck bright honour from the pale-faced moon' (*1 Henry IV*, I.iii.202), while Hal *appears* to be a wastrel, spending his time in the taverns and stews (brothels) of Eastcheap, where he is only likely to hear Falstaff's cynical 'catechism' on the subject of honour (V.i.127–39). The contrast makes the confrontation between the two men at the battle of Shrewsbury a fitting climax to *1 Henry IV*. It may not be true to the facts in the chronicles, but it is true in a symbolic way to the history of Prince Hal, which in many ways is the central subject of that play.

The (un)reliability of dramatised history is also an issue that lies behind Cleopatra's decision to commit suicide. She shudders at the prospect of seeing herself traduced on the stage:

> The quick comedians
> Extemporally will stage us, and present
> Our Alexandrian revels: Antony
> Shall be brought drunken forth, and I shall see
> Some squeaking Cleopatra boy my greatness
> I'th' posture of a whore.
>
> (V.ii.216–21)

It is a moment of extreme self-consciousness in the theatre, since what Cleopatra fears is exactly what we have seen in Shakespeare's play – a drunken Antony and a capricious minx of a Cleopatra, who would have been played by a boy ('squeaking') at the Globe. In one sense, therefore, what Cleopatra fears seeing is the truth about herself – the stage being too accurate a mirror to nature. On the other hand, if we look at the world as she at least sometimes seems to do, she may be right to see this as a travesty. In resolving to kill herself, she orders: 'Show me, my women, like a queen: go fetch / My best attires. I am again for Cydnus, / To meet Mark Antony' (227–9). She plays her final scene as the god-like royalty which, for all their palpable human weaknesses, Antony and Cleopatra see in each other and which Shakespeare flickeringly shows to us too, most famously in Enobarbus's description of their meeting at Cydnus: 'The barge she sat in, like a burnished throne, / Burned on the water . . .' (II.ii.187–241). The fascination of Shakespeare's play has a lot to do with its capacity to show both sides of this famous romance – Antony drunken and Cleopatra whorish, yet at the same time beings above such things, incarnations of Mars and Venus. So what Cleopatra fears from 'the quick comedians' is both the truth and yet not the truth, at least not *her* truth and so not the whole truth.

So Shakespeare was aware that all history – the spoken word, the written chronicle, on the stage itself – could tell lies. And he was conscious that, however faithfully he might try to follow the facts as he found them in his sources, the medium itself might distort reality. The Prologue and Chorus of *Henry V* return to this theme repeatedly:

> O for a Muse of fire, that would ascend
> The brightest heaven of invention;

A kingdom for a stage, princes to act
And monarchs to behold the swelling scene!
(Prologue, 1–4)

The 'wooden O' (1.13) of the theatre itself belittles the grandiose scale of the subject, laying the whole conception open to Jonson's scorn.[11] But one of the differences between Shakespeare and Jonson as dramatists was their view of the audience and its role in bringing the plays to life. Jonson constantly appeals to the 'understanders', to the 'judging spectators', looking for an informed critical response. Shakespeare, here and elsewhere, appeals not for critical judgement but for imagination, which can overcome the inadequacies of the theatre, the actors and his own poetry: 'let us, ciphers to this great accompt, / On your imaginary forces work' (Prologue, 17–18); 'Still be kind, / And eke out our performance with your mind' (Chorus to Act III, 34–5).

None of this, however, exactly answers the specific problems posed by *Richard III*. However much we respond to the call to 'piece out our imperfections with your thoughts' (Prologue to *Henry V*, 1.23), the resulting 'history' poses problems. None of the 'distortions' which cause modern disquiet arise from the dramatic adaptation, simple errors or problems created by the medium; they are all present in the sources which Shakespeare followed and are not of his own invention. The psychological portrait of Richard in the play is a faithful transcript of the one we find in Holinshed's *Chronicles*, reinforced and padded out with details from other histories which he consulted, such as that of Edward Hall (1548); this in turn derives from a more subtle artist than Holinshed himself, Sir Thomas More, whose incomplete life of Richard III is incorporated into both Holinshed and Hall, essentially unaltered. It offers a penetrating but far from impartial picture of the man:

As he was little of stature, so was he of body greatly deformed, the one shoulder higher than the other, his face small but his countenance was cruel, and such, that a man at the first aspect would judge it to savour and smell of malice, fraud and deceit: when he stood musing, he would bite and chew busily his nether lip; as who said, that his fierce nature in his cruel body always chafed, stirred, and was ever unquiet: beside that, the dagger that he wore he would, when he studied, with his hand pluck up and down in the sheath to the midst, never drawing it fully out: his wit was pregnant, quick and ready, wily to feign, and apt to dissimul[at]e.[13]

Already here are the key features of Shakespeare's version: wit, restlessness and dissembling, spiced with suggestions of something inhuman, something devilish. It seems that something of this passage was translated into Burbage's performance even though details are not incorporated in the play. Samuel Rowlands, probably thinking of Shakespeare's play, described 'gallants' who would 'like Richard the usurper, swagger, / That had his hand continual on his dagger'.[14] Shakespeare tells us that Richard had a dagger (III.i.110) but says nothing about this characteristic habit; he presumably passed on the idea to Burbage in rehearsal.

Sir Thomas More's prejudice can be traced to the fact that he spent some of his youth in the household of Cardinal Morton (the Bishop of Ely in Shakespeare's play) who was an opponent of Richard. But that does not account for the unanimity with which later chronicles like Hall, Holinshed and Shakespeare himself subscribed to More's version of the man and events. The fact is that this version was politically acceptable both to More's master, Henry VIII, and to all his children, including Queen Elizabeth. The reason is not hard to find: the Earl of Richmond who defeated Richard at Bosworth was Henry Tudor who, as Henry VII, started the Tudor dynasty. In reality his claim to the throne was not the strongest possible, but he prospered and encouraged the idea of a strong and stable monarchy as a necessary defence against the chaos and carnage of the Wars of the Roses which had preceded him, culminating in the tyranny of Richard III. Not unnaturally, his successors did their best to keep the idea alive. Shakespeare's *Richard III* is thus suspect in its apparent subscription to what is often called 'the Tudor myth of history'; it is propaganda rather than history. The accusation is difficult to refute, but needs to be put into context.

Firstly, there is no question of Shakespeare having been *commissioned* by the government or its supporters to write the play as it is. There is some evidence that the authorities might occasionally encourage plays on particular themes, to influence public opinion, but this would be on matters of immediate moment rather than broad propaganda support for the regime. Similarly, we should not assume that censorship forced Shakespeare to write in this way on this theme. Elizabethan political censorship could certainly be very strict,[15] but it would probably be a mistake to think of it as ideologically rigorous in ways that we know it to be in, say, Eastern European countries today – except in matters of religion (a concern which partly explains why the censorship of printed books was in the hands of the Archbishop of Canterbury and the Bishop of London). In other respects its main aim was to eliminate material that was critical or defamatory of those in power, or questioned their prerogatives. Thus, for example, when John Stubbs surreptitiously distributed *The Discovery of a Gaping Gulf* (1579), puritanically denouncing Elizabeth's apparent intention to marry the Duc d'Alençon, he and his publisher paid for it with their right hands.[16] And the government ruthlessly suppressed the unlicensed, Presbyterian-inspired 'Martin Marprelate' satires that attacked the hierarchy of the Church of England in 1588–89. But the system could be remarkably tolerant of matters which, while potentially controversial, were not seen as a direct threat to the current regime. For example, although the authorities kept an eye on Christopher Marlowe and his activities, there is no evidence that his *plays* were ever tampered with. As we have seen, the evidence to be derived from *Sir Thomas More* is inconclusive, but the very fact that a serious attempt was made to write a play about a man who resisted Queen Elizabeth's father and died a Catholic martyr points to the possibility that Shakespeare *could* have offered a more sympathetic account of Richard III, had he felt so inclined, with reasonable expectations of its being performed. Sir George Buc himself, the Master of the Revels who was responsible for censoring and licensing the last of Shakespeare's plays, wrote a history of Richard III, praising him as a virtuous and much maligned prince.[17] That was, admittedly, in the reign of James I, a generation after Shakespeare's play, when matters might have been seen differently. But James's claim to the English throne (stemming from Margaret, daughter of Henry VII) depended every bit as much as did Elizabeth's on the legitimate deposition of the last Plantagenet.

So censorship alone does not explain the consistent vilification of Richard III in the sixteenth century, to which Shakespeare broadly subscribed. To challenge this would, in Shakespeare's case, have been to fly in the face of what by then was a popular myth and, moreover, to have rejected what, as we have seen, was an outstanding ready-made dramatic character. It would also, in all probability, have reduced what we may call the providential dimension of the story, which there is some reason for supposing would have attracted Shakespeare quite apart from its convenience in terms of the 'Tudor myth'. It was the Italian historian, Polydore Vergil, whose *History* (1534) offered the most sophisticated view of recent English history as a divinely-ordained process of sin (the deposition and murder of Richard II, the last legitimate Plantagenet king), expiation (the interminable warfare of the fifteenth century, culminating in the tyranny of Richard III) and redemption (the accession of the Tudors and their unification of the Houses of York and Lancaster). This work was commissioned by Henry VIII himself as a justification of the Tudor dynasty; Vergil blackened Richard's name with several crimes not hitherto attributed to him, though he tried to protect his integrity as historian by noting that these were all a matter of rumour or hearsay. Vergil's providential patterning of events is reflected, though with less sophistication, in the later chronicles of Hall and Holinshed, and it echoes, as we shall see, throughout Shakespeare's two tetralogies of English history plays.

The idea of a providential patterning of human affairs is one that recurs time and again in every kind of play that Shakespeare wrote, often completely divorced from contemporary political implications. In the romantic comedies it is the heroines, in particular, who tend to recognise time as a redemptive force that will do more to resolve men's difficulties that their own efforts. As Viola puts it in *Twelfth Night*: 'O Time, thou must untangle this, not I' (II.ii.39). Faced with the possibility of treachery in the duel, Hamlet insists: 'We defy augury. There is a special providence in the fall of a sparrow. If it be now, 'tis not to come; if it be not to come, it will be now; if it be not now, yet it will come. The readiness is all' (V.ii.208–11). *Macbeth* is a play of prophecies misunderstood and yet fulfilled. The late tragi-comedies are pre-eminently concerned with characters driven by forces which they do not understand and over which they have no control;[18] these forces bring misery, confusion and even death but at times seem concerned for men's greater good, as Gonzalo enthuses in *The Tempest* (see p. 147). People have tried to read into such instances Shakespeare's belief in fate, destiny or – in a Christian context – providence. But the evidence is at best equivocal. He also suggests that people can put too much faith in such beliefs, particularly when they use them to justify their actions. Edmund in *King Lear* mocks Gloucester's belief in supernatural portents: 'An admirable evasion of whoremaster man, to lay his goatish disposition on the charge of a star' (I.ii.122–4). Lest we think the opinion of a self-confessed villain is to be discounted easily, we also have the example of Albany's over-facile belief in providential justice: 'This shows you are above, / You justicers, that these our nether crimes / So speedily can avenge' (IV.ii.78–80) is his reaction hearing the circumstances of Cornwall's death – a reaction which is hardly adequate to the deaths of Lear and Cordelia that follow. Lines taken out of context often lose the reservations with which they are hedged in the text. Brutus's famous lines about a 'tide in the affairs of men / Which, taken at the flood, leads on to fortune' (*Julius Caesar*, IV.iii.218–9) occur as he self-importantly overrules Cassius and insists that they march to Philippi, where the 'tide' turns disastrously against their cause. Gonzalo's ecstatic lines ignore the treacherous Antonio and Sebastian, who have mocked him before for his sententious optimism and show no sign of reforming contritely to suit Prospero's 'miracle'.

It is perhaps safer not to try to reduce such matters to a consistent philosophy on Shakespeare's part but to observe simply how often his drama reverts to situations where individuals are caught up in events at the limits of their free and purposeful action. Such situations often underlie the famous occasions where Shakespeare invokes the image of the actor (the man performing a role written by someone else) as a metaphor of human experience. Everyone knows, for example, Jaques's lines in *As You Like It*: 'All the world's a stage, / And all the men and women merely players . . .' (II.vii.139 *ff*) and Macbeth's harrowing image in the 'Tomorrow, and tomorrow, and tomorrow' soliloquy of life as 'a poor player / That struts and frets his hour upon the stage / And then is heard no more' (V.v.24–6).[19] We should not fall into the simple trap of assuming that lines so often quoted necessarily reflect Shakespeare's own thinking. Jacques's pose as the melancholic philosopher has a good deal of affectation about it, and the end of his speech (the seventh age of man as 'second childishness and mere oblivion, / Sans teeth, sans eyes, sans taste, sans everything') is directly challenged by the entrance at that point of Orlando carrying faithful old Adam. Macbeth, of course, is speaking as a man unmoved by news of his own wife's death, staring despair in the face. The important thing is that the issue of fate or providence clearly fascinated Shakespeare, whatever he made of it philosophically or religiously. We may, therefore, suspect that it was this, as much as the contemporary political implications of the 'Tudor myth of history', that drew him to the 'providential' patterns in his English history tetralogies.

If these patterns may be said to culminate in *Richard III*, they undoubtedly originate in the events depicted in a play written later (c.1595), *Richard II*. The deposition of Richard II by Henry Bolingbroke, Henry IV, and later his murder by Henry's followers, are events of great consequence. Richard II is depicted as a vain and capricious king, who indulges himself and his favourites at the expense of the country, with results graphically outlined in John of Gaunt's famous death-bed speech: 'This royal throne of kings, this sceptr'd isle . . .' (II.i.31–68). He is, nevertheless, the 'deputy elected by the Lord' and 'Not all the water in the rough rude sea / Can wash the balm off from an anointed king' (III.ii.57; 54–5). From the Tudor point of view, as expressed most centrally in the homilies, it was the subjects' duty to serve whomever God had placed in sovereignty over them. We are all fallen beings, heirs of Adam and Eve's original sin, and so need to be kept in order by kings and their ministers. If God sends us a weak or evil monarch, it is punishment for our sins and to be suffered with patience (a prime Tudor virtue, in all spheres); such a monarch will find retribution in heaven and should not be resisted on earth – a compelling, self-justifying and, from a ruler's point of view, very comfortable doctrine. So the deposition of Richard is a moment of high drama in the play, a moment when the role of king and the only legitimate actor of that role are divorced; it was so politically sensitive that the texts published in Elizabeth's lifetime (one in 1597, two in 1598) were not allowed to print the scene (IV.i.154–318).[20] It is an interesting reflection on the priorities of the censors both that they allowed the play to be printed at all and that, while they cut the deposition, they allowed the murder itself to stand. That has palpable overtones of a martyrdom about it. The combined deposition and murder amount to a Second Fall for England, a theme expressly introduced in a scene (III.iv) where the gardeners ('Thou old Adam's likeness, set to dress this garden') compare their husbandry to the ruling of the kingdom. The scene exemplifies an underlying principle of construction in any Shakespeare play: sequences are arranged so as to invite us to compare one scene with another. Here the symbolism is obvious, since the scene is an interlude, barely contributing to the narrative thrust of the play as a whole; in more mature plays the process of parallelism is more fluently integrated *within* the narrative structure.

Prior to the deposition, the Bishop of Carlisle warns what the 'Second Fall' will amount to, if Bolingbroke usurps the throne:

> if you crown him, let me prophesy,
> The blood of English shall manure the ground
> And future ages groan for this foul act;
> Peace shall go sleep with Turks and infidels,
> And in this seat of peace tumultuous wars
> Shall kin with kin and kind with kind confound . . .
>   (IV.i.136–41)

This is exactly what happens, in the Wars of the Roses, as depicted in the first tetralogy. But the threat of its happening hangs over the second tetralogy. Henry IV is a more business-like king than Richard II, but his reign is beset with troubles, not only rebellion but the apparent unfitness of his heir, Prince Hal, for the crown. Henry vows to make a pilgrimage to Jerusalem to expiate the guilt of Richard's murder, but the cares of office never allow him to undertake it. This is ironically underlined by his death in the Jerusalem Chamber at Westminster. Even when Hal proves, against appearances, to be the great warrior king, Henry V, he cannot shake off the threat of divine retribution for his father's acts. His determination to lay the responsibility or blame for all his actions – on the Church, on those who plot against him, on the citizens of Harfleur, above all on the French Dauphin – may be seen as the fundamental insecurity of a man who, despite the talents for leadership he has fostered in an apparently mis-spent youth with Falstaff, has no divine sanction for the office he holds. Before his great triumph at Agincourt, Henry prays desperately:

> Not to-day, O Lord,
> O, not to-day, think not upon the fault
> My father made in compassing the crown!
> [He lists the pious works he has done in Richard's name.]
>   More will I do:
> Though all that I can do is nothing worth,
> Since that my penitence comes after all,
> Imploring pardon.
>   (IV.i.278–80; 289–92)

It is a moment reminiscent of the great tragedies, when the most resourceful of men recognises his impotence in the face of an inscrutable providence – a theme which, as I have suggested, Shakespeare was to explore repeatedly. In this instance, providence smiles on his efforts, but the play's Epilogue puts the short-lived triumph in a sobering context:

> Henry the Sixth, in infant bands crowned King
>   Of France and England, did this king succeed;
> Whose state so many had the managing
>   That they lost France and made his England bleed:
> Which oft our stage hath shown . . .
>
> (9–13)

And so we come full circle to *Richard III*, which we can now see not only as the nemesis of an individual but as the final working out of a providential process. The accession of Henry VII represents not only the replacement of an evil king by a good one but, by implication, the restoration of legitimacy to the English royal line. In dramatic terms, however, the emphasis is rather different. Richmond is always something of a cipher, never explored sufficiently to give him the real force of a personality. What we observe is less his victory that the disintegration of the apparently all-powerful Richard. The self-confidence of stage Machiavels is almost always misplaced; though cynically clear-sighted about other people's weaknesses, they prove to be blinkered about their own. In Richard's case, his career is like that of a rocket, gloriously powerful at the outset, but pulled to destruction by the inexorable laws of gravity. The turning point is his over-confident decision to do away with Buckingham, the man who had helped him to the throne. Thereafter he is never the force that he was. As a king, he is beset by worries of rebellion; as a man, he is haunted by a conscience he had earlier failed to acknowledge, so that by the time Richmond comes to claim the throne in the name of God, Richard is already a spent force. His famous death on the battlefield at Bosworth – 'A horse! a horse! my kingdom for a horse' (V.iv.7 and 13) – contrasts completely with the assurance of the man at the beginning of the play. The claim of the Machiavel to self-sufficiency, the ability to control his own destiny, is cruelly exposed as a sham. Later in his career Shakespeare was to explore almost

identical territory in *Macbeth*, where another usurping king and
tyrant struggles both with providence and with the disintegration
of his own personality; the difference is that he allows us to follow
the psychological process from within, almost to sympathise with
Macbeth, with an intimacy that the *grand guignol* style of *Richard
III* precludes.

Not until the end of his career did Shakespeare carry his account
of English history beyond Henry VII. After *Richard III* he reverted
to the earlier events depicted in the second tetralogy; these
concluded with *Henry V* (1599) and thereafter he abandoned the
English chronicle history play – though not the subject of history.
Apart from his Greek and Roman plays, he mined the quasi-
mythological history of 'Britain' for *King Lear* and *Cymbeline* and
the medieval history of Scotland for *Macbeth*. But he did not write
about 'modern' English history again until *Henry VIII*, which was
playing when the Globe burned down in 1613, under the more
cryptic title *All is True*.[21] That better befits its mode, which is that
of the late tragi-comedies rather than of the chronicle histories. In
keeping with the mysticism of those late works, the theme of
providence looms larger than ever, with an application to Shakespeare's own time that cannot be ignored. Archbishop Cranmer talks
prophetically over the baby who was to be Queen Elizabeth:

> She shall be
> (But few now living can behold that goodness)
> A pattern to all princes living with her
> And all that shall succeed . . .
> . . . In her days every man shall eat in safety
> Under his own vine what he plants, and sing
> The merry songs of peace to all his neighbours . . .
> . . . Nor shall this peace sleep with her; but as when
> The bird of wonder dies, the maiden phoenix,
> Her ashes new create another heir
> As great in admiration as herself,
> So shall she leave her blessedness to one
> (When heaven shall call her from this cloud of
> darkness)
> Who from the sacred ashes of her honour
> Shall starlike rise, as great in fame as she was,
> And so stand fixed.
>   (V.v.20–47)

The Tudor myth expands to incorporate Elizabeth's Stuart successor, in an act of calculated flattery. At some essential level for Shakespeare history doubtless was the working of God's will through men's lives. But he was well aware that life is indeed a 'cloud of darkness' and that what passes with men for history – the written and oral record – is too incomplete, if not also too distorted by the limited vision of those who create it, ever to be read at so absolute a level.

6

Sly's Dream – Romantic Comedy

The Comedy of Errors is probably amongst the earliest of Shakespeare's comedies. It is one of the slightest of his works, plumbing few depths either of characterisation or of thought, though it is great fun in the theatre, which perhaps suggests a young dramatist who knew something of his trade but as yet had little to say. It was certainly written by the Christmas season of 1594, when it was put on as part of the annual 'law-revels' at Gray's Inn; the performers were professional and may well have been the newly-formed Lord Chamberlain's Men. As an eye-witness records, in the *Gesta Grayorum*, the evening was a shambles; it was the first entertainment there after the plague and far too many people turned up. The guest of honour was so disgusted by the chaos that he and his train left before the play:

> After their departure the throngs and tumults did somewhat cease, although so much of them continued, as was able to disorder and confound any good inventions whatsoever. In regard whereof, as also for that the sports intended were especially for the gracing of the Templarians, it was thought good not to offer anything of account, saving dancing and revelling with gentlewomen; and after such sports, a *Comedy of Errors* (like to Plautus his *Menechmus*) was played by the players. So that night was begun, and continued to the end, in nothing but confusion and errors; whereupon, it was ever afterwards called, *The Night of Errors*'.[1]

This speaks volumes about the social and artistic status of a theatrical performace, and about the professionalism of the players who were able to go on under such conditions (which seem not to have been uncommon, even at Court or within the theatres). It is also striking that the writer spotted that the play was based on Plautus's *Menaechmi*, a comedy of mistaken identity centring on a

88

pair of twins – Renaissance lawyers knew their Latin comedies. He may also have realised that Shakespeare's major adaptation of the plot, doubling the confusion by adding twin servants to twin masters, was not pure invention either, but derived from Plautus's most popular play, the *Amphitruo*. Shakespeare, like most of his fellow dramatists, rarely *invented* plots, even when free of the constraints of historical sources: his skill lay in reworking existing plot-lines.

The choice of Plautus's plays as the basis for this comedy tells us something about Shakespeare's conception of the theatrical experience. Jonson told William Drummond that he 'had an intention to have made a play like Plautus' *Amphitrio*, but left it off, for that he could never find two so like others that he could persuade the spectators they were one' (427–30). Clearly this problem did not bother Shakespeare, who was again to exploit the mistaken identity of twins, Viola and Sebastian, in *Twelfth Night*. He was prepared to allow the audience's predisposition to believe to carry the inadequacies of make-up or disguise (which may have been considerable in the latter case, with Viola being played by a boy) in a way that Jonson would never sanction. Jonson always insisted upon realism in his drama: not a realism based on three-dimensional scenery, which did not exist on the Elizabethan stage, but one that kept character, action and setting within common-sense bounds of what was possible or likely. *The Alchemist* might develop a farcical concatenation of events which is unlikely in itself, but details of timing and motivation are meticulously accurate, and no single incident is inherently improbable. Shakespeare, however, was always a fantasist, in the sense of allowing imagination – his own, or that of the audience, or a fusion of the two – to get the better of such common-sense notions of reality. People point to the improbable happenings of the late plays like *Cymbeline* and *The Tempest* as if they were somehow uncharacteristic of Shakespeare's art; but from the outset his comedies plumb the unfathomable, magical dimensions of human experience, which he seems to suggest are mirrored in that willing suspension of disbelief of the audience which *can* occur in a theatrical performance.[2] There is a folk-tradition of witchery associated with twins, and Shakespeare deliberately underscores this by setting *The Comedy of Errors* in Ephesus, a city notorious for sorcery (see The Acts of the Apostles, XIX: 19).

It is the quasi-magical edge to his comedies of the 1590s that has led to their being dubbed 'romantic' – not in the modern sense of being about love and lovers (though that is comprehended within the term) but because they are invested with the spirit of super-natural freedom which characterises the medieval/Renaissance romances of chivalry and adventure.[3] They are fairy-tales of being lost and found, of being truly oneself only when disguised as someone else, of loving at first sight or not at all, in the most exotic of places, such as the magical 'green world' of the forest or 'Illyria' (*Twelfth Night*). Familiarity may have dulled our sense of just how *strange* they can be: the fairies and the night-time world of *A Midsummer Night's Dream*; the casket scenes in *The Merchant of Venice*; the god Hymen and the hermit who converts the wicked Duke in *As You Like It*, and so on. The modern, rational instinct is to treat such phenomena (as we do the ghosts in the tragedies) as metaphors or theatrical devices; this is a legitimate response, as long as it does not belittle them, rob them of their capacity to disturb us as perhaps they should. Fairies, for example, were not for Shakespeare's time the child-like creatures of Arthur Rackham-ish sentiment to which they have largely been consigned today; they were much more complex, and potentially malevolent.[4] The success of the famous Peter Brook production of *A Midsummer Night's Dream* in the early 1970s, which emphasised the arresting strangeness of that play, is a reminder of the need to take this dimension of these plays seriously.

The most persistent analogy that Shakespeare offers for this 'strangeness' is that of the dream, an experience at once unreal and yet more real than real – a paradox he explores not only in *A Midsummer Night's Dream* but also in the Induction to *The Taming of the Shrew*, with the comic action of Christopher Sly's 'dream'.[5] The story is that of 'The Sleeper Awakened', from *The Arabian Nights*, which Shakespeare probably knew from a number of retellings. Essentially, a ragged beggar (Sly) falls drunkenly asleep, in which condition he is found by a great lord, who determines to play a trick on him: to set him up in his own chamber with a group of his servants, all conspiring to convince him that he is in fact a nobleman, whose conviction that he is a drunken beggar is a delusion of insanity. The analogy between Sly's 'dream' and the experience of a theatrical performance is underlined in the lord's decision to have a boy, a page, play Sly's lady 'wife' – just as would happen on the Elizabethan stage. The page wittily side-steps Sly's demands for his marital dues (which would have punctured the laws of decorum, dramatic illusion *and* Sly's dream in one fell swoop had they been allowed to proceed too far) by insisting that the doctors feared that it would cause a recession into 'insanity'. A messenger then appears to announce that, as an alternative, his doctors: 'thought it good you hear a play / And frame your mind to mirth and merriment, / Which bars a thousand harms and lengthens life' (Induction, ii. 131–3). The play, 'a pleasant comedy', proves to be the tempestuous tale of Petruchio and Kate, *The Taming of the Shrew* itself. So Sly's 'dream' and the experience of watching a play become one and the same thing.

If we may abstract a little from this, Shakespeare seems to be saying that the experience of watching a play (or, at least, a comedy) involves a delusion, a loss of self; but it is a delusion within limits – the page-boy is not, and never can be, Sly's real wife, though within mutually respected conventions he can represent her. It we take the delusion too seriously, we will destroy it; if, however, we accept it in a spirit of 'mirth and merriment' it can be positively medicinal. It would be wrong to treat the business of Sly too solemnly, but it does epitomise a dramatic balance we find time and again in Shakespearean comedy. Again, the contrast with Jonson is helpful: the 'gulls' in *Volpone* and *The Alchemist* who succumb to the quasi-theatrical illusions devised for them by the tricksters are treated with a brisk contempt, which Jonson extends by implication to the majority of the audience watching his own plays. The experiences of watching a play and of being taken in by a confidence-trickster are, he suggests, all too similar – unless one has the 'understanding' to be the master, rather than slave, of the dramatic illusion. Shakespeare is never so censorious or dismissive; even the most foolish of fellows, like the ass-turned Bottom, retains a human dignity, receiving a kind of blessing in his delusion/dream: 'I have had a most rare vision. I have had a dream, past the wit of man to say what dream it was' (IV.i.203–5). The 'strangeness' of Shakespeare's 'romantic comedies' highlights human follies and weaknesses, and not least the lunacies of love, but does so in a spirit of compassion and 'merriment' that is ultimately benign.

This perhaps lays these plays open to the charge of being pure escapism: fantastic entertainments of and for themselves. This debate hangs around the question of how Sly's 'dream' ends. In the text as we have it, Sly's part finishes with the beginning of the play proper, he and his 'wife' becoming an audience-on-stage. But would he still have been there at the end, and if so what would have become of him? In the sources, the beggar always returns to his beggary, his glorious dream curtailed in time and space; some argue that it would have happened to Sly at the end of *The Taming of the Shrew*, in a missing scene.[6] On the other hand it would have been extravagant of Shakespeare to tie up two actors so long with nothing to do. There were precedents for such 'framing' characters, notably in *The Spanish Tragedy*; but there they are essential to our understanding of the action, commenting on it from time to time. Perhaps, therefore, Sly and his 'wife' slunk away to double up roles in the main plot and be forgotten in the 'merriment'; to bring them back at the end would simply be distracting and anti-climactic. But *not* to do so would (arguably) be irresponsible, in the sense that we would have been shown the glory of the dream (escapism) but not its proper limits. It is a wrangle without resolution, which usefully demonstrates how many issues supposedly of textual or theatrical scholarship boil down ultimately to matters of interpretation or evaluative judgement.

But it may help to put the 'escapism' of the romantic comedies into perspective if we consider them in the context of the models on which Shakespeare was drawing. He inherited the mode of romantic comedy from a number of predecessors, including Robert Greene and Robert Wilson.[7] But the 'upstart crow' did not merely copy the originals; he invested the form with characteristics of his own. The most striking of these is forcefully present at the opening of *The Comedy of Errors*, deriving neither from Plautus nor from more recent precedents – the possibility of death hanging over the characters of the play. *Egeon*: 'Proceed, Solinus, to procure my fall, / And by the doom of death end woes and all' (I.i.1–2). It is an odd note to find at the start or, indeed, anywhere in a comedy. Yet it recurs insistently throughout Shakespeare's romantic comedies. Just when *Love's Labour's Lost* seems to promise a conventionally happy ending, a messenger enters:

> *Princess*: Welcome, Marcade;
> But that thou interrupt'st our merriment.
> *Marcade*: I am sorry, madam, for the news I bring
> Is heavy in my tongue. The king your father –
> *Princess*: Dead, for my life!
> *Marcade*: Even so. My tale is told.
>
> (V.ii.706–11)

The fact or possibility of death interrupts the 'merriment' of virtually all the comedies. Shylock's bond of Antonio's flesh looms so largely over *The Merchant of Venice* that some people have had difficulty seeing it as a comedy at all. *Much Ado About Nothing* is dominated by witty word-play and farcical action, but even here one of the characters (Hero) is presumed dead for much of the time and the banter of Beatrice and Benedick suddenly takes a different turn when she orders him to 'Kill Claudio' – his best friend (IV.i.285). Orlando in *As You Like It* does battle with a lion, bloodying a napkin which causes Rosalind to swoon. Viola in *Twelfth Night* has to face the fact that her brother may be dead, in obvious contrast to Olivia who has obsessively mourned her own dead brother for seven years; Feste's song, 'Come away, come away, death' (II.iv.51–65), is apposite in several contexts.

In *Love's Labour's Lost* we are left in no doubt as to the significance of the irruption of death into the comedy; it is to test the mettle of comedy itself to the limit, as in the 'service' that Rosaline imposes on jesting Berowne:[8]

> You shall this twelvemonth term from day to day
> Visit the speechless sick, and still converse
> With groaning wretches; and your task shall be
> With all the fierce endeavour of your wit
> To enforce the pained impotent to smile.
>
> (V.ii.840–4)

Berowne blenches at the suggestion: 'To move wild laughter in the throat of death? / It cannot be; it is impossible: / Mirth cannot move a soul in agony' (845–6). But Rosaline insists that: 'A jest's prosperity lies in the ear / Of him that hears it, never in the tongue / Of him that makes it' (851–3). Wit or comedy that is merely self-conceit will fail when put to such a stern test; but a true comic spirit, attuned to the real needs of its audience, can be of real value. If Berowne is to win her love, his jests must measure up to this standard.

Most of the romantic comedies end in multiple marriages, and we may suppose that this will be the *ultimate* outcome of *Love's Labour's Lost* too. This may seem the final endorsement of fairy-tale and fantasy, the unequivocal happy-ever-after ending. Marriage perfectly embodies the concept of personal and social concord,

when divine harmony touches human lives, as the presence of
Hymen suggests at the end of *As You Like It*. But in these comedies,
if marriage is to be 'a world-without-end bargain' (*Love's Labour's
Lost*, V.ii.779), it must not be undertaken without a trial of the
individuals concerned, parallel to the testing of the comedy over-
all. Hence Portia and Nerissa's testing of Bassanio and Gratiano in
the ring-plot of *The Merchant of Venice*; Rosalind's 'instruction' of
Orlando in *As You Like It*; the sparring between Beatrice and
Benedick in *Much Ado About Nothing* that has finally to be forced
to a match; and so on. It is, as it were, a structural principle of
these comedies to weigh their characters in the balance. A few
(like Shylock in *The Merchant of Venice*, Don John in *Much Ado About
Nothing* and Malvolio in *Twelfth Night*) seem not to be capable of
redemption, or only barely so. But, for the most part, they pass
muster, if some less convincingly than others. This is the point of
Jaques's wry salute to the male lovers at the end of *As You Like It*.
He beqeathes:

> (*To Orlando*): You to a love that your true faith doth merit;
> (*To Oliver*): You to your land and love and great allies;
> (*To Silvius*): You to a long and well-deserved bed;
> (*To Touchstone*): And you to wrangling, for thy loving voyage
>   Is but for two months victualled. So, to your pleasures:
> I am for other than for dancing measures.
>
> (V.iv.182–7)

Orlando has proved himself to be the true romantic lover; Oliver's
love for Celia is no less honourable, but is placed soberly in the
context of worldly ambitions; Silvius, the parody of a pining
Petrarchan lover, has at long last got what he thinks he wants;
and Touchstone's reason for choosing a mate is that of the animals.
Jaques the melancholic is dispassionate enough to put them all
into this perspective; but such detachment is two-edged. In opting
'for other than for dancing measures' he is claiming a kind of
superiority to the harmony of the dance, in which the rest of the
characters (here preparing to resume their proper places in society)
align themselves with the divine order of the music. It must be
doubtful if the play as a whole endorses that claim.

In such ways the romantic comedies temper escapist fantasies
and in turn temper those who would temper them. So it is that
Shakespeare writes for a theatre apparently able to sustain intense

flights of fantasy ('Titania waked, and straightway loved an ass', (*A Midsummer Night's Dream*, III.ii.34) while at the same time being merely a 'wooden O', where actors earn a living and audiences pay to watch 'the two hours' traffic of our stage' (*Romeo and Juliet*, Prologue, 11).[9] It is not that we are sometimes in our senses and sometimes out of them (as Bottom is) but that we simultaneously attend to what is necessarily real (time, death, the physical properties of the stage) and to what is romantically impossible. Part of the explanation of the capacity of Shakespeare's comedies to submit to such a wide variety of interpretations must lie in this inbuilt dual perspective of the fantastic and the real. The precise balance between the two is always a matter for the individual judgement of all those involved in staging, watching or reading them. Shakespeare seems to make a provocative point about this in the titles of his later romantic comedies, which followed a vogue in the late 1590s for off-handed flippancy. *Twelfth Night* seems to allude to the Christmas season, though there is no such reference in the text; its sub-title, 'Or What You Will', may well have been Shakespeare's preference all along (supply your own title, supply you own make-believe) but he was forestalled by John Marston's *What You Will*. *As You Like It* can be interpreted variously as polite or cynical deference to the taste of the audience for which this play is designed to cater. *All's Well that Ends Well*, similarly, is balanced on a provocative edge between complacency and cynicism. *Much Ado About Nothing* is both a precise reflection of its own plot, which hinges on a non-event that spawns prodigious consequences, and a wider comment on the ambiguous something/nothing quality of all these comedies, in which the status of the dream and the dreamer is so crucial. Each of these tacitly mocks its audience for attending to such empty vanities which are, however, perhaps not so meaningless if we all recognise our own God-given roles as dreamers, each of us as foolish or as blessed as Sly and Bottom in our dreams.

The 'romantic' freedom of Shakespeare's comedies is not merely a matter of self-reflective theatrical ingenuity; it is rooted in their subject-matter, which is predominantly Courtly. *The Comedy of Errors* begins at the Court of the Duke of Ephesus. *A Midsummer Night's Dream* begins (as does the very late *Two Noble Kinsmen*) in the Court of the Duke Theseus (the slayer of the Minotaur) in Athens. *Love's Labour's Lost* revolves around the King and Court of Navarre. *As You Like It* moves between the Court of Duke

Frederick and that of the banished Duke Senior, in exile in Arden. *Twelfth Night* opens in Duke Orsino's Court of self-love in Illyria. *All's Well That Ends Well* and *Measure for Measure* revolve around the royal Courts, respectively, of France and Vienna. Even where there is no royal Court as such, its characteristics are invoked: *Much Ado About Nothing* largely takes place in the house of the Governor of Messina, deputy to the Prince of Arragon (Don Pedro), who happens to be visiting at the time of the action; in *The Merchant of Venice*, Portia's house in Belmont (quite distinct from the commercial intrigues of Venice itself) has all the grace and sophistication of a royal Court, while all the power and majesty is vested in the court-of-law, over which the Duke/Doge presides.

There is a clear link between 'romance' and courtly society. The two most substantial and influential romances of the Elizabethan period, Sir Philip Sidney's *Arcadia* and Edmund Spenser's *The Faerie Queene* were both of and for the Court: the former written by a courtier for his sister and their aristocratic circle, the latter written by a man trying to establish himself in Court circles. The strange and wonderful tales of knights and princesses, hermits and fierce beasts, reflect in essence the neo-Platonic moral dilemmas and quasi-chivalric perplexities of Renaissance aristocrats, far removed from the practicalities of trade or the realistic need to make a living. That is not to say, of course, that wealth was unimportant, though most courtly literature took the stability of landed money (and the question of who owned it) for granted and focused on 'higher' matters. Shakespeare normally follows the conventions in this respect, though in *As You Like It*, the displaced courtiers are brought face-to-face with the greasy realities of sheep-rearing and cheese-making on which their 'civilised' society depends – matters which pastoral romances normally glossed over. And in *The Merchant of Venice* he takes the unusual step of foregrounding money matters – not only in the dealings of the merchant, Antonio, and the usurer, Shylock, but also in the status of Portia; quite apart from her spiritual grace (which is always the pre-eminent virtue of aristocratic ladies in courtly literature), he reminds us that she has a money-value, which is of interest to her suitors, and not least to Bassanio, who has already managed to lose his own fortune. These practicalities are, however, subsumed in a tale of benign providence working in and around the lady of Belmont: the curious terms of her father's will ('Your father was ever virtuous, and holy men at their death have good inspirations', says Nerissa, with a placid faith, I.ii.26–7); Bassanio's reading of the riddles of the caskets; and the complex moral dilemmas of the ring-plot (often overshadowed these days by our uneasy conscience about Shylock) – these are all pure romance. This is easier to appreciate if we compare the play as a whole to that later comedy about the mercantile 'splendours' of Renaissance Venice, Ben Jonson's *Volpone*, where not a glimmer of romantic sentiment is allowed to twinkle. Indeed, the courtly provenance of Shakespearean comedy as a whole is underlined if we compare it with the characteristic works of slightly later contemporaries, like Dekker, Jonson and Middleton, whose attention is on the low-life of London streets rather than on never-never worlds of Belmont and Illyria. The unusual emphases of *The Merchant of Venice* and *As You Like It* serve to indicate that Shakespeare could be as critical of the conventions of courtly literature as he was of escapist comedy (which to an extent overlap). But all the comedies and tragi-comedies he was to write (excluding only *The Merry Wives of Windsor*, for all its other courtly connections) were firmly based on them.

Elizabeth's Court was, both practically and symbolically, the centre of power and influence in the country and had, as we have seen, particular links with the acting profession; it was not a place but a collection of several thousand people attending upon the monarch and following her, for the most part, in her moves from one palace to another – Whitehall, Richmond, Greenwich, Hampton Court, Nonsuch, Windsor – and in her progresses about the country. The Queen both ruled and reigned and the principal politicians were her Privy Councillors. The Court was the principal fount of patronage and centre of fashion; it prided itself on being the focus of the nation's civilisation and culture, the upholder of the ideals and aspirations of the Renaissance. Human nature being what it is, the reality often fell far short of the ideal projection, but the Queen insisted on a high standard of behaviour and obedience from her courtiers; and a Court that fostered within its own ranks talents as remarkable as those of Sir Philip Sidney, Sir Walter Ralegh and Sir Francis Bacon had some right to think of itself as a leading force in the arts and sciences. Precepts of what a courtier should be like, such as those propounded by Sir Thomas Elyot in *The Book named the Governor* (1531) and Baldassare Castiglione in *Il Cortegiano* (Englished by Sir Thomas Hoby as *The Book of the Courtier*, 1561), urged the cultivation of an all-round talent and balanced personality, a blending of active, contemplative and passionate qualities. So the ideal courtier should not just be a soldier, or a scholar, or a poet, but all three, equally versed in 'manners, arms and arts',[10] an achievement the Elizabethans recognised (at least, after his death) in Sir Philip Sidney. It is an ideal against which Shakespeare constantly measures the aristocrats in his comedies, and elsewhere.

It is no accident, in this regard, that the action of *A Midsummer Night's Dream* takes place in the context of the wedding of Theseus and Hippolyta. Theseus is one of the chivalric heroes of classical mythology, the slayer of the Minotaur; Hippolyta, the Queen of the Amazons, was a woman he defeated in battle; but he in turn has been defeated by his love for her:

> Hippolyta, I wooed thee with my sword,
> And won thy love doing thee injuries;
> But I will wed thee in another key,
> With pomp, with triumph, and with revelling.
>
> (I.i.16–19)

So the man of action is tamed by love and celebrates the fact with a Renaissance marriage, all manners, arts and 'merriment'; this marriage is a model against which to measure the other pairings that struggle towards perfection in the Athenian woods. In *Love's Labour's Lost*, the King of Navarre's plan that 'Our court shall be a little academe, / Still and contemplative in living art' (I.i.13–14) is superficially a worthy one, until we appreciate how impractical it is. To devote oneself to contemplation to the exclusion of love, not to mention the neglect of affairs of state, is an unbalanced ambition. At the most practical of levels, Elizabeth's England knew full well that marriage and diplomacy were indistinguishable at Court. Academic study alone will not lead to a balanced view; Prospero in *The Tempest* (c. 1611) was to lose his dukedom for attending too much to his books. Nothing so serious occurs here, but it is made clear that the king's scheme is fundamentally *unnatural* and the 'merriment' of this play (as of most Shakespearean comedy) is dedicated to restoring a natural balance in human affairs: hence the conclusion of the play with the songs of Spring and Winter, the cuckoo and the owl, evoking the cycle of the seasons, to which humanity is bound like the rest of creation, for all its airs and graces.

The corrective standard of nature applies not only to the true courtiers but also to those who emulate their scholarship, like Don Armado and the pedant Holofernes. In each case, their 'fantastical' inflated language is a measure of how far they have strayed from a balanced perspective, both on themselves and on the world; words have become a substitute for and impediment to reality. This is an important consideration in weighing the significance of a principal attribute claimed by many of Shakespeare's courtly characters, which is wit:

> *Armado*: Now, by the salt wave of the Mediterranean, a sweet touch, a quick venew of wit! Snip, snap, quick and home! It rejoiceth my intellect. True wit!
> *Moth*: Offered by a child to an old man – which is wit-old.
>
> (V.i.54–7)

'Wit' has changed its meaning a good deal down the ages. For the Elizabethans it was a marriage of intelligence and imagination, all the better for having at least the appearance of spontaneity (qualities most familiar today in Donne's poetry), and it was a prime attribute of a courtier. Many characters pretend to it in Shakespeare's comedies, but far fewer actually possess it; in the main, they mistake the style for the substance. The constant function of the page-boy, Moth, is to puncture the pretensions to wit of Don Armado and his associates, by being so much sharper and to the point than they are, the rejoinder here being a fair example: he injects not only the obvious comment about the disparity in age between himself and Holofernes (whose 'wit' is the subject of this interchange) but also a subtle insult, since 'wit-old' implies 'wittol', the term for a complacent cuckold. The cuckold, the man who cannot control or possess his own wife, is a stock figure of fun in Elizabethan comedy, an image of something pathetically out of place in the 'natural', property-owning order of things; we find his mythical horns throughout Shakespeare's plays, most notably in *Othello*, where he took the unusual step of making suspected cuckoldry the mainspring of tragedy rather than of comedy. Moth's role helps us to understand Shakespeare's point about Berowne, who is easily the wittiest character in the play, constantly demonstrating a supposed superiority over the idiocies around him; but it brings him no obvious rewards. On the contrary, it provokes Rosaline's challenge that he should use it to bring smiles to the faces of the sick and dying – a test to distinguish true wit from mere affectation or self-conceit. The need to make that distinction is raised repeatedly in the comedies, famously in the duel of wits between Beatrice and Benedick in *Much Ado About Nothing*. In later comedies the focus of wit shifts interestingly from the courtiers themselves to men paid by them to be witty, professional 'fools', a development I shall pursue in the next chapter.

The question of wit modulates into the more serious issue of judgement when the plays confront the role of the Court, or the monarch, as the arbiter of law and justice. Egeon in *The Comedy of Errors* is sentenced to death by the laws of Ephesus and the Duke tells him: 'I am not partial to infringe our laws' (I.i.4). The discord which sends the lovers in *A Midsummer Night's Dream* into the confusions of the woods stems from the legal consequences of Hermia's refusal to obey her father and marry Demetrius; Duke Theseus decrees her options: 'Either to die the death, or to abjure / For ever the society of men' (I.i.65–6). *Love's Labour's Lost* begins with what Berowne calls 'A dangerous law against gentility' (I.i.126), banning women from the Court and its environs. The action of *The Merchant of Venice* hangs on Shylock's determination to have the letter of the law and his bond, by which the Duke and the court is bound. In *Twelfth Night* a significant part of the action turns on the fact that Antonio, Sebastian's loyal friend, is liable to instant arrest under Orsino's law, for the dubious crime of being too conspicuously successful in fighting against Illyria. In *Much Ado About Nothing* the 'nothing' devised by Don John is so wickedly successful because those ultimately responsible for the law – the Prince and his young nobles – are less vigilant than they should be, while the inane officers of the watch, Dogberry and Verges, discover the plot with no difficulty, but totally fail to understand the significance of what is going on. Repeatedly, then, the law presents an absolute standard against which human failings are to be measured, and which not even the monarch can alter arbitrarily; often, however, the law seems too harsh or inflexible to be an instrument of true justice, and the 'merriment' of comedy needs to find some way of averting the severest penalties. This is the central issue of *The Merchant of Venice*. Interestingly, these issues of law and human frailty, justice and judgment, become of paramount importance in *Measure for Measure* (c. 1604) and *All's Well That Ends Well* (c. 1603), which, though nominally romantic comedies, are often thought too extreme and problematic for such a label.

In many ways the law is too insenstive a tool for measuring human beings, but its rigidity is a constant reminder of ultimate standards by which we are all to be judged. The issue is rarely as critical in the comedies as it is in the histories and tragedies, but the royal princes in these plays act (within human limits, though the Duke in *Measure for Measure* strains those limits to breaking-point) as the agents of God. It is in the nature of these plays to imply an Ultimate Spectator, one to whom our follies and vanities are only too well known. The 'fairy' dimension of *A Midsummer Night's Dream* is an obvious example: 'Lord, what fools these mortals be!' (III.ii.115) is Puck's all-embracing comment. In *Love's Labour's Lost*, the king and lords of Navarre appear one by one, and unwittingly reveal to the others (present in hiding) the secret that they have fallen in love, contrary to their vows. The king, Longaville and Dumain each in turn reveal their secrets to a growing audience. Only Berowne sees all without making a public confession, and he revels in the power this gives him: 'Like a demi-god here sit I in the sky, / And wretched fools' secrets heedfully o'er-eye' (IV.iii.74–5). He is wrong, of course, to feel so secure and superior; a higher audience than himself will not allow his secret to remain hidden. There is a 'law' in Shakespeare's comedies to the effect that those who think of themselves as superior to their fellows must eventually be confronted with their own short-comings: obvious examples are Malvolio in *Twelfth Night* and Beatrice and Benedick in *Much Ado About Nothing*, but even exemplary characters like Portia in *The Merchant of Venice* and Rosalind in *As You Like It* are made to suffer at times for the apparent ease with which they rise over other people's difficulties.

These questions of courtly wit and judgement help to explain Shakespeare's comic use of the play-within-a-play.[11] Such on-stage theatricals are common in Elizabethan drama, moments of significant disjunction, liable to result either in a comic debacle or tragic chaos. The pageant of the Nine Worthies in *Love's Labour's Lost* brings face-to-face the polished wit of the courtiers and the affected, pedantic or plain ignorant 'wit' of Armado, Holofernes, Costard and the others. The result is a travesty of the kind of decorous entertainments Elizabeth often encountered on her progresses; the actors are ludicrously inept and their audience refuse to take them seriously, constantly interrupting:

Holofernes: Judas I am –
Dumaine: A Judas?
Holofernes: Not Iscariot, sir.
                    Judas I am, ycleped Maccabaeus.
Dumaine: Judas Maccabaeus clipt is plain Judas.
Berowne: A kissing traitor. How, art thou proved Judas?
                                                    (V.ii.588–93)

It is very funny, no doubt, but it raises significant issues. The
theme of the tableau is far from arbitrary: the Nine Worthies are a
pantheon of heroes from the classical, Hebrew and Christian eras
and, as such, are models for Navarre's courtiers to emulate. But
there is no evidence that they are conscious of this: their 'wit' is
all bent on making fun of the 'players' rather than taking on board
the import of their show. This underlines how far they fall
short of some ideals, so that Holofernes's complaint: 'This is not
generous, not gentle, not humble' (621) is perhaps more pointed
than, in the heat of the comedy, we are likely to appreciate.
'Generous' here means 'befitting noble persons'; 'gentle' means
'befitting those well-born'; 'humble' means 'considerate, not arro-
gant'. For once, every Holofernes word strikes home. The courtiers
are, in every sense, forgetting themselves, frustrating the tableau's
aim of reminding them who they *might* be. It is evidence that the
ladies are right to put them to a sterner test before agreeing to
marriage.

Throughout Shakespeare's career, the device of the play-within-
a-play is similarly pointed, though to different ends, be it Hamlet's
'Mousetrap', the various dumb-shows in *Pericles*, or the masque of
Iris, Juno and Ceres in *The Tempest*. The other comedy which uses
this device to even more hilarious effect is *A Midsummer Night's
Dream*. Here again, the 'tedious brief scene of young Pyramus / And
his love Thisby' offers great scope for the Athenian courtiers to air
their 'wit' at the expense of Quince, Bottom and their fellows, but
it is more restrained than the debacle in Navarre and disturbs the
'performance' less. Theseus himself sets the 'generous' tone. When
Hippolyta protests: 'This is the silliest stuff that ever I heard', he
observes: 'The best in this kind are but shadows; and the worst are
no worse, if imagination amend them' (V.i.208–10). His observation
takes us to the heart of *this* play-within-a-play, which explores the
whole nature of dramatic imagination and suspension of disbelief,
the experience of 'the dream'. The incongruities of Bottom playing

Pyramus, Snout the Wall and Snug the Lion ('A very gentle beast, and of good conscience', 224) take us into the mysteries of romantic comedy itself, which are finally blessed by the fairies.

In comedies that lack the mannerist self-consciousness of the play-within-a-play, those mysteries are commonly focused on the plays' remarkable heroines, notably Portia in *The Merchant of Venice*, Rosalind in *As You Like It* and Viola in *Twelfth Night*.[12] These leading 'breeches' roles – all three of them go into disguise as young men – are extremely unusual. They do not occur in the romantic comedies of Greene and Wilson, nor are there any real equivalents in the all-boy Courtly comedies of Lyly. The likes of Jonson and Middleton were closer to the conventional models in making their comic female roles, particularly the younger ones, relatively minor – for the most part, sexual and financial pawns in worlds dominated by men. Broadly speaking, this was a fair reflection of the actual legal and social standing of women in Tudor England, though it was not always accepted without question. There was also a practical argument in favour of minimising female roles on the Elizabethan stage, in as much as they had to be played by boys or young men. Having lost the tradition, there is no way of knowing how this struck audiences at the time: did they take it for granted, or was there something epicene or parodic about it? Was there any incongruity about Marlowe's Faustus asking of the boy who played Helen of Troy: 'Was this the face that launch'd a thousand ships'? Does it show Shakespeare's confidence in the convention, or the opposite, that his Cleopatra should talk of the actors 'boying' her greatness? At this remove, all the evidence is ambiguous, though it is clear (not least in Shakespeare's comedies) that it was an issue about which the players were self-conscious. It seems reasonable to suggest that, however well trained the boys might have been, they would not have been as sophisticated and dominant on stage as the likes of Burbage and Kempe.[13] But against that is the evidence of the challenging female roles that Shakespeare himself wrote – not only the great comic heroines, but Goneril and Regan, Lady Macbeth and Cleopatra. Around 1596–1601 and 1605–7, the periods respectively of the dominant comic and tragic female roles, his company perhaps had particularly gifted players of female parts.

In the absence of external explanations, we can only discuss Shakespeare's unusually resourceful comic heroines in terms of their function within his plays. The recurrent make-believe business of having the boy/actor playing a girl, in disguise for long periods as a young man, allows endless scope for sexual teasing, but it also focuses in a particular way the imaginative, dream-like quality of romantic comedy. It is significant in this respect that Shakespeare never 'cheats' his audience: *we* always know who is in disguise and why, and we enjoy sharing vicariously in the fantasy of their advantage over the other characters on stage. Unlike Jonson's *Epicoene* or Beaumont and Fletcher's *Philaster*, the final 'revelations' come to us as the working-out of careful processes, not as ironic surprises. We see the most important action of these plays as it were through the eyes of these disguised heroines: the courtroom confrontation of Shylock and Antonio, the love-entanglements of Arden, the perversities of Illyrian society. And this obviously has an effect. The courtly world of 'romance', where the women were adored icons, was normally very much male-dominated. So to find the ladies of France putting the courtiers of Navarre in their place, or a girl arguing better than the best lawyers of Venice, or another teaching her hero-lover (Orlando) the rules of love, or another shaking Orsino's Illyria out of its self-conceit was more than a good joke: it turned the expected on its head. Just as much as a play-within-a-play, the convention forces a reconsideration of perspectives and priorities; make-believe becomes a way of testing what is real and proper, of reinvigorating and redefining the values of the Court. This is the serious business of Shakespearean romantic comedy.[14]

7

The Turn of the Century

On 7 September 1598 *Palladis Tamia: Wit's Treasury*, by Francis Meres, was entered in the Stationers' Register. It contains 'A Comparative Discourse of our English Poets, with the Greek, Latin, and Italian Poets', and is still remembered because it mentions Shakespeare several times, as a lyric and love poet and as being among 'our best for tragedy' and 'best for comedy'. Crucially, Meres offers this comparison:

> As Plautus and Seneca are accounted the best for comedy and tragedy among the Latins: so Shakespeare among the English is the most excellent in both kinds for the stage; for comedy, witness his *Gentlemen of Verona*, his *Errors*, his *Love Labours Lost*, his *Love Labours Won*, his *Midsummer's Night Dream*, & his *Merchant of Venice*: for tragedy his *Richard the 2. Richard the 3. Henry the 4. King John, Titus Andronicus* and his *Romeo and Juliet*.[1]

In several instances this is the earliest record of the plays he lists, proving that they must have been staged by that date. The catalogue is tantalising both for what it includes and for what it leaves out. Is *Love Labours Won* a lost play (we do not hear of it again) or is it an alternative title for a known play? *The Taming of the Shrew* is a good candidate, but *Much Ado About Nothing* is not impossible. Does the absence of the *Henry VI* plays strengthen the case for their not being written by Shakespeare, but only revised by him? Does the bare *Henry the 4.* imply that only Part 1 had been staged by this date? These matters are imponderable because we do not know how well-informed Meres was or how exhaustive he intended to be, but his catalogue, supplemented by the plays I have associated with it (plus, as I shall suggest, *Henry V* and so, logically, *2 Henry IV*) probably represents Shakespeare's total dramatic output before he moved to the Globe.

The Globe itself was not radically different from the theatres that had existed before it, though numerous contemporary references to 'the great Globe on the Bankside' confirm that it was the most splendid playhouse built to that date. Being built with the main timbers of the old Theatre, its dimensions and probably the size of the stage were broadly similar. Since all of Shakespeare's subsequent plays (with the possible exception of *Troilus and Cressida*), and a number of works by Jonson and others, were specifically written for performance there, we may deduce some of its features. For example, the tiring-house wall must have contained at least two main doors to allow for complex entrances and exits, but no one has demonstrated that any of these plays called for more than that. *Pericles* (admittedly not a very satisfactory text) specifies: 'Enter Pericles at one door, with all his train; Cleon and Dionyza at the other' (IV.iv.22). More vexatious is the question of whether there was also a separate 'discovery space', a curtained recess within the tiring-house wall or booth sticking out from it, possibly between the two doors. A number of episodes do seem to call for the possibility of characters being expeditiously revealed or concealed. As *Othello* ends, Lodovico says, 'The object poisons sight;/Let it be hid' (V.ii.364–5), referring to Othello and Desdemona both dead on her bed. This suggests a curtaining-off rather than a removal; something similar may be implied in the order to cover the faces of Goneril and Regan towards the end of *King Lear*: clearing a body-strewn stage at the end of a tragedy was always a problem. In *The Tempest*, 'Prospero discovers Ferdinand and Miranda playing at chess' (at V.i.171). The question is whether such scenes required a specific 'discovery space' or whether they might not have been managed within one of the door-ways, suitably curtained over (which might also have served, for example, as the 'arras' behind which Polonius is stabbed). We do know, however, that the actors must have had access to the area below the stage, whence the Ghost in *Hamlet* cries out (I.v.), a scene which is more effective if the audience is not aware in advance of his presence. In the same play, the requirement for Hamlet to leap into Ophelia's grave suggests that there was a capacious trap-door, which could be opened up as necessary (and may have been adapted for the 'quaint device' of the vanishing banquet in *The Tempest*, III.iii.52). Above the stage, presumably within the 'heavens' canopy, there was some sort of tackle that facilitated spectacular descents, notably the descent of Jupiter 'sitting upon an eagle' in *Cymbeline*. Such devices are a marked feature of Shakespeare's last plays and people often associate them with the Blackfriars theatre rather than the Globe. But those plays were staged interchangeably in both theatres (see Chapter 9) and the Globe must have had some such equipment, though it may not have been as sophisticated as that in the indoor house. *Antony and Cleopatra*, written before the Blackfriars was annexed, calls for the Guard to 'heave Antony aloft to Cleopatra' (IV.xv.37), which would have been more practicable with some lifting-gear. This scene also demonstrates that the Globe had an upper acting gallery, probably adjacent to the lords' room (which Jonson mentions the Globe as having 'over the stage' in *Every Man Out of His Humour*).

One of the last plays probably *not* to be performed first at the Globe was *Henry V*. We can date the play quite closely from the parallel it draws between Henry in France and Essex's Irish expedition:

> Were now the general of our gracious empress,
> As in good time he may, from Ireland coming,
> Bringing rebellion broached on his sword,
> How many would the peaceful city quit
> To welcome him!
>
> (Chorus to Act V, 30–4)

The Earl left London on 27 March; on 28 September, the expedition an utter failure, he returned secretly and against the Queen's orders, bursting into her bedchamber at Nonsuch unannounced and smeared with mud. It was the beginning of the end for a man already in debt and further losing the confidence of the Queen. There have been attempts to read into the plays of this period Shakespeare's attachment to the Earl and his cause but nothing conclusive has emerged.[2] Shakespeare's old patron, the Earl of Southampton, was one of Essex's most enthusiastic supporters; but there is no evidence that Shakespeare maintained links with him after 1594. Even this compliment to Essex – the only *explicit* reference to the Earl in Shakespeare's works[3] – is more guarded than it appears out of context. Shakespeare describes the analogy between Essex and Henry as 'a lower but . . . loving likelihood' and stresses that the enthusiasm for the king's French victories ('Much more, and much more cause') was greater than anything that would greet the Earl. And he carefully underlines the queen's supremacy by styling her 'our gracious empress'. This is surely discreet patriotism rather than hero-worship.

The fact that he alludes to Essex at all, however, suggests that the play was written closer to March than to September, since rumours of disaster began to circulate quite early in the summer. It is this which has led some scholars to the conclusion that *Henry V* was probably not first staged at the Globe and that its famous 'wooden O' describes the less illustrious Curtain, where the Lord Chamberlain's Men performed until the new theatre was ready. In a legal document of 16 May 1599, the Globe is described as *de novo edificata*, newly built; that may only mean that the super-structure was in place, not that it was ready for use, though it just about leaves open the possibility that *Henry V* was Shakespeare's first composition for the new playhouse. The first of his plays that we can be reasonably sure was performed there is *Julius Caesar*, seen by Thomas Platter on 21 September.[4] Whichever play had this particular honour, in general terms the move to the Globe certainly coincided with a major development in Shakespeare's writing career. He abandoned English chronicle histories, based largely on Holinshed,[5] and turned for the first time to a new and influential source: Sir Thomas North's translation of *Plutarch's Lives of the Noble Grecians and Romans*, first published in 1579. This was to be the principal source of three subsequent plays: *Antony and Cleopatra, Coriolanus* and *Timon of Athens*.

Plutarch offered a very different style of history from that in the English chronicles – no providential sweep or detailed factual record, but biographical sketches heavily moralised, most of them arranged in Graeco-Roman pairings (e.g. Theseus and Romulus, Alexander and Caesar) so as to facilitate a relative assessment of virtues and vices. We can only surmise why Shakespeare now found this attractive. Possibly he felt that he had played out the vein of English medieval history after mining it for the best part of a decade. And it may have presented an interesting challenge to examine men and affairs outside the framework of Christian attitudes and assumptions, something he was to do frequently hereafter, not only in plays based on Plutarch (e.g. *King Lear, The Winter's Tale*). But it may also have been politic for Shakespeare to abandon English history for Roman at this juncture. In February 1599 Dr John Hayward's book, *The First Part of the Life and Reign of King Henry IV*, (which dealt with the deposition of Richard II) caused a stir, not least because of its florid dedication to Essex. The Attorney-General drew up a list of items demonstrating that it had been conceived with particular 'application' to current events, and Hayward was confined to the Tower. In June the Privy Council decreed that no English histories were to be printed without the permission of its own members[6] – their potential 'application' to current events was now too provocative to be allowed. There is no record of similar restrictions on stage-plays, though possibly it was made known that English histories would not be welcome there either. At all events, classical history may for the moment have seemed a more judicious alternative, though soon it was to prove no less suspect of 'application' than the English variety, as Jonson's *Sejanus* and Daniel's *Philotas* demonstrated.

Indeed, if discretion was what prompted this new departure in Shakespeare's career, his choice of topic was an odd one. Julius Caesar never was emperor of Rome (as the play carefully underlines) but he was not far short of being, and a play built around his assassination must have seemed daring. The idea of a monarchy being *created* or *eliminated* by a military/political process (an issue implicit in all the Roman plays) was obviously a contentious one anywhere in Renaissance Europe. Whether we should ascribe the daring to political sympathies or to an instinct for good box-office, there is no way of knowing. But whatever Shakespeare's interest in the politics of ancient Rome, his concern for verisimilitude did not extend to details: *Julius Caesar's* glaring anachronisms include chimney pots, striking clocks and books with leaved pages. They might not have been apparent to the average Elizabethan, but they made purists like Jonson wince. It was this play that sprang to his mind when he weighed up Shakespeare's talents and their limitations:

I remember, the players have often mentioned it as an honour to Shakespeare, that in his writing (whatsoever he penned) he never blotted out line. My answer hath been, would he had blotted a thousand. Which they thought a malevolent speech. I had not told posterity this, but for their ignorance, who chose that circumstance to commend their friend by, wherein he most faulted. And to justify mine own candour (for I loved the man, and do honour his memory – on this side idolatry – as much as any). He was (indeed) honest, and of an open, and free nature: had an excellent fancy; brave notions, and gentle expressions: wherein he flowed with that facility, that sometime it was necessary he should be stopped: *sufflaminandus erat*; as Augustus said of Haterius. His wit was in his own power; would the rule of it had been so too. Many times he fell into those things, could not escape laughter: as when he said in the person of Caesar, one speaking to him; 'Caesar, thou dost me wrong'. He replied: 'Caesar did never wrong, but with just cause': and such like; which were ridiculous. But he redeemed his vices, with his virtues. There was ever more in him to be praised, than to be pardoned.[7]

If Shakespeare did write those lines, they were changed before they reached print; the offending passage appears as: 'Know, Caesar doth not wrong, nor without cause/Will he be satisfied (III.i.47–8). The lines Jonson quotes are not inherently ludicrous, though Caesar's argument may be ethically indefensible; to claim that a man might do things that were themselves wrong in the interests of a supposed higher good might be a perfect encapsulation of tyranny. The play as we have it is ambivalent about Caesar: he is vain and ambitious, but also shrewd, aware of his own deficiencies; he is not self-evidently the tyrant that the original lines would suggest, which may be why Jonson thought them out of place.

The issue Jonson raises is, however, wider than the particular instance, and goes beyond the rankling envy that some suppose lies behind this passage. He called his own plays 'poems' and thought of them as works of art which would have a life in print beyond their life on stage; he thought of his two surviving tragedies, *Sejanus* and *Catiline*, as serious treatments of history and allowed no clumsy anachronisms to mar their credibility. So Jonson perhaps had some cause to question the judgement of the actors, in awe of this man who turned out play after successful play and 'never blotted line'. From their point of view, Shakespeare was the consummate professional, crafting commercial plays that translated readily on to the stage: why worry about small details no audience would notice, or the odd ill-considered line? Jonson had a point; if their (and presumably Shakespeare's own) view of what he was doing had gone unchallenged – if Jonson's own example had not been followed – few of his works would have survived, and hardly any of them in decent texts. But Jonson was wrong to assume that his own kind of perfectionism was the only way to turn commercial drama into art. Shakespeare could be slap-dash about details (giving Bohemia a sea-coast in *The Winter's Tale* is another example that provoked Jonson)[8] but his professionalism extended in other directions, far beyond producing merely efficient stage-pieces. We may relate the lasting success of his plays to the practical effects of this professionalism.

Julius Caesar here provides a different kind of example. Unlike the preceeding English histories, with Falstaff, Pistol and their associates, it is not a play best remembered for its comic characters. This must partly be a question of the Roman *gravitas* of the subject-matter, which Shakespeare apparently wanted to respect even if his concern did not extend to finding out that Roman citizens would not have had 'sweaty nightcaps', as Casca says they did (I.ii.244). But he does not neglect comedy altogether. There are perhaps three scenes, though none of great substance, which have a marked comic element: the opening scene in which a cobbler trades puns with the tribunes, Flavius and Marullus; III.iii., the scene in which Cinna the poet is mistaken for Cinna the conspirator and torn to pieces (black comedy indeed, but there does seem to be deliberate humour in the questioning that produces the tragically wrong name); and the strange business on the night before Philippi when a character designated merely as 'a Poet' bursts in on Brutus and Cassius, bent on healing the 'grudge between 'em' (IV.iii.124–38). It is my contention that these scenes represent Shakespeare's solution to the problem of accommodating not one but two leading comic actors in a play where their principal qualities were not heavily in demand. This theory may not be accepted in its entirety, but there can be no doubt that the scenes show Shakespeare thinking carefully and professionally about the relationship between styles of comedy and of serious drama.

To take the last first. The text as we have it is almost unintelligible. The Poet's appearance adds nothing to the plot or to our knowledge of the characters. The explanation surely lies in Brutus's line: 'What should the wars do with these jigging fools?' (137). The 'jig' was the extremely popular forte of the Lord Chamberlain's Men's established leading comic, Will Kempe. John Marston suggested that 'the orbs celestial will dance Kempe's jig' (*Scourge of Villainy*, 1598), while Everard Guilpin proclaimed how 'Whores, beadles, bawds, and sergeants filthily chaunt Kempe's jig' (*Skialetheia*, 1598) – testimony to the vogue of Kempe's dance-cum-ballads, which were not always in the most decorous of taste. The explanation for the 'Poet' scene is surely that Shakespeare devised a pause in the action for Kempe to go on and do his 'turn', an interlude before the battle which (as the dialogue suggests) is entirely divorced from the more serious action. If so, there is every likelihood that it was one of the last roles that Shakespeare devised for him, since around this time he left the company, selling his share in the Globe. He had apparently left by February–March 1600, when he famously morris-danced from London to Norwich for a wager. In the published account of his 'nine days' wonder' he says how 'I have danced myself out of the world' – not improbably a pun about leaving the Globe. There is reason to suppose that he did not depart on the best of terms with at least some of his fellows. Kempe also addressed 'the impudent generation of ballad-makers and their coherents' (whom he accuses of lying about what really happened) as 'my notable Shakerags', very probably a gibe at Shakespeare.[9] Shakespeare in turn may well have had Kempe in mind when he has Hamlet lecture the players: 'And let those that play your clowns speak no more than is set down for them, for there be of them that will themselves laugh, to set on some quantity of barren spectators to laugh too, though in the mean time some necessary question of the play be then to be considered. That's villainous and shows a most pitiful ambition in the fool that uses it' (III.ii.36–42). This strikes an obvious chord with the treatment of the 'jigging fool' in *Julius Caesar*, whose irrelevance is actually made the point of the scene.

The two Shakespearean roles that we *know* Kempe played are Peter, the servant to Juliet's nurse, in *Romeo and Juliet* and Dogberry in *Much Ado About Nothing*. We know this because, in the printed texts, Kempe's own name appears once or twice in the speech-prefixes, in place of the roles he was playing. It was not uncommon for playwrights to write in the names of actors who would take particular roles, which indicates how carefully they tailored their product to suit the resources of those who were going to perform them; usually the evidence of this would be edited out before a play was printed. These particular survivals into print probably reflect the unique status of the principal comic character, 'clown' or 'fool', who was always to an extent independent of the play-script: Kempe was always Kempe, whatever role he was formally assigned to. Shakespeare seems to have accommodated this by confining his appearances to set-pieces: Peter in *Romeo and Juliet* is a minor, incidental role as scripted, with entrances but very little to say in II.iv. and v. and an irrelevant sequence with the musicians in IV.v; in any of these Kempe could have indulged in 'business' without seriously disrupting the action. Dogberry is a much more substantial comic role ('O that I had been writ down an ass!' IV.ii.78–9), but his part is carefully confined to three scenes of broad comedy with his fellow officers of the watch, apart from the denoument where the villains are brought to justice. He is a bumbling counterpart to the likes of Beatrice and Benedick, and a reflection upon them, but he is never allowed to interfere in their scenes. Nevertheless, it might well have irritated Shakespeare if Kempe had thought himself, his 'business' and his own witticisms more important than this fine comic creation.

If we look at the other two 'comic' scenes in *Julius Caesar*, and particularly the opening one, we find something very different. The cobbler is a quibbler, a player with words, a man of sardonic wit (but *not* an aristocrat). My candidate for this role would be Robert Armin, who took over from Kempe as the principal comedian with the troupe; for a time, around 1599, they were apparently both members. There is no record of the parts Armin played (except that he took over Dogberry) but roles of a particular and distinctive style emerge in Shakespeare's works from the time that he joined the company – all, as it were, extensions of that cobbler. Two famous cameo examples are the gravedigger in *Hamlet* and the porter in *Macbeth*. The most intriguing possibility is Iago in *Othello*, a desperately serious role set in a sardonically comic mode; in 1694 (too late to be trusted) Charles Gildon recorded: 'I am assur'd from very good hands, that the person that acted Iago was in much esteem for a comedian, which made Shakespeare put several words and expressions into his part (perhaps not agreeable to his character)'.[10] But the principal examples are all, strikingly, cast in type as *professional* fools or clowns: Touchstone in *As You Like It* ('A fool, a fool!' chortles Jaques. 'I met a fool i'the forest, / A motley fool!' II.vii.12–13); Feste in *Twelfth Night*;[11] Lavatch in *All's Well That Ends Well*; Pompey the Clown in *Measure for Measure*; and the Fool in *King Lear*. They are all what Feste calls himself, 'corrupter(s) of words' (III.i.35), not dropping clumsy malapropisms like Dogberry, but deliberately exploiting the elasticity of language to comment on what happens around them; they have the verbal skills of the nobility who employ them, but not the same interests or values; they are outside observers masquerading as members of the community, and inclined to sardonic detachment as a result. As Viola says of Feste:

> This fellow is wise enough to play the fool,
> And to do that well craves a kind of wit.
> He must observe their mood on whom he jests,
> The quality of persons, and the time;
> And like the haggard [*untrained hawk*], check at every feather
> That comes before his eye. This is a practice
> As full of labour as a wise man's art;
> For folly that he wisely shows, is fit;
> But wise men, folly-fall'n, quite taint their wit.
>
> (III.i.58–66)

The passage is sometimes thought of as Shakespeare's personal tribute to Armin for being a comedian skilled and disciplined enough to carry off these roles. Possibly Armin contributed something to the writing of them; he was the author of a comic work, *Fool Upon Fool*, and of at least one play, *Two Maids of Moreclacke* (1609). At all events, the cooperation between Shakespeare and Armin appears to have been fruitful. This kind of professional attention to his resources, while very different in emphasis from Jonson's perfectionism, is no less a component of genius. The careful disposition of different styles of comedy has certainly been a factor in keeping Shakespeare's plays alive.

However we explain it, the nature and quality of the comic strategies in Shakespeare's plays certainly changes around the turn of the century: we see no more buffoons like bully Bottom and Dogberry, and fewer obvious droll 'turns' like Launce and his dog in *The Two Gentlemen of Verona*, Peter in *Romeo and Juliet* or Launcelot in *The Merchant of Venice*. None of these is merely there, as critics used to say, for comic relief; they are all thematically related to the wider action of the plays in which they appear. But from now on the comedy tends to be more fluidly integrated within the action, relating to it more subtly and indirectly. The undistinguished cobbler in *Julius Caesar*, once more, is a good example, as is the black comedy of the death of Cinna the poet. The former takes us directly into the confusion of the holiday crowds awaiting Caesar's 'triumph', while the latter graphically demonstrates the chaos that the assassination opens up. Both are brief, yet pointed: the comedy in both scenes circles around the question of identity – how the individual relates to the name/trade he bears. This is a major issue in the play at large; both 'Caesar' and 'Brutus' are names that exist independently of the persons who bear them. The comedy is thus brisk and economical, rather harder edged than in most of the earlier plays.

These qualities are writ large in the characters of the professional fools who are not confined to set-pieces but 'licensed' to wander around the plot, casting a disenchanted eye on virtually everything and cutting across the 'upstairs/downstairs' divisions of society generally observed in the structure of the earlier plays. Feste, for example, is employed in the household of the Lady Olivia, where he comments both about her excessive grieving and (more bitterly) Malvolio's pretensions; but he also entertains the self-absorbed Duke Orsino, with mordant if oblique advice, and crosses verbal swords with Viola: he touches more aspects of the play even than she does, and is well placed to end it with a doleful song ('For the rain it raineth every day'). It detaches the audience from Illyria, preparing them to face the reality outside the theatre. His constant presence as a paid sceptic (he makes a point of extracting maximum payment) subjects the fantasies of romantic comedy to a scrutiny they can barely withstand, and it may be no accident that *Twelfth Night* (c. 1601) is the last play we can unequivocally describe as a romantic comedy. Feste's immediate successors (the foul-mouthed cynic, Thersites, in *Troilus and Cressida*, Pompey and the worldly-wise Lavatch) are significant ingredients in the more disturbing comedy of their plays. Beyond those so-called 'problem comedies,' there is an echo of Feste from the storm on the heath in Lear's Britain, when the Fool sings a last verse of that doleful song:

> He that has a little tiny wit,
>   With heigh-ho, the wind and the rain,
> Must make content with his fortunes fit
>   Though the rain it raineth every day.
>   (III.ii.74–7)

It perfectly sums up the disenchanted opportunism of this breed of fools, though it is ironic coming from the one Fool who shows something like personal loyalty to his master, in spite of all.

It is often observed that the plays Shakespeare wrote from c. 1600–c. 1608, including the great tragedies and 'problem' comedies (virtually everything he wrote for the Globe, in effect, until the company also started using the Blackfriars), are darker in tone than the plays that went before. We can hypothesise many extrinsic reasons for this – the old Queen's reign concluding with conspiracy, uncertainty and economic recession; the unprepossessing nature of her successor and the lax morality of his Court; religious dissension; more conspiracies, and so on – but the change in comic style and the freedom of comment (often bawdy and irreverent) that came with it are important factors, and these may have been suggested to Shakespeare by some of the professional competition he began to face around this time. Ben Jonson really established his reputation in the theatre with *Every Man In His Humour* (1598) and *Every Man Out Of His Humour* (1599), which were staged by the Lord Chamberlain's Men. Both are markedly unromantic in subject-matter and style, fixing on contemporary urban vanities and affectations in the manner of Aristophanes, and dividing the world between manipulators, 'gulls' and witty gallants in the style of Latin comedy. Jonson eventually came to see these as the plays where he established a personal idiom distinctively different from (and, in his view, superior to) what then held sway on the public stage, which pre-eminently meant Sheakespeare.[12] But if Jonson was reacting to Shakespeare's established presence, there is evidence to suggest that Shakespeare in turn reacted to this new challenge. Parts of *The Merry Wives of Windsor*, for example, seem to reflect the styles of acerbic 'citizen comedy' pioneered by Jonson and Chapman, while *Troilus and Cressida* has a satirical venom and misanthropic tone which is not found in earlier Shakespeare plays.

The latter work may also be anomalous in Shakespeare's career in other ways, perhaps symptomatic of the changes and challenges of that period. The title was entered in the Stationers' Register on 7 February 1603, 'as it is acted by my Lord Chamberlain's Men', but no edition was apparently produced then; on internal evidence the play was probably not written much more than a year earlier. In 1609 different printers did produce a quarto text, whose title page proclaimed 'The History of Troilus and Cressida. As it was acted by the King's Majesty's servants [as the company became] at the Globe. Written by William Shakespeare'. This text was withdrawn and reissued, with a new title-page, which omitted the reference to the Globe, and a preface, 'A Never Writer, to an Ever Reader. News,' describing it as 'a new play, never staled with the stage, never clapper-clawed with the palms of the vulgar', and recommending it to a sophisticated, witty readership. Which version is to be believed? The first suggests that the play was written in the normal way by Shakespeare for his company, and presented at their usual theatre. The second does not deny that the play was performed (cf. the Stationers' Register entry) but implies that it was not performed at the Globe or any other public theatre where it might be seen by 'the vulgar'. As we shall shortly see, Shakespeare's company are not known to have performed in the more exclusive 'private' theatres before 1609. This opens up the possibility that the play was written and performed in some other exclusive context – an Inns of Court audience being perhaps the likeliest. We have seen that Shakespearean plays were staged at both Gray's Inn and the Middle Temple, in the latter instance (at least) by his own company. What is not on record is that plays performed there by professional companies were ever specially written for them or not also staged commercially. The unusual style of *Troilus and Cressida*, with heavily rhetorical (and often sardonic) debates that might have engaged Elizabethan lawyers, has further fuelled speculation that the play is an exception along just such lines. All of this depends very heavily, however, on a preface which was clearly not sanctioned by Shakespeare or his company, and may simply have been an unscrupulous sales 'puff'. Of all Shakespeare's plays, this is perhaps the one with the best claim to have been commissioned for performance outside the public theatre, but even the evidence for this falls well short of being conclusive.[13]

At the end of 1599 or the beginning of 1600 there was a fundamental challenge to the virtual monopoly of playing enjoyed by the Lord Chamberlain's Men and the Lord Admiral's Men, and this definitely had an effect on Shakespeare's writing. The so-called 'private' theatres, defunct since around 1590, were successfully revived in the Blackfriars and by old St Paul's Cathedral. They operated under the privileges attached to the choir-schools of the Chapel Royal and St Paul's, which entitled them to demonstrate their skills in music, dancing and recitation. While music and dancing remained a marked feature of their repertoires, in practice these children's companies were just as much professional troupes as their adult rivals, trained and run by managers who saw an opening in the theatrical market; the boy performers became increasingly distinct from the choristers and many continued to act even after their voices broke, so that 'children' was something of a misnomer by the time their vogue diminished, c. 1608. Their theatres were private only in the sense of being enclosed (and so candle-lit) and notably smaller than their 'public' competitors; it is generally estimated that the Blackfriars (the larger of the two) held a maximum of around 600, against the 2500 of the Globe, but everyone was seated (some even on the stage itself) and people paid distinctly more to get in. And these theatres had one great advantage over the Globe and the Fortune – they were in the centre of London itself, protected by their choir-school warrants.

The Blackfriars enterprise, in particular, must have been galling to the Lord Chamberlain's Men since the theatre was actually owned by the Burbage brothers. Their father had bought the building in 1596 and probably finished converting it before his death the next year. But the Privy Council forbade its use as a theatre, following a petition from local residents who objected to having a 'common playhouse' in their midst; one signatory was their own patron, the younger Lord Hunsdon, whose enthusiasm for the actors did not extend to having them on his own doorstep.[14] Apparently the Children of Her Majesty's Chapel Royal met no such objections, when they leased the theatre from the Burbages four years on. Their success is most famously attested in *Hamlet*, where Rosencrantz explains why the (adult) players are on tour:

Rosencrantz: Nay, their endeavour keeps in the wonted pace, but there is, sir, an eyrie [*nest*] of children, little eyases [*young hawks*], that cry out on the top of question and are most tyrannically clapped for't. These are now the fashion, and so berattle the common stages (so they call them) that many wearing rapiers are afraid of goosequills and dare scarce come thither.

Hamlet: What, are they children? Who maintains 'em? How are they escoted? Will they pursue the quality no longer than they can sing? Will they not say afterwards, if they should grow themselves to common players (as is most like, if their means are no better), their writers do them wrong to make them exclaim against their own succession?

Rosencrantz: Faith, there has been much to do on both sides, and the notion holds it no sin to tarre [*incite*] them to controversy. There was, for a while, no money bid for argument unless the poet and the player went to cuffs in the question.

Hamlet: Is't possible?

Guildenstern: O, there has been much throwing about of brains.

Hamlet: Do the boys carry it away?

Rosencrantz: Ay, that they do, my lord – Hercules and his load too.

(II.ii.331–54)

The passage reflects the rivalry that promptly grew up between the 'private' theatres and 'the common stages'. It was not the boys themselves but their managements and writers who incited an antagonism that captured public attention. From the start the 'private' theatres gained a reputation for sophisticated satirical drama, engaging writers like Jonson, Chapman and Marston who had already shown a talent in that direction: these were the 'goosequills' who made the ordinary playgoer quake for fear that he would be derided if he attended the 'public' theatres. It was perhaps inevitable to begin with that much of the satire should be aimed at those within the theatre itself (though after the accession of James I it took on a much more political edge): it developed into a 'War of the Theatres', with 'much to do on both sides'. This is not the place to review that episode of theatrical history,[15] except to point out that it was not in the end simply a matter of 'private' theatre against 'public' – by the time Jonson wrote *Poetaster* (early in 1601) for the Blackfriars he was taking on virtually all comers, and the Lord Chamberlain's Men joined forces with the Children of Paul's to commission *Satiromastix* (by Thomas Dekker, probably with help from Marston) to get their own back.[16] The 'little eyases', in fact, are probably the dominant Children of the Chapel Royal in the Blackfriars rather than the boys' companies generally.[17] There was a good deal of box-office 'hype' about all this. And there is no knowing what part, if any, Shakespeare himself took in it, despite the third *Parnassus* play (c. 1602) performed at St John's College, Cambridge, where 'Burbage' and 'Kempe' appear on stage (IV.iii), and the latter says:

> Few of the university men pen plays well, they smell too much of that writer Ovid, and that writer *Metamorphosis*, and talk too much of Proserpina and Jupiter. Why here's our fellow Shakespeare puts them all down, aye and Ben Jonson too. O that Ben Jonson is a pestilent fellow, he brought up Horace giving the poets a pill, but our fellow Shakespeare hath given him a purge that made him beray his credit.

Horace giving the poets a pill is *Poetaster* (see V.iii), and the purge ought to be *Satiromastix*, but there is nothing to associate Shakespeare personally with that play. Possibly the *Parnassus* author, up in Cambridge, was misinformed; the use of Kempe (who was certainly with the Earl of Worcester's Men by 1602) undermines his credibility. People have looked in Shakespeare's own plays for the purge (one suggestion is Ajax in *Troilus and Cressida*) but nothing convincing has emerged. University gossip, then as now, was perhaps not to be relied upon.

The children's companies did not, in the end, pose a serious threat to Shakespeare's career, despite the claim that the boys carry it away 'Hercules and his load too', referring to the sign of the Globe.[18] But *Hamlet*'s very existence may owe something to the challenge from the 'private' theatres. Despite the continuing popularity of *The Spanish Tragedy* and *Titus Andronicus*, revenge tragedy seems not to have interested Shakespeare or other dramatists, on the whole, in the 1590s; perhaps, like Western movies in recent years, it seemed old-hat and bad box-office. But it was revived almost simultaneously at the turn of the century by Shakespeare in *Hamlet* and by John Marston, an iconoclast among dramatists, in *Antonio's Revenge*, written for the Children of Paul's. That play has virtually all the characteristics of revenge tragedy, as conveniently summarised by Horatio at the end of *Hamlet*:

> So shall you hear
> Of carnal, bloody, and unnatural acts,
> Of accidental judgements, casual slaughters,
> Of deaths put on by cunning and forced cause,
> And, in this upshot, purposes mistook
> Fall'n on th'inventors' heads.
>
> (V.ii.369–74)

But Marston does not merely replicate the conventions as he found them; he rings the changes on them, perhaps exploiting the effect of having children aping their elders. In particular, he abandons the pattern established with Hieronimo and Titus that the revenger must die himself, for having taken God's law into his own hands. Antonio finally wreaks revenge, but calmly, almost cynically, denies moral culpability and is not punished at all. Marston delights in tantalising the audience and perhaps shocking them; his Prologue archly warns anyone unfit to face up to 'common sense of what men were, and are' to 'Hurry amain from our black-visaged shows;/We shall affright their eyes'.

Whichever dramatist led in reviving revenge tragedy,[19] it is apparent that both plays are marked by a theatrical self-consciousness which the reopening of the private theatres seems to have fuelled. *Hamlet* (c. 1600/01) does not adopt the same spirit as *Antonio's Revenge*, but it does similarly infuse the old conventions with new life. We know that an old play of *Hamlet* existed, probably written by Kyd. It is mentioned as early as 1589, and we get a taste of its quality from Thomas Lodge's *Wit's Misery* (1596), which describes a countenance 'pale as the vizard of the ghost which cried so miserally at the Theatre like an oyster wife, *Hamlet, revenge*'; if Lodge was any judge, it was an old pot-boiler. Shakespeare probably used it as a source, as he was shortly to use the old chronicle play of *King Leir*, but we may presume on the same analogy that he changed the original out of all recognition. Without more knowledge of the *Ur-Hamlet*, as it is sometimes called, we cannot say how specifically he may have changed what would have been a familiar plot, but some of the ways in which the *Hamlet* we know stands out from the genre as a whole are apparent. The first audiences may well have been surprised, for example, that 'The Mousetrap' leads to nothing more conclusive than Claudius's discomfiture; it is in the confusion of the theatricals at the end of *The Spanish Tragedy* that Hieronimo achieves his long-delayed revenge and causes total havoc – a precedent that was to be honoured in subsequent examples of the revived genre, like *The Malcontent* (c. 1604) and *The Revenger's Tragedy* (c. 1607).[20]

The complexity of Shakespeare's *Hamlet* is not to be explained away, of course, as a re-treading of the ground he had crossed years ago in *Titus Andronicus*. Doubtless many factors had a bearing on it, most of which lie outside the scope of this book. It is relevant to observe here, however, that in the process of re-vamping the old play and thinking through the challenge posed by new playwrights and new theatres, Shakespeare recapitulated many of the most striking features of his own drama to that date – not simply repeating himself, but forging a new synthesis. As in so many of the English histories, the tension focuses on a 'free' individual caught up in an uncontrollable providential process: 'The time is out of joint. O cursed spite/That ever I was born to set it right' (I.v.188–9). As in the comedies, behaviour is measured against the canons of courtliness and chivalry: 'O, what a noble mind is here o'erthrown!' says Ophelia of the mad or seeming-mad Hamlet. 'The courtier's, soldier's, scholar's, eye, tongue, sword . . . quite, quite down!' (III.i.150–4). The Renaissance paragon, who had combined 'manners, arms and arts', is shattered by the events that have overtaken him and the play follows Shakespeare's established comparative/contrastive mode in tracing the alternative modes of behaviour that he *might* now adopt: young Fortinbras, the man of cold-blooded action; Laertes, the man of hot-blooded action; Horatio, the sceptical scholar; Claudius, the smiling Machiavel; Polonius, the over-devious politician; Rosencrantz and Guildenstern, the time-servers, and so on. Repeatedly, as Hamlet oscillates between such possibilities, he takes on the characteristics of the professional fools in the comedies, wittily crossing swords with the likes of Rosencrantz and Guildenstern, Polonius and Osric, though always with a degree of ironic detachment. Meanwhile, the true fool, Robert Armin, would have played the gravedigger, who digs up the skull of the old court jester, Yorick. Many in the audience must have 'identified' the latter as the legendary comic, Richard Tarlton (died 1588), who was said to have 'made Armin his adopted son, to succeed him'; if so, it must have been a very charged moment on stage.

Shakespeare seems to have built the role of Hamlet around the established strengths of Richard Burbage, his leading tragedian, recapitulating them as much as his own skills. Burbage is known to have played the 'original' mad revenger, Hieronimo in *The Spanish Tragedy*. One contemporary praises him as the ideal Romeo, and it is recorded that he proposed to play *Love's Labour's Lost* before Queen Anne, in which he would probably have played the King – roles encapsulating the distracted young lover and the idealistic courtier–scholar. We know he had played Richard III, all guile and venom; he died sword in hand, as Hamlet does, and Macbeth was to do later, so we must assume that he handled the weapon at least competently. It is even possible that *Hamlet* glances knowingly at Burbage in the role, during that climactic duel, when Gertrude observes of Hamlet: 'He's fat, and scant of breath' (V.ii.276) – ostensibly a reference to her son being out of training, but meshing with the fact that Burbage is known to have been short and stout. Certainly, Burbage impressed audiences in the role, as is witnessed by this extract from 'The Elegy on Burbage', written after his death in 1619:

He's gone and with him what a world are dead,
Which he reviv'd, to be revived so.
No more young Hamlet, old Hieronimo.
Kind Lear, the grieved Moor, and more beside,
That lived in him, have now for ever died.
Oft have I seen him leap into the grave,
Suiting the person which he seem'd to have
Of a sad lover with so true an eye,
That there I would have sworn, he meant to die.
Oft have I seen him play this part in jest,
So lively, that spectators, and the rest
Of his sad crew, whilst he but seem'd to bleed,
Amazed, thought even then he died in deed.[21]

This accords with the fullest account of Burbage's quality as an actor, written by Richard Flecknoe in the Restoration: 'he was a delightful Proteus, so wholly transforming himself into his part, and putting off himself with his clothes, as he never (not so much as in the tiring-house) assum'd himself again until the play was done . . . never falling in his part when he had done speaking; but with his looks and gesture, maintaining it still unto the height'.[22] Burbage was an exceptional talent and it must have been particularly pointed to have him lecture the players in *Hamlet* on how to: 'Suit the action to the word, the word to the action . . . hold, as 'twere, the mirror up to nature' (III.ii.15–21), implied rebuff to Kempe or no. The play is fraught in so many ways with reflections on Shakespeare's own career and the careers of those involved closely with him. To mention one final example: Polonius boasts to Hamlet of once having been a good actor. 'I did enact Julius Caesar. I was kill'd i'th'Capitol; Brutus killed me' (III.ii.99–100). It is believed that the part of Polonius, like that of Caesar, was played by John Heminge, who seems to have specialised in playing older men; and Burbage played both Hamlet and Brutus. So this is a public/private joke between the two actors about their recent performances in Shakespeare's *Julius Caesar*. But it is not without a function: it foreshadows the fact that Burbage is again going to 'kill' Heminge when Hamlet stabs Polonius – a small effect, but typical of the self-referentiality that informs *Hamlet*, making it a work of intense professional recapitulation.

It is much more difficult to say in what ways, if any, *Hamlet* relates to the eclipse of the Earl of Essex. No man in England better fitted some facets of Hamlet: 'Th'expectancy and rose of the fair state, / The glass of fashion and the mould of form, / Th'observ'd of all observers' (III.i.152–4); he was a prince in all but name and had been cheated, as some would see it, of his expectations. But there is nothing more concrete to associate him with the play, which we cannot precisely date in relation to his rebellion. Shakespeare's company *was*, however, very specifically associated with the rebellion itself. The uprising, on 8 February 1601, was Essex's last, desperate attempt to regain power. He hoped for a popular insurrection in his name, but it never materialised, and Cecil, Ralegh and others easily out-manoeuvred the rebels. The Privy Council subsequently investigated every aspect of the affair, including the fact that Essex's followers had commissioned the Lord Chamberlain's Men to perform a play on Saturday 7 February. Augustine Phillips, one of Shakespeare's associates, was interrogated on 18 February, recording that:

> on Friday last was sennight or Thursday, Sir Charles Percy, Sir Josceline Percy and the Lord Mounteagle with some three more spoke to some of the players in the presence of this Examinate to have the play of the deposing and killing of King Richard the Second to be played the Saturday next, promising to get them 40sh. more than their ordinary [share of the profits] to play it. Where this Examinate and his fellows were determined to have played some other play, holding that play of King Richard to be so old and so long out of use that they should have small or no company at it. But at their request this Examinate and his fellows were content to play it the Saturday and had their 40sh. more than their ordinary for it, and so played it accordingly.[23]

We do not *know* that this was Shakespeare's *Richard II*, though it is probable; a play written c. 1595 might well have been 'out of use' by 1601.[24] But there must have been an element of disingenuousness about Phillips' defence. The company knew full well that the play had only been published with the deposition scene missing; and they must have known that Dr Hayward was in prison on account of his own version of essentially the same subject. Shakespeare's play (or any other old work on this theme) may have been disinterested history when it was written, but it had been overtaken by events and charged with particular significance. So there were stronger reasons for not staging *Richard II* than its presumed unprofitability; but Phillips apparently did not mention them nor was he pressed on the matter. And it may have weighed in the latters' favour that the performance itself sparked off no disturbances, nor perhaps was intended to. Essex himself was not present and could not have led any insurrection stemming from it. Most likely the motive for staging the play was to steel the resolution of the conspirators, rather than to spark off action, which came the next day.

Something about the play nevertheless rankled with the Queen, since she commented on it that August to William Lambarde, her Keeper of the Books in the Tower of London: ' "I am Richard II," she said; "know ye not that?" Lambarde made a fitting remark on the wicked imagination of a most unkind gentleman, "the most adorned creature that ever your Majesty made". "He that will forget God", answered Elizabeth, "will also forget his benefactors. This tragedy [of Richard II] was played forty times in open streets and houses" '.[25] The last remark perhaps refers to the play's original popularity, when it was said Essex himself often attended performances, 'with great applause giving countenance and liking to the same'.[26] But the remark also smacks of hysteria. She was an old and increasingly lonely woman, little more than a year from her death, which must have contributed to many of the theatrical tensions of the time. But the Lord Chamberlain's Men seem not to have suffered for their indiscretion, though the theatres may have been closed briefly after the rebellion – a standard precaution at times of crisis. This might have been when the company took *Hamlet* to Oxford and Cambridge, as the 1603 quarto tells us they did; equally, however, their touring might have been during the heavy plague of 1603 itself: they would not leave the Globe unless they had to.[27] At all events, they were certainly in London on 24 February 1601 and all was forgiven, since they performed that night at Court, the night before Essex's execution. History does not record what play they staged, or what the atmosphere was like.

8

The New Reign

The old Queen died on 24 March 1603, and her 'cousin of Scotland', who had already reigned there as James VI for thirty-six of his thirty-seven years, was proclaimed her successor. The transition of power was smoother than most people had dared to hope, given that no aspirant had a clear-cut claim to the throne; it was master-minded by Sir Robert Cecil, who, elevated to the peerage as Earl of Salisbury, was to be the king's first minister until his death in 1612. In most respects James I suffered by comparison with his predecessor: an unprepossessing figure who ruled over an openly venal Court, where the Scots he brought south with him were much resented; he had a passion for deer-hunting that seriously disrupted the business of government, and an uncircumspect predilection for handsome young men, several of whom did not repay the trust and favours he lavished upon them; throughout his youth he had been a pawn in the factional politics of Scotland, which seems to have left him almost neurotically insecure, favour-ing padded doublets as a defence against assassins' knives; some people unkindly linked this with the pacifism of his foreign policy, which brought about an unpopular peace with Catholic Spain, the national enemy for more than a generation. Nothing marked the change of reigns more symbolically than the eclipse of Sir Walter Ralegh, last surviving of Elizabeth's favourites, in 1604; distrusted by James and seen as a rival by Cecil, he was found guilty on very dubious charges of treason and consigned to the Tower, where he remained for the rest of Shakespeare's life. He had never been popular in himself, but he represented opposition to Spain and remained a living link with the Armada and Elizabeth's hey-day.

Against the king's deficiencies must be weighed several signifi-cant virtues. James had two sons and a daughter, who ensured the succession, and in his person he had united the crowns of the British Isles. He had pretensions, moreover, as an intellectual in the best manner of Renaissance princes, having written various volumes of poetry, together with a treatise on kingship (*Basilikon Doron*) and another on witchcraft (*Demonology*). He and his wife,

Queen Anne, had a passion for drama, not merely as diverting entertainment but as fitting reflection – in the French and Italian manner – of royal magnificence; James had himself written a masque. Elizabeth had always enjoyed theatricals, but mostly let other people pay for them; she had been too careful with money ever to indulge heavily in such items at Court. But James and Anne had no such inhibitions. In 1604 the first of their Court masques, Daniel's *The Vision of the Twelve Goddesses*, was performed at Hampton Court, with the Queen herself taking part: it was a feature of these elegant and costly allegorical entertainments that courtiers took the (mute) leading roles, while professional actors took the speaking and singing parts. The following year Ben Jonson and Inigo Jones – poet and architect/stage-designer – devised *The Masque of Blackness*, the first of what became virtually annual collaborations throughout the reign.

Shakespeare himself never wrote a Court masque, though masques and masque-like elements were to be features of his last plays. But he and his company were affected immediately by the intensified royal interest in the theatre. On 19 May 1603 they received letters patent taking them under direct royal patronage as the King's Men.[1] By these, James licensed and authorised 'these our servants Lawrence Fletcher, William Shakespeare, Richard Burbage, Augustyne Phillipes, John Heminge, Henrie Condell, William Sly, Robert Armyn, Richard Cowly, and the rest of their associates freely to use and exercise the art and faculty of playing comedies, tragedies, histories, interludes, morals, pastorals, stage-plays, and such others like as they have already studied or hereafter shall use or study, as well for the recreation of our loving subjects, as for our solace and pleasure when we shall think good to see them, during our pleasure'. The document specifically permitted them to perform their works 'within their now usual house called the Globe within our County of Surrey, as also within any town halls or moot halls or other convenient places within the liberties and freedom of any other city, university, town or borough whatsoever within our said realms and dominions'.[2] Their principal rivals, the Lord Admiral's Men and the Earl of Worcester's, were also taken under royal patronage as, respectively, Prince Henry's and Queen Anne's Men, but the king's personal patronage sealed their status as the premier troupe of the day.

This must have been of immediate benefit to them, because the London theatres were closed on the death of the Queen (as a mark of respect and a precaution) and it is doubtful whether they opened again before the worst plague in years descended upon the city. Being unable to perform there, they probably went on tour; none of the officials they encountered would lightly have ignored the king's warrant. On 2 December they were summoned from Mortlake to appear before the king at Wilton in Wiltshire, the house of William, Earl of Pembroke. He was reputedly the richest man in England and was eventually (with his brother, Philip, Earl of Montgomery) to be joint dedicatee of the Shakespeare First Folio. By 1623 Pembroke was Lord Chamberlain and there was doubtless an element of circumspect self-interest in the choice of dedicatees made by Shakespeare's old colleagues. But the terms of the dedication suggest that Pembroke and Montgomery had both known and patronised Shakespeare, as well as enjoying his plays: 'since your L[ordships] have been pleas'd to think these trifles something, heretofore; and have prosecuted both them, and their author living, with so much favour; we hope, that . . . you will use the like indulgence toward them, you have done unto their parent'. Pembroke did not become Lord Chamberlain until 1615, the year before Shakespeare's death, so this can hardly refer to formal dealings between them in respect of Court theatricals; moreover, when Richard Burbage died, on 20 May 1619, Pembroke wrote of how he had declined to see a play performed for the French ambassador, 'which I being tender-hearted could not endure to see so soon after the loss of my old acquaintance Burbage' - which suggests that his relations with at least some of the King's Men were more than merely formal.[3] It says something about the rise in status of the theatrical profession in the Jacobean era that one of the country's grandest aristocrats should write so affectionately about an actor, albeit such a notable one. Despite attempts to link Pembroke with the sonnets, the visit of the King's Men to Wilton in 1603 is the most tangible connection we know of between him and Shakespeare – assuming that the latter was in the party; but it seems certain that their acquaintance was more extensive than that.

Besides the visit to Wilton, the King's Men were called upon eight times to perform at Court in the winter of 1603/4 – more often than in any single season before the old Queen. And this set the pattern for the years to come. In 1604/5 they performed eleven times, and here we know the plays chosen; besides the lost *The Spanish Maze*, and Jonson's two *Humour* plays, the great preponderance were by Shakespeare: *The Merry Wives of Windsor, Othello, Measure for Measure, The Comedy of Errors, Love's Labour's Lost, Henry V* and *The Merchant of Venice.* In subsequent years, during Shakespeare's lifetime, they never performed less than eight times during a winter season, more usually at least twelve times, and on two occasions (1611–12 and 1612–13) twenty times.[4] Occasionally there might also be Court performances at other times of the year, as when the King of Denmark visited in the summer of 1606 and the King's Men performed three times. The usual fee on each of these occasions was £10, which must have added significantly to the company's income. Nevertheless it was not sufficient, in itself, to sustain them. In that first year of royal patronage (8 February 1604), as the plague raged on, Burbage was granted £30 'for the maintenance and relief of himself and the rest of his company being prohibited to p[re]sent any plays publicly in or near London by reason of great peril that might grow through the extraordinary concourse and assemble of people to a new increase of the plague, till it shall please almighty God to settle the city in a more p[er]fect health, by way of his Majesty's free gift'.[5] Something similar happened in the severe plague season of 1608–9, when they were granted £40, the money being accounted as rehearsal fees, so that the actors might be ready to perform at Court at Christmas. The King's Men were technically Grooms of the Chamber in his household, and as such should have attended the coronation, but owing to the plague this was conducted with as few persons present as possible. A belated procession through the streets was held on 15 March 1604 and the Grooms were each granted a regulation four and half yards of scarlet cloth for their livery, though they did not apparently take part in the procession, which encountered a variety of theatrical spectacles devised by Ben Jonson and Thomas Dekker. They did, however, act in an official capacity later in the year (9–27 August), when they were called upon to form part of the retinue that attended upon Juan Fernandez de Velasco, Duke of Frias and Constable of Castile, the Spanish Ambassador Extraordinary, who was in England to conduct peace negotiations.

Given the much closer affiliation to the Court that his company now enjoyed, it is not surprising that some have seen in the plays that Shakespeare wrote from this time on a greater preoccupation with issues and tastes current there, and specifically with the known interests of the king himself. We need, however, to keep this in perspective. It would be surprising if Shakespeare had not chosen his subjects with careful attention to their likely appeal for his company's patron. But the *ex gratia* payments we have already noted underline the fact that the King's Men were still primarily dependent on their income from public performances at the Globe. When this was cut off by the plague they were apparently not able to get by even on the increased number of Court performances, supplemented by whatever they were able to make from touring the provinces. So Shakespeare was still primarily in the business of pleasing the paying London public, and it is unrealistic to suggest that the plays of this period were so tailored to the special conditions of Court performance and a royal audience that their meaning hinges critically upon an imaginative re-creation of those conditions.

For example, *Othello* (of all Shakespeare's plays, the one that broaches most closely on contemporary history, though the plot itself is fictional) probably owes something to the king's known interest in the Christian struggle against the Muslim Turks; in his youth, James had written a 'celestial poem', *Lepanto*, to celebrate the great sea-battle of 1571 in which a Christian fleet organised by the Venetian republic and captained by Don John of Austria virtually destroyed Muslim sea-power. Clearly the play evokes that period and the tensions that led up to the battle; the Mediterranean is where conflicting religions meet, a cosmopolitan mixing-pot where an alien like the Moor might plausibly make his mark. But it is difficult to see how the primary themes of deception and tragic jealousy could be construed as having particular appeal to the king. As we have noted, *Othello* was indeed performed at Court, in 1604–5; so was *Measure for Measure*. Josephine Waters Bennett has argued in detail the case for the latter play as one carefully devised to appeal to King James's known interests in the law and religion, and to his image of himself (mirrored in the role of the Duke) as the all-seeing judge and arbitrator.[6] The apparently irreconcilable conflict of 'absolutes', between Isabella's determination to remain chaste and what she must do to preserve her brother's life, is one that might intrigue a would-be Solomon. It is worth noting, however, that it was another play – on similar themes, but written long before James came to the throne – *The Merchant of Venice*, that was actually called for a second performance, 'repeated on Shrove Tuesday by the King's command'. If *Measure for Measure* really was a deliberate attempt to curry royal favour it was not, by those criteria, a spectacular success.

The case for such plays having been composed *primarily* for a royal audience remains, in that most useful of Scottish verdicts, 'not proven'. The evidence is perhaps best read as yet another example of Shakespeare's sheer professionalism. The theatricals which Dekker and Jonson devised for the belated coronation procession indicate that those dramatists had done their homework, finding out themes and motifs relating to the new monarch. Shakespeare must have done the same for his plays, but at the same time chose material that would be perfectly acceptable and comprehensible at the Globe. *King Lear* is a good example of how carefully he seems to have addressed both 'popular' and 'privileged' audiences. The idea for the play could have come to him from one of several sources, or from a number of them cohering in his mind. Perhaps the sorry fate of Brian Annesley sparked things off; he was a courtier who, around 1603, went mad and his daughters (one called Cordell) squabbled over his treatment and the division of his estate.[7] This might have reminded Shakespeare of the old chronicle play of *King Leir*, dating back to 1594 and probably earlier; it is not impossible that Shakespeare himself had acted in it back then. Or it could have been the belated publication of that play, in 1605, that gave him the idea – though, equally, the publication of the old play might have been in response to Shakespeare's new one. We cannot date the first version of Shakespeare's play (which was revised at some point, as the two surviving versions of the text indicate)[8] more closely than to within a year of 1605. Once the idea was in his head, however, he went back (for the first time in five years or so) to his favourite source-book, Holinshed's *Chronicles*; there the story of Lear hovers between myth and history in the early, pre-Christian stories of 'Britain' after its supposed conquest from a race of giants by Brute the Trojan. His followers included Corineus, who wrestled with the giant Gogmagog and threw him off Dover Cliff at a point later know as Gogmagog's Leap – an anecdote which Shakespeare seems to have transmuted into Gloucester's would-be suicidal leap near Dover Cliff. Corineus was rewarded by Brute with Cornwall. Cornwall and Albany (Scotland) figure in several early versions of the Lear story; but it was Shakespeare's idea to add Kent, both in the person of the king's loyal adviser (called Perillus in the old play) and in setting so much of the action near Dover, so invoking all three of the traditional triangular 'points' of old Britain.

Shakespeare was not content, however, only with the versions of the story in Holinshed and the old play. It is apparent from details that he looked at Spenser's *The Faerie Queene*, whence he derived the modern version of Cordelia's name and the fact that she died by hanging. He also consulted John Higgins's account in the immensely popular compendium of stories of the fall of princes, *A Mirror for Magistrates* (1574). Still not satisfied with the conception of the whole work, he hit on the idea of introducing a second plot, to parallel the story of Lear. The characters we know as Gloucester, Edgar and Edmund were based on Sidney's story of the Paphlagonian king in his prose romance, *Arcadia* (published 1590), though the names he gave the half-brothers derived from Anglo-Saxon history, which Shakespeare was apparently thinking about at this time – he could have spotted them in later sections of Holinshed or in the works of William Camden, such as *Britannia* (published in Latin, 1586) or *Remains* (1605). For Edgar's mad-talk in the role of Poor Tom, and especially details of the devils he mentions, Shakespeare went to Samuel Harsnett's *Declaration of Egregious Popish Impostures*, a particularly nasty attack upon diabolism and the Jesuits, which is intriguing in view of the possibility of Shakespeare's Catholic upbringing. Harsnett was the unhappy chaplain to the Bishop of London who had licensed Dr Hayward's *History of the Reign of Henry IV* – the object of so much suspicion at the time of Essex's downfall; it transpired that he had not bothered to read it. The *Declaration*, with its hysterical account of Catholic missions to England in the 1580s, was obviously an attempt to make amends with his masters. Shakespeare derived a more sceptical turn of mind on religious matters in the play from the *Essays* of the French philosopher, Montaigne, and particularly his *Apology for Raymond Sebonde*, which he apparently knew from the translation by John Florio (published 1603).

It is a disparate array of sources. But we can begin to put into perspective what Shakespeare made of them if we consider *King Lear* alongside *The Triumphs of Reunited Britannia* by Anthony Munday. This was a show devised to celebrate the inauguration of the new Lord Mayor of London for 1605, Sir Leonard Holliday. The Lord Mayors' Shows, performed in the streets on pageant-wagons, were the most splendid annual free theatricals in Jacobean London; when King James was finally pushed by his Spanish allies into executing Ralegh, in 1618, he chose the day of the Lord Mayor's Show in the hope of keeping the crowds as small as possible. Much of Munday's 1605 show is given over to praising Sir Leonard Holliday, with a succession of forced puns of his name, but his broader, patriotic theme, early in the new reign, is the reunification of Britain by the merging of the crowns of England and Scotland in the person of King James: 'reunification' in the sense that this restores Britain to the state it supposedly enjoyed when Brute first conquered the kingdom. Munday had consulted Holinshed too, a few pages before those Shakespeare drew on, and rehearsed the story of how the three-pointed island had been divided between Brute's sons, which resulted in discord and civil war; the mythological characters involved eventually step out of time to celebrate the fact that the chaos they created has been reduced to order by the 'new Brute', King James.

There is no narrative overlap between Munday's show and *King Lear* (though the former does briefly introduce Corineus and Gogmagog, on whose story the latter apparently draws) but there are very suggestive parallels: the mistake Brute made in dividing the kingdom between his sons is repeated in Lear's division of it between his daughters, treachery and civil war ensuing in each case; both works point up the natural, triangular unity of Britain. Munday's show is artless in the extreme, apparently confident that its audience will be familiar with the mythology it deploys and not surprised to find it put to contemporary, patriotic uses. *King Lear*, it goes without saying, is an immeasurably more complex drama; but it is difficult not to conclude that the original audience must have understood some of its elements in the same terms that they were expected to understand *The Triumphs of Reunited Britannia*. Shakespeare does not draw explicit links with the present, as Munday does, though the folio text does include a passage in which the Fool (imitating the mythological prophecies of Merlin, to which Munday also artlessly alludes) steps oddly out of time: 'This prophecy Merlin shall make, for I live before his time' (III.i.95). In this version of the play, at least, Shakespeare seems to have been alerting the audience to ways in which his material might transcend the historical context to which it apparently belongs.

This suggestion would be compounded by the radical alterations that Shakespeare makes to the ending of the Lear story. Those familiar with Holinshed's version or that in the old chronicle play would know that Lear was actually restored to the throne, and that Cordelia did not die until some years later; above all, there was no Edgar who became King of Britain in their wake (apparently obliterating the subsequent line of Brute's descendants, including such figures as Cymbeline and Arthur).[9] The change is justified in terms of Edgar's growth in stature in the second half of the play, but it remains a perplexing deviation from 'history'. The explanation would appear to be that he represented the historical King Edgar (944–75), who is one of the Anglo-Saxon kings of England with a claim to having been a king of all-Britain, since it was said that several lesser kings, including the King of Scotland, acknowledged their allegiance to him by personally rowing him on the river at Chester. His claim to be a king of kings was reflected in the coronation service which Archbishop Dunstan devised for him, and which has been the basis of the coronation service used for all subsequent English monarchs. This may all seem very arcane history to the modern reader, but there are reasons for supposing that it would not have been so for the average Jacobean play-goer. The details are all in Holinshed and Camden, for example, and Thomas Heywood claimed as a principal virtue of the theatrical profession in this time that it had made common people aware of the history of their country: 'plays have . . . taught the unlearned the knowledge of many famous histories, instructed such as cannot read in the discovery of all our English chronicles: and what man have you now of that weak capacity, that cannot discourse of any notable thing recorded even from William the Conqueror, nay from the landing of Brute, until this day, being possessed of their true use'.[10] Heywood exaggerates and ignores the fact that many Elizabethan so-called history plays are only tenuously related to the 'chronicles' on which they are based. But it is true that such works must have familiarised the play-going public with many characters and incidents that we can no longer assume every school-boy knows. An old play like *A Knack to Know a Knave* (c. 1592), for example, would have told them about Edgar and Dunstan, though it involves them in a lot of apocryphal nonsense.

In short, it is not unrealistic to assume – on the evidence of the uses to which mythological history was put in *The Triumphs of Reunited Britannia* – that Shakespeare's audience would have seen in the transition from old Lear to the 'godson' whom he himself named Edgar (II.i.91) a passage from the age of fables to something more securely historical; and that they would also have seen a foreshadowing of the reign of King James, which had *finally* resolved the divisions of the kingdom. Given what Munday thought he could get away with for the broadest of audiences, we must assume that 'Shakespeare's audience' in this context did not only mean its better-educated members at Court, but also the general public at the Globe. It remains possible, nevertheless, that some would have discerned an additional dimension in the play, not least when it was presented at Court on St Stephen's Day, 1606. Between 1604 and 1607 the king pressed the idea of uniting the parliaments of England and Scotland under his recently (re)united crown. The English House of Commons resisted the move, just as they refused to acclaim James as King of Great Britain – a title he had to accord himself by proclamation. A play so centrally concerned to demonstrate the folly of a disunited kingdom may well have been seen as support for the king's policy.[11] What is now beyond knowing is whether this specific 'courtly' dimension of *King Lear* was part of its original conception, or indeed whether it had any bearing on Shakespeare's revision of the play. The union of the crowns was a non-controversial fact, widely celebrated in the popular literature of the day, such as Munday's show. The union of the parliaments was an altogether thornier issue, most likely to be glanced at – as in Ben Jonson's Court masque, *Hymenaei* (early 1606) – where the support of the audience could be taken for granted. *King Lear* seems to straddle the two extremes, its politics capable of both general and specific application, depending on the complexion of the audience.

For rather different reasons we must also be sceptical about claims that *Macbeth* was written to appeal to King James. At first sight this is an attractive proposition. It is Shakespeare's only foray into Scottish history (mainly derived, once more, from Holinshed) and is embellished with witchcraft, a subject in which the king was intensely interested, as his *Demonology* demonstrates. It also contains a passage (IV.iii.140–59) on the quasi-magical practice of royal 'touching' for the King's Evil (scrofula), by which King James set great stock. There is a scene, moreover, in which the implications of ancient history for the (Jacobean) present are strongly under-lined, even more clearly than in *King Lear*. In IV.i. the witches present to Macbeth *'A show of eight Kings and Banquo, last [King] with a glass in his hand'* (stage direction, line 111). The 'glass' is a magic one, for in it Macbeth sees future kings beyond the eight in this pageant: 'and some I see/That twofold balls and treble sceptres carry' (120–1). This is generally understood to refer to Kings of Scotland also being crowned as Kings of England, though the precise implications are not altogether clear. It is even possible that the 'glass' might have 'proved' its magic qualities, in a Court performance, by being turned on King James himself.

But here doubts begin to accumulate. In the first instance, there is no record of there ever having been a Court performance at all. Given our general lack of information on such matters we should not make too much of this omission. There were certainly many occasions when the King's Men did appear at Court and we do not know what they performed; one of these (when King James entertained his brother-in-law, the King of Denmark, at Hampton Court on 7 August 1606) has been advanced as particularly suitable for a performance of *Macbeth*,[12] but the earliest record we actually have of the play being staged relates to 1611, when Dr Simon Forman saw it at the Globe. Two circumstantial clues as to when it was written perhaps emerge in allusions to equivocation (II.iii.8ff) and to the hanging of traitors (IV.ii.49ff); these are generally taken to refer to the executions of those implicated in the Gunpowder Plot of November 1605 and specifically that of Father Garnet (hanged 3 May 1606), at whose trial equivocation had become a burning issue. Possibly so, though Shakespeare had mentioned equivocation without any such connotations in *Hamlet* (V.i.129). Such allusions, if accepted on these terms, would bolster the widely-held assumption that the play as a whole is related to the Gunpowder Plot, underlining the horrific consequences of the assassination of a king, such as Britain had been so narrowly spared. They would date the play (or, more precisely, the version of the play that has survived) squarely in 1606. The problem here is that the sole text of *Macbeth* that has survived, that of the 1623 folio, is manifestly unsatisfactory on several counts. There are suspicions that several passages, including a good deal of the witch material, are not by Shakespeare himself. Even the pageant of the eight kings, which we have already discussed, poses problems. The stage direction seems to imply that it is Banquo who holds the 'glass', but this is contradicted by the text itself, where it is clearly the eighth king. The two murderers whom Macbeth instructs to kill Banquo are mysteriously joined about their business by a third. Some of these problems may be accounted for by a revision of the text, which may or may not have been connected with a special performace at Court – when the allusions to the Gunpowder Plot and even the joint monarchies of Scotland and England (reinforced by the fact that the forces which finally overthrow

Macbeth come with the help and blessing of King/Saint Edward
the Confessor of England) might have been added to an existing
script.

Above all, the play is markedly shorter than any other history
or tragedy Shakespeare wrote, and many of its scenes seem
unnaturally brief. One explanation for this would be censorship.
The Master of the Revels may simply have found too much of
the subject matter of a royal murder and usurpation unfit for
production – though, if so, it is surprising that he should (apparently) have left the harrowing business of the murder itself intact.
But it is equally possible that Shakespeare was experimenting with
a particularly brisk, hard-edged style for this inhuman story.
Looked at in this light, the theory of the play having been written,
or constructively revised, to appeal to King James seems most
doubtful. *Macbeth* might be described as intensely orthodox politically; it makes no bones about the murder of a legitimate king
being a sin against God and nature, and shows the inexorable
destruction of those responsible. As such it probably caught the
mood of pious relief that the government encouraged in the
wake of the thwarted Gunpowder Plot. Yet the subject itself is a
shocking one, and in following the action primarily through the
consciousness of Macbeth himself Shakespeare comes close to
human, if not moral, ambiguity. What Macbeth does is wrong, but
to follow the man through his crimes makes us painfully aware of
what he suffers in the process. All this might be thought odd fare,
awkwardly unreassuring, for a king so nervous about his own
safety. Furthermore, we might expect Shakespeare to have gone
out of his way to paint a more creditable picture of Banquo (the
founder of the royal line from which James himself was ultimately
descended) if he was really anxious to impress his royal patron.
All in all, it must be said that Shakespeare could have found more
appealing episodes in Scottish history, or have treated this one in
a rather different manner, if pleasing King James was his first
priority.

We perhaps ought to consider *Macbeth* in the context of another
play performed by the King's Men, which we know incurred
official displeasure. In December 1604 they staged *Gowry*, which
is no longer extant but apparently dealt with the Gowrie Plot
against King James in 1600. A Court gossip wrote: 'whether the
matter or the manner be not well handled, or that it be thought
unfit that Princes should be played on the stage in their lifetime, I

hear that some great councillors are much displeased with it, and so 'tis thought shall be forbidden'.[13] The incident suggests that the King's Men did not treat their royal patronage over-deferentially; they could not have been so naive as to suppose that a play (however tactfully handled, and even passed by the Revels Office) about an attempt barely four years since on the king's own life would not meet with objections. On the other hand, they doubtless knew that it would attract large crowds if they could get it staged, in which they obviously succeeded, at least for a time. *Macbeth*, being based on ancient history, would not be open to precisely the same objections. But it might have been written with precisely the same motives. The fact is that any play which might be seen as appealing to the *known* tastes and interests of King James could equally be seen as appealing to audiences curious about their royal master. In Britain today *anything* about royalty attracts crowds, audiences and readers; there is no reason to suppose that the Jacobean public was, in this respect, any different from a modern one. And no one was better placed to exploit this curiosity than the King's own players, who had one foot in Court life and another in the commercial world of the theatre. A play about Scottish history with modern royal 'applications', including witchcraft, might well titillate the audience at the Globe more than the King who was perceived as its indirect subject. This is not to say that it might not have been acceptable at Court (possibly revised and trimmed under the gaze of the Master of the Revels) but that is not the same thing as having been written for a very specific royal audience.

King Lear and *Macbeth* both reflect a shrewd professionalism, alert both to the issues of the day and to the needs of various audiences. But this can hardly be the whole story. We cannot rediscover the factors that drove Shakespeare to transcend his material, to write *King Lear* rather than *The Triumphs of Reunited Britannia* or *Macbeth* rather than some less harrowing Scottish history. But we have some possible clues. The use of material from the *Declaration of Egregious Popish Impostures* in *King Lear*, for example, takes the play into dimensions never touched in earlier versions of the story; Harsnett's virulent anti-Catholicism and lurid 'exposure' of diabolism seems to have touched Shakespeare and certainly contributes to the exhaustive and exhausting philosophical range of the play. In the case of *Macbeth*, Shakespeare must have been struck by the fact that the principal persons involved in the

Gunpowder Plot had Warwickshire connections. The leader, Robert Catesby, was the son of Sir William Catesby of Lapworth, who had given refuge to the Jesuit Campion about the time that John Shakespeare may have subscribed to his Spiritual Testament. Shakespeare possibly knew Catesby who, along with other plotters (Tresham, Grant and Winters) was a cousin of the Bushell family; the Bushells were certainly known to Shakespeare and his daughter, Judith, was to be related to them when she married in 1616. The plotters were reported to frequent the Mermaid Tavern. The romantic vision of Shakespeare as a convivial regular at the famous hostelry in Bread Street, along with Jonson, Ralegh, Donne and Beaumont is, sadly, a nineteenth-century fiction. (Ralegh, as we have noted, was in the Tower at this time). Nevertheless, Shakespeare did know the landlord, who witnessed the last property transaction he made, so he probably visited the tavern on occasions. Certainly one man he knew also knew the plotters. Ben Jonson was seen in their company not long before the plot's discovery, and was employed by the Privy Council in their investigations immediately after it. One way or another, the Gunpowder Plot must have struck very close to home for Shakespeare. The issues of regicide, providence, religious faith, political deviousness and fanaticism, which were all evoked by it, were inevitably in his mind as he wrote *Macbeth*.

It is more difficult to isolate the pressures that prompted Shakespeare back into his most sustained contemplation of classical history at around this time, with *Antony and Cleopatra*, *Coriolanus* and *Timon of Athens*. The first of these shares with *King Lear* and *Macbeth* (and most of the late tragi-comedies) a fascination with imperial destinies, albeit not those of Britain; human weakness, folly and vice all contribute, by some perverse miracle, to the possibility of a more secure and splendid future.[15] Shakespeare's Antony and Cleopatra are beings past their prime, he frequently drunk and vacillating, she vain and capricious. At the same time, however, they may have qualities which transcend these limitations. Enobarbus is a crucial character here, resisting Egypt's enchantments yet also communicating to his fellows and to the audience something of Cleopatra's unique charm: 'Age cannot wither her, nor custom stale / Her infinite variety' (II.ii.236-7). They see Venus and Mars in themselves, and their tragedy rides a strange line between divine transfiguration and squalid comedy. It all takes place, however, against the assurance that 'The time of universal peace is near'. These are Caesar's own words (IV.vi.5). As Augustus he will reign over the golden epoch of the Roman Empire, an era to be remembered for its peace, prosperity and poets, and to be blessed by the birth of Christ. The deaths of Antony and Cleopatra are a necessary prelude to all that. No such dimension is apparent, however, in either *Coriolanus* or *Timon of Athens*. These two plays seem self-consciously smaller in conception, focused on protagonists who in their different ways are misfits in their societies, honoured individuals but only up to a point. Both plays remorselessly, and with a singular lack of softening comic perspective, explore what happens when these men are alienated and turn against the societies that bred them. *Coriolanus* appears to be similar in temperament to the 'absolutist' tragedies of George Chapman, the *Bussy* and *Byron* plays, while the unsatisfactory text of *Timon of Athens* appears to have features in common with satirical, dystopic plays of the period, such as *Volpone* and *The Revenger's Tragedy* (both of which were performed by the King's Men c. 1606/7). They are singularly bleak, at one with a disenchanted mood reflected often in the drama of the period.

9

'Tales, Tempests and such like drolleries'

The last major redirection of Shakespeare's career took place in 1608. The Children of the Revels, then occupying the Blackfriars theatre, were in disgrace for staging Chapman's politically-pointed *Byron* plays, and their financial backers decided to sell back the lease of the building to the Burbages. On 9 August Richard Burbage set up a new syndicate of seven sharers in the Blackfriars, who would each contribute to the annual rent of £40 and divide the profits among them. Among the sharers were four other actors from the King's Men, including Shakespeare, but one of these, William Sly, died only five days later and his share was redistributed among the remaining partners. The King's Men intended to use the Blackfriars as their winter house, retaining the Globe for use in the summer, but taking advantage of the indoor theatre when the light and the weather were so much poorer. Apparently the objections to use of the building by 'common players' no longer applied. As with the Globe, the ownership and profits of the 'house' were distinct from the profits of the acting company that used it, even though some of the personnel involved were the same. Thus, when the King's Men were finally able to take advantage of their new facility – not until late in 1609, because of the plague – Shakespeare derived two incomes from his involvement with the Blackfriars, in addition to payment for his plays.

It is widely assumed that the new theatre had a bearing on the style and nature of the plays that Shakespeare wrote from now until the end of his career. It is a critical commonplace to talk of Shakespeare's 'late' or 'last' plays – broadly, *Pericles*, *Cymbeline*, *The Winter's Tale*, *The Tempest* and (depending on the view of how much he had to do with them) *Henry VIII* and *The Two Noble Kinsmen* – as a separate sub-species of Shakespearean drama; and also to assume that the peculiar characteristics of these works relate both to the theatrical conditions of the Blackfriars and to the more select nature of its audiences compared to those of the Globe and

141

other 'public' theatres. The part of the Blackfriars building used as a theatre – the Parliament Chamber of the Upper Frater – was significantly smaller than the Globe (46 feet by 66 feet) and laid out on a different basis: a rectangle, with the tiring-house at one end and the stage before it, spanning the whole 46 feet breadth. Audience capacity was correspondingly lower – some 600–700 compared with the possible 2500 at the Globe – but the entire audience was seated, whether in the pit or in the galleries built on all the walls other than that of the tiring-house, and they paid handsomely for the privilege: a minimum of sixpence, against the penny entry fee at the Globe. Those who paid most of all sat on the stage itself, a privilege not recorded in the public theatres, but a noted feature of private ones, where gallants were willing to pay both to see and be seen.[1]

There were three boxes in the second storey of the tiring-house façade, at the rear of the stage; one was the lords' room, one was apparently for action 'above' when needed, and one was a music room. The consort of musicians who accompanied performances at the Blackfriars became famous in their own right. In 1604 the King's Men somehow acquired Marston's play, *The Malcontent*, originally performed by the children at the Blackfriars. For the Globe production John Webster wrote an Induction, in which members of the company appeared as themselves to explain their appropriation of the play and the changes they had made:

> *Sly*: What are your additions?
> *Burbage*: Sooth, not greatly needful; only as your salad to your great feast, to entertain a little more time, and to abridge the not-received custom of music in our theatre.

Music was probably used only for specific dramatic purposes – songs, dances and ceremonial purposes – in performances at the Globe, but the Kings's Men kept up the house-tradition of more extensive and elaborate music when they started playing at the Blackfriars. This may be reflected in the heavy use of music in a play like *The Tempest*, where the stage-directions call for a striking amount of atmospheric music: 'Enter Ariel with music and song'; 'Solemn and strange music'; 'then, to soft music, enter the Shapes again'; 'Soft music. Enter Iris'; 'Solemn music'. The musicians perhaps also contributed to some of the more unorthodox sound effects required; the characters in Prospero's masque are required to vanish 'to a strange, hollow, and confused noise' and Spirits in the shape of dogs pursue Caliban, Stephano and Trinculo while a 'noise of hunters [is] heard'. But it is not clear if Shakespeare's own plays were affected by the tradition of inter-act music in the 'private' theatres, marking the nominal five-act structure of the plays in a way that was not known in the public theatres. Being indoors, the auditorium required artificial lighting, provided by suspended candelabra. We cannot be certain, however, how adaptable the lighting was during performances. The entire hall was probably lit to an extent, and not just the stage, though the lighting there may have been brighter; the actors may also, on occasion, have intensified the lighting with mirrors and coloured reflectors, such as we know were used in Court masques. Two scenes in particular might be thought to have exploited some degree of controlled artificial lighting. In *Cymbeline* (II.ii.), Iachimo emerges from the chest in Imogen's bed-chamber and, with only a flickering taper for light, examines the decorations and the sleeping Imogen herself. At the end of *The Winter's Tale*, Hermione reappears, pretending to be a statue and only acknowledging that she is alive when a flourish of music revives her, a sequence most effective when the lighting can spin out the uncertainty.

Here, however, we must enter several substantial *caveats*. Firstly, although *Pericles* is often classified with these other late plays, it was published before the King's Men began performing at the Blackfriars; the 1609 quarto explicity states that 'it hath been divers and sundry times acted by his Majesties Servants, at the Globe on the Bank-side'.[2] Secondly, *The Winter's Tale* was one of the plays seen by the astrologer/doctor, Simon Forman, and recorded in his *Book of Plays*. He saw it on 15 May 1611, at the Globe. He also saw *Cymbeline* without mentioning where or when, though again the Globe seems likely.[3] Thirdly *Henry VIII* was certainly performed at the Globe. So, in the three instances where specific information exists about the staging of the 'late' plays, they were all performed at the Globe. We have no concrete evidence that *any* of Shakespeare's plays were actually performed at the Blackfriars during his lifetime, though it is inconceivable that some of them were not. But we must beware of making over-easy equations between the late plays and the nature of the Blackfriars theatre. We cannot even assume that the plays from *Cymbeline* (c. 1609) on were written to be performed *firstly* in the indoors theatre and only later adapted for the Globe.[4] Shakespeare probably wrote the plays with the expectation that they might be staged at either of his company's houses, just as he had long anticipated that they might be staged at Court or on tour, as well as at the Globe. The statue-scene in *The Winter's Tale* would doubtless be very moving, intimately lit by candlelight, but audiences also accepted it, as Forman did, by daylight.

If the plays might be produced at either house it is also difficult to argue that their style and subject-matter was slanted to appeal more to the audiences of the Blackfriars who, paying so much more than the groundlings at the Globe, might be supposed more sophisticated, better educated, less unruly, possibly influenced by Court tastes and fashions. There did come to be a clear distinction between the audiences at the two houses by the 1630s; by then the King's Men's profits from the Blackfriars substantially outweighed those from their operations at the Globe, and their artistic endeavour was clearly biased towards the indoor house (whose productions by then were devised with a strong presumption of Court presentation, while the Globe catered for more popular tastes).[5] But it is an unwarranted assumption to suppose that such distinctions and expectations were apparent from the moment the company acquired the use of the Blackfriars, or that Shakespeare ever subscribed to them. John Webster indicated the way things were to develop when he complained about the reception of *The White Devil* after its performance (c. 1611) at a public theatre, probably the Red Bull: 'it was acted in so dull a time of winter, presented in so open and black a theatre, that it wanted . . . a full and understanding auditory' (Epistle, 'To the Reader', printed 1612) but made no such complaint after *The Duchess of Malfi* was performed at the Blackfriars (1613–14). Significantly, in the epistle prefacing *The White Devil*, Webster aligned himself firstly with 'that full and heightened style of Mr Chapman, the laboured and understanding works of Mr Jonson, the no less worthy composures of the both worthily excellent Mr Beaumont and Mr Fletcher; and lastly (without wrong last to be named), the right happy and copious industry of Mr Shakespeare, Mr Dekker and Mr Heywood, wishing what I write may be read by their light'. That is, Webster associates himself with dramatists who were already aiming for an élite audience; he is civil to Shakespeare, but categorises him as a popular playwright, one who writes to entertain a broad public. If Shakespeare had changed tack with his 'late' plays, Webster for one had not noticed.

Another explanation suggested for the new style apparent in these plays is to be found in the names, Francis Beaumont and John Fletcher, in the middle of Webster's list: that Shakespeare was influenced by the remarkably successful plays these younger dramatists produced together, including *Philaster* and *A King and No King*, both of which were staged by the King's Men.[6] These are tragi-comedies, not in the sense of indiscriminately mixing serious and comic material, but in their deliberate blending of tragedy and comedy as prescribed by the Italian dramatist, Guarini, for his play, *Il Pastor Fido*.[7] Fletcher (probably here writing alone) acknowledged his debt to Guarini in *The Faithful Shepherdess*, to which he prefaced an explanation of its form: 'A tragi-comedy is not so called in respect of mirth and killing, but in respect it wants deaths, which is enough to make it no tragedy, yet brings some near it, which is enough to make it no comedy, which must be a representation of familiar people, with such kind of trouble as no life be questioned; so that a god is as lawful in this as in a tragedy, and mean people as in a comedy. Thus much I hope will serve to justify my poem, and make you understand it; to teach you more for nothing, I do not know that I am in conscience bound'. This is too rough-and-ready to be very helpful, and Fletcher's formula specifically rules out deaths, which Shakespeare does not observe (e.g. Cloten in *Cymbeline*; Antigonus and Mamillius in *The Winter's Tale*). But it does point to some qualities apparent in Shakespeare's late plays as well as in those of Beaumont and Fletcher, notably the intermingling of gods or god-like agencies in a broad spectrum of human affairs (such as the descent of Jupiter in *Cymbeline*, the oracle of Apollo in *The Winter's Tale* and the masque of 'Iris', 'Juno' and 'Ceres' in *The Tempest*) and the suggestion of endings that work out for the best, though in unpredictable ways.

The classic Shakespearean example of this is the closing scene of *Cymbeline*, in which revelation follows breathless revelation, untying no less than twenty-five plot complications in defiance of any normal standards of plausibility. Scholars have long recognised that it is related in some way to Beaumont's and Fletcher's first great success, *Philaster*; the plays seem to echo each other in themes, plot situations and even in specific lines. The difficulty is in determining in which direction the indebtedness lies, though the majority of recent scholars think that Shakespeare led and

Beaumont and Fletcher followed.[8] Bearing in mind, additionally, that *Pericles* certainly antedated both plays, there is as strong a case for saying that Shakespeare instigated the form of tragicomedy that was to become identified with the younger dramatists as that he followed their lead. Leaving aside questions of influence and borrowing, however, Shakespeare's late plays and the tragiccomedies of Beaumont and Fletcher do have a good deal in common. In particular, they both draw on themes and styles associated with courtly romance literature, the kinds of tales of lost princes and disguised princesses, cultured shepherds and idealistic lovers, thwarted passions and magical confusions, which are best known to modern readers in Sidney's *Arcadia* and Spenser's *The Faerie Queene*. As we noticed before, this was essentially the mode of Shakespearean comedy in the 1590s, and it would be a mistake to draw an absolute critical distinction between these two phases of his career.[9] Heminge and Condell (who stuck to traditional Elizabethan categories of comedies, histories and tragedies, with no separate category of tragi-comedy) certainly did not recognise any such distinction, setting *The Tempest* at the head of the comedies and concluding that section with *The Winter's Tale* (though they unaccountably included *Cymbeline* among the tragedies).

Nevertheless, it is appropriate to describe the late plays as 'romances' (though contemporaries did not use that term for plays) or as 'tragi-comedies' (even if they do not exactly fit the prescriptions of Guarini and Fletcher). 'Tragi-comedy' was broadly concerned with finding a theatrical equivalent for prose and verse romances – not merely translating their stories for the stage but doing so in a way that preserved the essential qualities of their style and outlook. The early comedies contained elements of the supernatural (*A Midsummer Night's Dream*), divine interventions (*As You Like It*) and curious betrothal rites (*The Merchant of Venice*). But the presence (among other things) of such resourceful characters as the heroines and the witty fools gives most of those plays a solid point of contact with what Rosalind calls 'this working-day world', where the normal laws of cause-and-effect operate *most* of the time. The late plays seem determined to break that point of contact, to establish play-worlds in which the mysterious and magical dimensions of romance can operate on their own terms. The plays signal this in acknowledging that what they portray is, literally, incredible. 'Strange' is a term that recurs resonantly. Early in *Cymbeline*, two anonymous gentlemen discuss the unlikely

events that have overtaken the royal family of Britain and determine
the play's action:

> 2. *Gentleman*: That a king's children should be so conveyed,
> So slackly guarded, and the search so slow
> That could not trace them!
> 1. *Gentleman*:   Howsoe'er 'tis strange,
> Or that the negligence may well be laughed at,
> Yet is it true, sir.
>
> > (I.i.63–7)

There is a correlation between a possibly laughable strangeness
and the truth. In the final act of *The Tempest*, Alonso harps
repeatedly on the strangeness of it all: 'This must crave / (An if
this be at all) a most strange story' (V.i.116–17); 'These are not
natural events; they strengthen / From strange to stranger' (227–8);
'This is as strange a maze as e'er man trod' (242); 'This is a strange
thing as e'er I looked on' (290, speaking of Caliban). *The Tempest* is
unusual in this context, in that the audience knows – almost from
the beginning – about Prospero and his magical powers; they may
marvel at what he can do, but they are not bewildered by it. In
the other late plays the audience, like the characters, are in the
same position as Alonso, confused and disturbed by the action of
the play, until a semi-miraculous resolution emerges and provides
an explanation (of sorts) of all that has gone before. This emerges
most resonantly in *The Tempest*, where Gonzalo proclaims:

> Was Milan thrust from Milan that his issue
> Should become kings of Naples? O, rejoice
> Beyond a common joy, and set it down
> With gold on lasting pillars: in one voyage
> Did Claribel her husband find at Tunis,
> And Ferdinand her brother found a wife
> Where he himself was lost; Prospero his dukedom
> In a poor isle; and all of us ourselves
> When no man was his own.
>
> > (V.i.206–13)

This is not the only tone heard at the end of the play. Antonio and Sebastian, notoriously, are not impressed by Prospero's wonders, and Prospero himself defuses some of the enthusiasm. To Miranda's 'O brave new world/That has such people in't!', he cautions (gently? wearily? cynically?) "Tis new to thee' (184). Nevertheless, Gonzalo's wondrous amazement is perhaps the dominant tone in the closing moments of the play. He is in a state of what the Jacobeans called 'admiration' – wonder, amazement, marvelling, responses beyond the confines of reason. It is associated specifically with Miranda ('wondrous one'), as Ferdinand signals when he calls her 'Admired Miranda' (III.i.37). And the implication is that we in the audience are expected to respond to the play (and to all the other late plays) with the same measure of astonishment and 'admiration' that we see aroused in these characters.

This (rather than sour grapes) surely lies behind the attack that Ben Jonson launched against these plays in *Bartholomew Fair*. In the Induction he declares that he 'is loath to make nature afraid in his plays, like those that beget *Tales, Tempests*, and such like drolleries'. In the body of the play itself he satirically parodies *The Two Noble Kinsmen*.[10] Jonson objected to the plays' departure from realistic principles and their attempts to involve the audience emotionally in their mysteries, which were at odds with his own demand that audiences in the public theatres should judge rationally the entertainment they were paying for. In this, it is apparent that Jonson was drawing a distinction between plays performed in the commercial theatre and masques, like his own, which were performed at Court. The masques that Jonson devised for performance at Court used complex machines, lighting effects and (by 1611, the date of *Oberon*) ingenious perspective scenery, mainly devised by Inigo Jones, that were not to be seen on public stages in Britain until the 1630s; and this costly paraphernalia was deployed essentially to inspire in the spectators a sense of 'admiration'. Jonson appears to have thought this appropriate in theatricals of state, which both mirrored and magnified the Court to itself and to neighbouring states. But different principles applied in the commercial theatre, and the attack on Shakespeare is at heart an objection to his colleague's failure to observe decorum in this matter.

Shakespeare's late plays were not as sumptuous or theatrically innovative as Jonson's Court masques; the cost would have been prohibitive. But they approximated to them in some respects; it was part of their 'strangeness'. The dream of Posthumus in

Cymbeline, for example, employs many masque-like features, as the stage-directions suggest: 'Solemn music. Enter, as in an apparition, Sicilius Leonatus, father to Posthumus, an old man attired like a warrior; leading in his hand an ancient Matron, his wife and mother to Posthumus, with music before them. Then, after other music, follow the two Leonati, brothers to Posthumus, with wounds as they died in the wars. They circle Posthumus round as he lies sleeping' (V.iv. between 29 and 30); 'Jupiter descends in thunder and lightning, sitting upon an eagle. He throws a thunderbolt. The Ghosts fall on their knees' (between 92 and 93). The emphasis is upon music, ritual and spectacle, rather than realistic dramatic action. *The Tempest* contains its own masque, that of Iris, Juno and Ceres, which Prospero invokes to celebrate the betrothal of Ferdinand and Miranda; there is no indication that this employed anything very elaborate in the way of staging, but the whole sequence – culminating in the dance of the Nymphs of spring and the Reapers of autumn (eliminating winter) – is a masque-like ritualised triumph of theatrical art over the truths of everyday life. There is evidence, moreover, that the King's Men sometimes appropriated items from actual Court masques and incorporated them in their plays. *The Winter's Tale* calls for 'a dance of twelve Satyrs' (IV.iv.335/6), which was presumably the 'antic dance, full of gesture, and swift motion' performed by the satyrs in Jonson's *Oberon*. It is also probably not coincidental that Shakespeare, notoriously, wrote a part for a bear in this play ('Exit, pursued by a bear') when *Oberon* called for two bears to draw Prince Henry/Oberon's chariot.[11] Such transferences would be relatively easy for the King's Men since they usually performed the speaking, singing and comic parts. Something similar also happened with *The Two Noble Kinsmen*, which incorporates characters and a dance (III.v.121–58) from Francis Beaumont's *Masque of the Inner Temple and Gray's Inn*, written as part of the festivities for the 1613 marriage of the Princess Elizabeth.

Does the heavy emphasis on romance material and masque-like elements suggest that Shakespeare was deliberately pitching his late plays at Court audiences who would be familiar with, and appreciate, these conventions? Again, the evidence is double-edged. Audiences accustomed to the sophisticated machinery of an Inigo Jones stage or the dazzling finery of Court masquers might be disappointed by relatively pale reflections of such things at the Globe or the Blackfriars. It is perhaps more realistic to think of the

King's Men aiming to offer their paying customers a glimpse of
the kind of things going on at Court, which most of them would
not otherwise have a chance to see. They would thus be turning
to direct commercial advantage their royal commission. Jonson's
attacks on these plays would, I suggest, be more comprehensible
in such a context. This is a question that needs to be borne in mind
in relation to a number of theories about the late plays as
allegories concerning the royal family or contemporary politics – the
emergence of Henry, Prince of Wales, as a potential champion of
Protestant Europe, or nostalgic evocations of Queen Elizabeth
focusing on her namesake, Princess Elizabeth. The whole vogue
for romance might be seen as an idealisation of Elizabeth's Court
as it was graced by Sidney and glorified by Spenser – so different,
the implication might run, from that presided over by King James.[12]
Such suggestions are arguably more credible if the plays were
aimed primarily at an audience eager for reflected images of the
Court, rather than at the Court itself.

In saying as much, I recognise that I am questioning the prevalent
assumption that these plays enjoyed a special popularity – alongside the tragi-comedies of Beaumont and Fletcher – at Court. We
do know that in 1611, for example, *The Winter's Tale, The Tempest*
and *A King and No King* were all performed there by the King's
Men. And, in the fraught Christmas season of 1612–13, between
the death of Henry, Prince of Wales, and the wedding of the
Princess Elizabeth to Frederick, Elector Palatine of the Rhine
(known as the Palsgrave), the King's Men performed twenty times,
with an apparent emphasis on this style of play: *The Winter's Tale,
The Tempest* and *A King and No King* were all given again, and
Philaster was called for twice. We must beware, however, of reading
too much into these snippets of information. For most of the
Elizabethan/Jacobean period we do not know the titles of plays
that were performed at Court; in the main, only the record of
payments survives. Portions of the Revels Accounts in 1611,
however, and of the Chamber Accounts in 1612/13 do unusually
mention the titles, but it must be unwise to generalise too much
from this very incomplete picture. This must be particularly true of
the latter case, since the circumstances were so strained. Prince
Henry died on 6 November, when negotiations for the marriage
of his sister to the Palsgrave were already quite advanced. The
Court plunged into hysterical grief and then, after Christmas,
indulged in the most crowded programme of courtly theatricals of

the entire period – not only the twenty plays staged by the King's Men, but six others by different companies, fireworks, a river triumph and no less than three newly-created masques in the week of the wedding itself, all within eight weeks. The impression one gets is of the Court drawing on all its resources (including the greater part of the King's Men's current repertoire) to translate mourning into the necessary festive spirit. The actual choice of plays may well have been fortuitous. Burbage and his men also performed, for example, *Much Ado About Nothing, Othello, Julius Caesar* and versions of the *Henry IV* plays, so it would be wrong to get the impression that tragi-comedy totally monopolised Court performances, or that it was somehow more 'of the Court' than other forms of drama, at least at this date.[13]

By the same token, I am sceptical of the arguments that associate these late plays (excepting possibly *Henry VIII*, which I shall discuss later) *specifically* with the events of 1612/13. The death of Prince Mamillius and the subsequent marriage of Perdita to Florizel strikingly parallel what happened to the royal family, and perhaps some people did notice the analogies when *The Winter's Tale* was performed at Court the second time; but the play had already been staged there, a year before, when none of this could have been anticipated – and there is no basis for assuming that Shakespeare revised the text to heighten the parallels. The case relating to *The Tempest* is superficially more attractive. The text of the play as we have it is both very good and yet curiously unsatisfactory: good, in that it has unusually detailed stage directions, and preserves well the dense, eliptical verse which is characteristic of late Shakespeare (and apparently baffled some of the typesetters employed on other works, like *Pericles*); unsatisfactory, in that it leaves several loose ends, such as the suggestion of Antonio having a son (I.ii.439), which is not followed up elsewhere, the sketchy existence of characters like Adrian and Francisco, and several apparent non-sequiturs in the dialogue. Numerous arguments have been advanced to the effect that the play as we have it is a slightly imperfect revision of an earlier text – either of a play from very early in Shakespeare's career (which is pure speculation) or of the play that we know was given at Court on 1 November 1611. If it were the latter (so the argument runs), might it not have been occasioned by relations between the Princess and the Palsgrave – most specifically, might it not have been prepared for 27 December 1612, when these two formally plighted their troth before King

James, an occasion mirrored in Prospero's masque for Miranda and Ferdinand? Were the supposed revisions made to accommodate the masque as a late feature? None of this is inherently implausible, but the speculation is out of proportion to the given facts. The masque is thematically related to the rest of the play, and the inconsistencies in the text are really no greater than we find in many other Shakespeare plays. In several instances (the ending of *Timon of Athens*, which provides two contradictory epitaphs for Timon at V.iv.70–3, is a good example) the printed texts reflect what were either the author's provisional workings or changes generated in rehearsal/performance, and either explanation might cover *The Tempest* as readily as the theory of a 'special' Court performance.[14] The wedding of Princess Elizabeth and the Palsgrave (the only wedding within the immediate royal family during Shakespeare's lifetime) was indeed marked by intensive theatrials and it was only natural that these should include a preponderance of works by the most consistently popular playwright of his generation, including some of his most recent successes. There is no need to imagine any more intensive involvement.

It is often argued that Shakespeare's late plays are less interesting or challenging than (say) the great tragedies, engaging less of his artistic energies. This is ironic because it is in these plays that Shakespeare develops some of his most sustained insights into the relationship between art and nature, as in the argument between Perdita and Polixenes about flowers and gardening in *The Winter's Tale* (IV.iv.77–108) and all the premises of Prospero's magic. To an extent the myth of a 'falling off' is one created by hindsight. We know that Shakespeare was to be dead by 1616, and that he probably wrote nothing for the stage after 1613. It is easy to slip into the assumption that he was an old man, in semi-retirement, slowing down. From there, it is only a short step to the caricature provided by Lytton Strachey early this century, where he condemned the late plays as poor, careless works written by a man 'bored with people, bored with real life, bored with drama, bored, in fact with everything except poetry and poetical dreams'.[15] The dislodging of this myth has not been made any easier by the existence of a sentimental counterpart in the theory that Prospero in *The Tempest* represents Shakespeare himself, and that the abjuring of his 'rough magic' and his prayer to the audience in the Epilogue to be released amount to his own farewell to the stage –

a harmless theory, as theories go, but it does ignore the fact that Shakespeare had a hand in at least two, and very possibly three, plays after the *The Tempest* is known to have been staged.[16] It is also salutory to recall that, when the King's Men began to use the Blackfriars, Shakespeare was all of forty-five years old, only just a grandfather (see below), and there is no extrinsic evidence that either his health or his spirits were failing. Whatever we make of the role of tragi-comedy in the over-all development of Jacobean drama, there is no doubt that it represented an exciting new challenge in the years either side of 1610 – and that Shakespeare rose to the challenge, either leading the way himself or responding promptly to the competition. There can be no suggestion of him sitting on his laurels, repeating old triumphs or sinking into his dreams.

Nevertheless, there is some evidence that Shakespeare's contacts with the theatre did steadily decline in the last decade of his life. There is, for example, no record him acting after 1603. As so often, the lack of record is hardly conclusive proof, but Jonson assiduously listed in the 1616 folio of his *Works* the principal actors in the first productions of his plays. Shakespeare's name does not appear there after *Sejanus*, though the King's Men staged *Volpone, The Alchemist* and *Catiline* during the relevant period. There might be no significance in absence from any one such list (as it was missing from *Every Man Out of His Humour*) but that it was missing from all three surely tells us something. Moreover, in the years before his retirement, there was a falling-off of Shakespeare's dramatic output. From a steady average of two plays a year before 1608, he only managed about one a year until 1613, the last year in which he appears to have written anything. Within such a process of winding down, it would be natural to spread the burden of the plays he did work on with colleagues, and the evidence suggests that this is what Shakespeare did. Among the works performed at Court by the King's Men in 1612/13 was a lost play, variously described as *Cardenno* and *Cardenna*, and successful enough to be repeated there the following June. That too was probably a tragi-comedy, based on material in *Don Quixote*. It was entered in the Stationers' Register in 1653 as 'The History of Cardenio', ascribed jointly to Fletcher and Shakespeare. Evidence as late as that is hardly reliable, but it would fit a pattern. *The Two Noble Kinsmen* (performed after February 1613 since it borrowed from Beaumont's masque for the royal wedding) was published in 1634 as 'by the memorable worthies of their time; Mr John Fletcher, and Mr William Shakespeare. Gent.' This has more authority than the *Cardenio* entry, since the play was printed from the repertoire of the King's Men while they were still a flourishing concern. And modern scholarship generally confirms what the title-page tells us.[17] Many modern scholars also see Fletcher's hand in *Henry VIII*, though this goes against the evidence of the 1623 folio, where Heminge and Condell printed it as Shakespeare's own work – perhaps a relative rather than an absolute judgement. Fletcher certainly succeeded Shakespeare as the King's Men's 'ordinary poet' and, while he wrote some plays unaided, he was an inveterate collaborative writer – later working extensively with Field, Middleton, Massinger, Daborne, Shirley and possibly others. So it seems reasonable to think of Shakespeare collaborating quite extensively with him in his final active year in the theatre, 1612–13.

Whether it was a collaborative work or not, there must be a possibility that *Henry VIII* was written specifically for the marriage of Princess Elizabeth and the Palsgrave – or, at least, to echo its glory. This marriage would have been sufficiently important to warrant a play being specially commissioned. And the play is odd enough (a belated return to the cycle of English history, albeit in a very different style from that of the old chronicle histories) to invite special explanation. It is a play of reconciliations, culminating in Archbishop Cranmer's prophecy of the greatness of the reigns of the infant Elizabeth (after whom the princess was named) and of King James, whose marriage of his daughter to a Protestant champion was diplomatically significant:

> He shall flourish
> And like a mountain cedar reach his branches
> To all the plains about him. Our children's children
> Shall see this, and bless heaven.
>
> (V.v.52–5)[18]

Court records make no mention of the play, though it could have been the unnamed work that the King's Men prepared for a performance on 16 February, only to have it cancelled at the last minute in favour of a masque. The fact that Wotton described the play as 'new' (see below) might be explained by the actors keeping it off the stage until all possibility of a special first performance at Court had passed. A more simple explanation is that the play may have been an attempt to cash in with commercial audiences on the mood created by the wedding.

The symbolic, if not necessarily literal, end of Shakespeare's theatrical career is linked with this play (apparently then known as *All Is True*) and can be dated with unusual precision: 29 June 1613. On that day the Globe burned down. The most famous of numerous contemporary accounts of this misfortune is a laconic one penned by Sir Henry Wotton:

> Now, to let matters of state sleep, I will entertain you at the present with what has happened this week at the Bank's side. The King's players had a new play, called *All Is True*, representing some principal pieces of the reign of Henry VIII, which was set forth with many extraordinary circumstances of pomp and majesty, even to the matting of the stage; the Knights of the Order with their Georges and garters, the Guards with their embroidered coats, and the like: sufficient in truth within a while to make greatness very familiar, if not ridiculous. Now, King Henry making a masque at the Cardinal Wolsey's house, and certain chambers [cannon] being shot off at his entry, some of the paper, or other stuff, wherewith one of them was stopped, did light on the thatch, where being thought at first but an idle smoke, and their eyes more attentive to the show, it kindled inwardly, and ran round like a train, consuming within less than an hour the whole house to the very grounds. This was the fatal period of that virtuous fabric, wherein yet nothing did perish but wood and straw, and a few forsaken cloaks; only one man had his breeches set on fire, that would perhaps have broiled him, if he had not by the benefit of a provident wit put it out with bottle ale.[19]

Fire destroyed the rival Fortune theatre in 1621. In 1623 it burnt out Ben Jonson's library, prompting an 'Execration upon Vulcan', where he recalls the burning of the Globe as if he had been an eye-witness:

> But, O those reeds! Thy mere disdain of them,
> Made thee [Vulcan] beget that cruel stratagem,
> (Which, some are pleased to style but thy mad prank)
> Against the Globe, the glory of the Bank,
> Which, though it were the fort of the whole parish,

Flanked with a ditch, and forced out of a marish,
I saw with two poor chambers taken in
And razed; ere thought could urge, this might have been!
See the world's ruins! Nothing but the piles
Left! And wit since to cover it with tiles.[20]

We do not know if Shakespeare himself saw it happen. As Jonson implies, the Globe was promptly rebuilt 'in far fairer manner than before' (Stowe's *Annals* (1615) – a tiled rather than a thatched roof being one prudent improvement), and was certainly open for business again by the June of 1614. The cost of this naturally fell upon the 'housekeeper' sharers – a hefty re-investment to set against the handsome profits of the previous fourteen years, but the speed of the re-building suggests that no one doubted continuing profitability.

There must be a strong possibility, however, that Shakespeare decided at this juncture to withdraw from the venture (and, conceivably, all his other theatrical investments), by selling his shares to the other remaining sharers. There is no record of this, if he did so. But, equally, there is no other record of what subsequently might have happened to his shares in the Globe or the Blackfriars. They are not mentioned in his will, though it is just possible that they were included among certain 'leases' bequeathed to his elder daughter, Susanna, and her husband, Dr John Hall. There is nothing, in fact, to connect Shakespeare with his old theatrical associations after the burning of the Globe, apart from bequests in the will 'to my fellows John Heminge, Richard Burbage and Henry Condell 26s 8d apiece to buy them rings' – a customary style of fond remembrance.

Although his work for the theatre was at an end, we need not imagine Shakespeare subsiding into quite as peaceful a domestic retirement as that dreamed up for him by his first biographer, Rowe: 'The latter part of his life was spent, as all men of good sense will wish theirs may be, in ease, retirement, and the conversation of his friends'. The example of Fletcher's previous regular collaborator, Francis Beaumont, should tell us that there were other good reasons for quitting the theatre than weary old age. Beaumont had achieved the ultimate ambition of all indigent young men in Jacobean comedies: he married an heiress, and retired to the country. Shakespeare had no rich widow, but he may well have felt that he had accrued a sufficient fortune from his profession, and that it was now time to live up to the title by which he styled himself – that of a gentleman. His life-style was doubtless comfortable, but not necessarily indolent. There is certainly record of him visiting London on at least one occasion in 1614, possibly in connection with property that he continued to own there, including a house in the Blackfriars district; he also owned considerable land and property in the Stratford region, whose affairs must have kept him busy – if not quite the careworn capitalist in Edward Bond's *Bingo*. Certainly, his status as a man of property meant that he was consulted about local affairs, such as proposals to improve the highways and (more contentiously) to enclose some common land. It is also recorded that a visiting preacher was entertained at New Place – the sort of duty that was likely to befall a Jacobean gentleman of means (though the corporation subscribed 20d towards the expenses).

Shakespeare's family apparently brought him mixed blessings. We hear nothing at all about his wife, apart from the notorious 'second-best bed' left to her in the will; and I shall not add to all the unavailing speculation as to whether this bequest, the only mention of her, more reflects usual Jacobean practice in will-making or a deliberate snub. Susanna was well married to the physician, John Hall, and they had presented Shakespeare with a grand-daughter, Elizabeth in 1608. But Judith was undoubtedly a worry. She did not marry until February 1616, when she was a matronly thirty-one. The marriage, being conducted in Lent without the requisite special licence, had the couple in trouble with the church authorities. Even worse, the following month (26 March), Judith's husband, Thomas Quiney, went before another ecclesiastical court to confess to fornication with a woman who had recently died in childbirth. It is hardly surprising, even allowing for the factor of seniority, that the Halls did much better out of Shakespeare's will than did the Quineys. And it is surely not fanciful to suppose that the whole business hastened Shakespeare's death, which occured on his supposed birthday, 23 April.

There is only anecdotal evidence of the precise cause of his death, written down some half a century later. It may be more reliable than some, since its author (the Stratford vicar, Thomas Ward) probably knew Judith Shakespeare/Quiney, who was still alive at the time. He noted that 'Shakespeare, Drayton and Ben Jonson had a merry meeting, and it seems drank too hard, for Shakespeare died of a fever there contracted'. Michael Drayton, another prominent man of letters, came like Shakespeare from Warwickshire, while Jonson was never averse to a convivial drink. It is not an implausible scenario. Whatever the illness was, even the ministrations of a physician son-in-law were unable to save him, and Shakespeare was buried on 25 April in the chancel of Holy Trinity Church, where he had been baptised fifty-two years earlier. A plain slab covers the grave, inscribed with a malediction (tradition holds it to be Shakespeare's own) against anyone who moves it or the bones within. There is also a rather more elaborate memorial, a half-length bust, installed some five feet above the grave. Gheerart Janssen's handiwork in this has not met with universal approval, but it is one of the only two images of Shakespeare sanctioned by those who knew him. Indeed, Janssen himself could well have known Shakespeare: his stonemason's shop was in Southwark, not far from the Globe.

The other image similarly sanctioned is the portrait engraved by Martin Droeshout and used as frontispiece to the First Folio of *Mr William Shakespeare's Comedies, Histories, and Tragedies*, where Jonson commended it with a brief verse. He also commemorated Shakespeare as 'not of an age, but for all time', in a justly famous elegy. The folio, which appeared at the end of 1623, was edited by Heminge and Condell, the two survivors of the trio of actors who had been remembered in Shakespeare's will – Burbage died in 1619. They included every play that modern scholarship now ascribes in good part to Shakespeare, except for *Pericles* and *The Two Noble Kinsmen*. (They did not, of course, print the non-dramatic poems, which lay outside their province.) In so doing, they preserved eighteen works that had never been printed before, and in many cases gave posterity better or interestingly different versions of those that had appeared previously. Their 'care, and pain' are the rock on which modern Shakespearean scholarship principally stands, and it seems fitting to end this account of the dramatist's career with the commendation 'To the great Variety of Readers' with which his longest-surviving professional colleagues prefaced the volume.[71]

It had been a thing, we confess, worthy to have been wished, that the author himself had lived to have set forth, and overseen his own writings; but since it hath been ordained otherwise, and he by death departed from that right, we pray you do not envy his friends, the office of their care, and pain, to have collected &

published them; and so to have published them, as where (before) you were abused with diverse stolen, and surreptitious copies, maimed, and deformed by the frauds and stealths of injurious impostors, that expos'd them: even those, are now offered to your view cured, and perfect of their limbs; and all the rest, absolute in their numbers, as he conceived them. Who, as he was a happy imitator of nature, was a most gentle expresser of it. His mind and hand went together: and what he thought, he uttered with that easiness, that we have scarce received from him a blot in his papers. But it is not our province, who only gather his works, and give them you, to praise him. It is yours that read him. And there we hope, to your divers capacities, you will find enough, both to draw, and hold you: for his wit can no more lie hid, than it could be lost. Read him, therefore; and again, and again. And if then you do not like him, surely you are in some manifest danger, not to understand him. And so we leave you to other of his friends [those who contributed memorial verses], whom if you need, can be your guides: if you need them not, you can lead yourselves, and others. And such readers we wish him.

Notes

Chapter 1

1. See R. A. Foakes and R. T. Rickert (eds) *Henslowe's Diary* (Cambridge, 1961).
2. The inferences to be drawn from this are still hotly debated. See S. Schoenbaum, *A Compact Documentary Life* (Oxford, 1977) pp. 302–4.
3. Ted Hughes sees this as a central motif in Shakespeare's writing. See his *A Choice of Shakespeare's Verse* (London, 1971) pp. 181–200.
4. See John Henry de Groot, *The Shakespeares and 'The Old Faith'* (New York, 1946); Peter Milward, *Shakespeare's Religious Background* (Bloomington and London, 1973); E. A. J. Honigmann, *Shakespeare: The 'Lost Years'* (Manchester, 1985) particularly Chapter X.
5. The term 'protestant' has to be used with circumspection; the Church of England declared itself to be a 'Catholic' church, but one that did not acknowledge the authority of the Pope or Rome. The Queen herself was basically a traditionalist in religious matters and never approved, for example, of married clergymen. Much of the agitation we broadly label as 'puritan' came from those within the Church of England who wished it to become more avowedly protestant, particularly along Calvinist lines.
6. See Alison Plowden, *Danger to Elizabeth: The Catholics Under Elizabeth I* (London, 1973).
7. Contemporaries were in as much doubt as later historians have been as to what really lay behind the Gunpowder Plot. That government agents knew about the plot beforehand, fomented it and stage-managed its 'discovery' is as likely as not, though whether they instigated the whole business is more debatable. See Francis Edwards, S. J., *The Marvellous Chance* (London, 1968), but also C. Northcote Parkinson, *Gunpowder, Treason and Plot* (New York, 1977) especially pp. 80–2.
8. This was not unusual for a man of his generation, however affluent. See David Cressy, *Literacy and the Social Order* (Cambridge, 1980).
9. Dispassionately reviewed by Professor Schoenbaum in *A Compact Documentary Life*, Chapter 5, 'John Shakespeare's Spiritual Testament'.
10. Cited in *A Compact Documentary Life*, p. 99.
11. The Shakespeare family name lent itself to creative adaptation in a period when such practices were common; William's family is not know to have used 'Shakeshafte', but it is not inherently improbable.
12. Cited in E. K. Chambers, *William Shakespeare: A Study of Facts and Problems*, Vol. II (Oxford, 1930) p. 254. This title is hereinafter referred to by *WS*.
13. He is listed in Jonson's 1616 *Works* as an actor in *Every Man In His*

160

Humour, first staged by the Lord Chamberlain's Men in that year.

14. See Chambers, *WS*, Vol. I, pp. 39–41; Mark Eccles, *Shakespeare in Warwickshire* (Madison, Wisconsin, 1961) pp. 82–3.
15. See *Conversations with William Drummond*, lines 244–6 and 313–15.
16. John Carey, *John Donne: Life, Mind and Art* (London, 1981) p. 15.
17. That Shakespeare's play could at least be thought to have *anti*-papal sympathies is demonstrated by the fact that, in 1745, Colly Cibber staged an adaptation called *Papal Tyranny in the Reign of King John*.
18. See Alfred Hart, *Shakespeare and the Homilies* (Melbourne, 1934) especially p. 67; also A. L. Rowse, *William Shakespeare: a Biography* (London, 1963) p. 43.
19. This is not the same thing as political neutrality. In most respects Shakespeare seems broadly conservative. He respects the institution of monarchy, though he criticises particular monarchs, and he repeatedly depicts the mob as a fickle and dangerous element in society. But his conservatism is never aggressively articulated like that of Jonson's.
20. See *2 Henry VI*, IV.ii.; IV.vi, vii, viii; note the recurrent puns on cloth-working. See Richard Wilson, ' "A Mingled Yarn": Shakespeare and the Cloth Workers', *Literature and History*, 12 (1986) pp. 164–80.
21. *Henry V*, V. Chorus, lines 29–34, though see Chapter 7, note 3.
22. See below, p. 125.
23. See below, p. 109.
24. See Lily B. Campbell, *Shakespeare's 'Histories': Mirrors of Elizabethan Policy* (San Marino, California, 1947).
25. Sylvester Jourdain's *Discovery of the Barmudas* (1610) and William Strachey's *True Reportory of the Wracke*, describing his shipwreck in Bermuda, which was still in manuscript when Shakespeare wrote his play.
26. Heminge's name illustrates one of the minor problems besetting Elizabethan scholars, that of spelling, which was by no means standardised, even in respect of a person's name. The name of Shakespeare's associate was spelled variously with one or two 'm's, 'n' for 'm', 'y' for the 'i', with or without a final 'e', and with or without a final 's'. Even in the 1623 folio which he himself edited it appears both as 'Heminge' (twice) and as 'Hemmings'. I have used the former version throughout.
27. That is not to imply that they always printed from manuscript copy, when a reasonable quarto already existed. But no folio text simply reproduces an existing quarto one; there are always amendments produced, presumably, by reference to play-house copies. Nor are these amendments always improvements. Adaptations in performance, possibly on tour or at Court, sometimes (as with the *Henry IV* plays) seem to have confused or corrupted Shakespeare's original versions. It would be convenient if we could simply regard the first folio texts of Shakespeare's plays as the 'best', but that is not possible.
28. See below, pp. 158–9.
29. Cited from the paperback edition (New York and London, 1961), p. 90.
30. Andrew Gurr, *Playgoing in Shakespeare's London* (Cambridge, 1987)

p. 190. See Martin Butler's incisive criticism of Cook's thesis in *Theatre and Crisis 1632–42* (Cambridge, 1984) Appendix II, 'Shakespeare's unprivileged playgoers 1576–1642', pp. 293–306.
31. See below, p. 128.
32. See Guy F. Lytle and Stephen Orgel (eds) *Patronage in the Renaissance* (Princeton, 1981); Phoebe Sheavyn, *The Literary Profession in the Elizabethan Age* (1909; revised by J. W. Saunders, Manchester, 1967) and Michael G. Brennan, *Literary Patronage in the English Renaissance. The Pembroke Family* (London, 1988).

Chapter 2

1. Cited in Chambers, *WS*, Vol. II, p. 188.
2. This is to assume that Shakespeare was sole author of the *Henry VI* plays, or at least of the third part. This is the consensus of recent scholarship, though the issue was once much disputed. E. K. Chambers assumed thoughout *The Elizabethan Stage* (Oxford, 1923) – hereinafter referred to by *ES* – that at least parts 2 and 3 of *Henry VI* are Shakespeare's reworkings of the anonymous *Contention of York and Lancaster*, as first mentioned in the Stationers' Register in March 1594. He changed his mind, however, by the time of his *William Shakespeare* (1930), see Vol. I, pp. 281–9. The modern opinion is that *The Contention* is actually a bad reconstruction of Shakespeare's own plays.
3. Extracts from the relevant statutes are given in Chambers, *ES*, Vol. IV. pp. 269–71, 324–5. See A. L. Beier, *Masterless Men: The Vagrancy Problem in England, 1560–1640* (London, 1985).
4. See the letters of successive Lord Mayors in Chambers, *ES*, Vol. IV. pp. 307–8, 316–17, 318, 321–2. See also below, p. 60.
5. See below, p. 124 and note 24.
6. *Henslowe's Diary*, pp. 182, 203. Roslyn L. Knutson has recently argued that the practice of revising old plays before a new production was not as common or as necessary as has sometimes been supposed: 'Henslowe's Diary and the Economics of Play Revision for Revival, 1592–1603', *Theatre Research International*, **10** (1985) pp. 1–18.
7. Shakespeare's name was attached to plays that it was most unlikely he had anything to do with, including *Arden of Feversham, A Yorkshire Tragedy, Mucedorus* and *Fair Em*; it is a measure of his popularity.
8. In *Pierce Peniless his Supplication to the Divell*.
9. Chambers, *WS*, Vol. II, p. 189.
10. *Timber, or Discoveries*, lines 811–15. The tradition of envious rivalry between Jonson and Shakespeare (envious on Jonson's part) is an invention of later generations; see R. Dutton, *Ben Jonson: To the First Folio* (Cambridge, 1983), pp. 23–4. Even Thomas Fuller's delightful description (*History of the Worthies of England*, 1662) of their witcombats, Jonson like a solid but slow Spanish galleon, Shakespeare like a lighter English man-of-war, all quickness of wit and invention, is too late to be trustworthy. See Schoenbaum, *A Compact Documentary Life*, pp. 257–8.

11. Chambers, *WS*, Vol. I, pp. 59–60.
12. See Honigman's *Shakespeare's Impact on His Contemporaries* (London, 1982), pp. 53*ff*, and *Shakespeare: The 'Lost Years'*, pp. 60–3.
13. Compare the dating of these plays proposed by Professor Honigmann in *Shakespeare: The 'Lost Years'* (pp. 128–9) with those in, for example Andrew Gurr, *The Shakespearean Stage, 1574–1642*, pp. 225–6 or J. L. Barroll, A. Leggatt, R. Hosley and A. Kernan, *The Revels History of Drama in English, III: 1576–1613* (London, 1975) pp. xix–xxi.
14. Following apprentice riots in the vicinity of the Theatre and Curtain in June 1584, William Fleetwood, a principal magistrate, reported how 'the chiefest of Her Highness's players advised me to send for the owner of the Theatre [presumably Burbage], who was a stubborn fellow, and to bind him. I did so; he sent me word that he was my Lo[rd] of Hunsdon's man, and that he would not come at me, but he would in the morning ride to my lord; then I sent the undersheriff for him and he brought him to me; and at his coming he stouted me out very hasty; and in the end I showed him my Lo[rd] his m[aste]r's hand and then he was more quiet; but to die for it he would not be bound'. Quoted from Chambers, *ES*, Vol. IV. p. 298. Burbage had by then left the service of the Earl of Leicester, and it is not clear how he was in the service of Lord Hunsdon, eventual patron of Shakespeare's company. The point is that, as the 'servant' of an aristocrat, he felt that he could defy a magistrate.
15. See K. Wrightson, *English Society 1580–1680* (London, 1982) p. 128.
16. Chambers, *ES*, Vol. II. p. 365 (the author's own translation).
17. See Gurr, *The Shakespearean Stage 1574–1642*, p. 196. See above, p. 14 on the vexed question of the social mix of these large audiences.
18. See Levi Fox, 'The Early History of King Edward VI School Stratford-upon-Avon', *Dugdale Society Occasional Papers*, No. 29 (1984) p. 8.
19. *Henslowe's Diary*, pp. 291–4. These, and the stage properties which he inventoried in 1598, remained Henslowe's own property; he leased them to the actors. No one appears to have established this relationship with Shakespeare's company. John Heminge acted as business manager (his is regularly the name that occurs in Court accounts as receiving payment on their behalf; see Chambers, *ES*, Vol. IV, Appendix B, pp. 165–83), but as their agent not as someone on whom they were dependent.
20. See Chapter 9, p. 155.
21. 'Cuthbert Coneycatcher', *The Defence of Cony-Catching* (1592). Quoted in Chambers, *ES*, Vol. III., p. 325.
22. Quoted in Chambers, *ES*, Vol. III. p. 339.
23. See G. E. Bentley, *The Profession of Dramatist in Shakespeare's Time 1590–1642* (Princeton, 1971) pp. 88–110.
24. See Gurr, *The Shakespearean Stage 1574–1642*, p. 102.
25. It is virtually certain that Shakespeare collaborated with John Fletcher. See below, pp. 153–4. The case for other collaborations, notably in *Timon of Athens* and *Pericles*, is often made, with Middleton a frequent candidate, but the evidence is inconclusive.
26. See J. L. Hotson, *The Death of Christopher Marlowe* (London, 1925).

27. *Shakespeare: The 'Lost Years'*, pp. 59–76.
28. The issue is muddied by the fact that Ferdinando's father, the fourth earl, also maintained a company of actors in the 1580s.
29. See Chambers, *ES*, Vol. II, p. 128.
30. Chambers, *ES*, Vol. IV, p. 313.
31. The dating of *Sir Thomas More* and its additions is a vexed problem, whether or not Shakespeare was involved. See the Malone Society reprint of the play, edited by W. W. Greg, reissued with a Supplement to the Introduction by Harold Jenkins (Oxford, 1961). The introductory matter thoroughly surveys the dating problem and the question of Shakespeare's involvement. References to the play are to this edition.
32. The manuscript of *Sir Thomas More* is in the British Library (MS Harley 7368). It is usually on display in the manuscripts exhibit in the British Museum. There are three main grounds for considering the addition to be done by Shakespeare: the likeness of the handwriting to the surviving signatures (though this has been much disputed); the use of the unusual spelling 'scilens' for 'silence', which Shakespeare used in the speech-prefixes for Justice Silence in *2 Henry IV* – at least, they appear in that form in the 1600 quarto; and the similarity of the theme of the passage to others in Shakespeare's works.
33. In the folio text the role is performed by Egeus, perhaps reflecting some occasion when there were less actors available.
34. Chambers, *ES*, Vol. II, pp. 87–8. The Lord Chamberlain's Men probably had such a patent, though it has not survived. When they were reincorporated as the King's Men in 1603, they received a patent, though oddly it makes no mention of the Master of the Revels (see Chambers, *ES* Vol. II, pp. 208–9). Presumably it was taken for granted that the King's own players were subject to the authority of his Master of the Revels.
35. Chambers, *ES*, Vol. IV, pp. 263–4.
36. Chambers, *ES*, Vol. II, pp. 285–7. Tilney retained the office until his death in 1610 and must have been responsible for the 'allowance' of the great majority of Shakespeare's plays, though his successor, Sir George Buc, seems to have been acting with the authority of the Master of the Revels as early as 1606/7.
37. See below, p. 80, about restrictions on printed matter.

Chapter 3

1. Eleanor Rosenberg's, *Leicester, Patron of Letters* (New York, 1955) is a comprehensive study of the patronage of the most influential of Elizabethan aristocrats, though Leicester was dead before Shakespeare (presumably) began writing. See also works cited in Chapter 1, note 32.
2. Chambers, *WS*, Vol. I, pp. 543–4.
3. There are biographies of both earls. G. B. Harrison, *The Life and Death of Robert Devereux, Earl of Essex* (London, 1937); A. L. Rowse,

Shakespeare's Southampton (London, 1965). See also G. P. V. Akrigg, *Shakespeare and the Earl of Southampton* (London, 1968).

4. Because of these connections, Shakespeare possibly knew Florio, who might thus be a source for some of his knowledge of Italy.
5. Maurice Evans (ed.) *The Countess of Pembroke's Arcadia*, by Sir Philip Sidney (Harmondsworth, 1977) p. 57.
6. Chambers, *WS*, Vol. I, p. 546.
7. Chambers, *WS*, Vol. II, p. 192.
8. J. B. Leishman (ed.) *Three Parnassus Plays* (London, 1949) p. 244.
9. See, for example, Leslie Hotson, *Mr W. H.* (London, 1964). Hyder Rollins's New Variorum edition of *The Sonnets*, 2 vols (Philadelphia, 1944) exhaustively reviews the theories to that date. His agnostic conclusions also hold true for subsequent theories.
10. See R. Dutton, *Selected Writings of Sir Philip Sidney* (Manchester, 1987), pp. 18, 24.
11. Letter to Sir Robert Ker, quoted in R. C. Bald, *John Donne: A Life* (Oxford, 1970) p. 7.
12. Ferdinando, Lord Strange, became Earl of Derby in September 1593, but died in April 1594 and so did not figure in Shakespeare's career after that date, though members of his family may have done.
13. See R. Levin, 'Another Possible Clue to the Identity of the Rival Poet', *Shakespeare Quarterly*, **36** (1985) pp. 213–14.
14. See S. Schoenbaum, 'Shakespeare, Dr Forman, and Dr Rowse', in *Shakespeare and Others* (Washington and London, 1985) pp. 54–79.
15. See F. A. Yates, *A Study of Love's Labour's Lost* (Cambridge, 1936); M. C. Bradbrok, *The School of Night* (Cambridge, 1936); Leslie Hotson, *Shakespeare by Hilliard* (London, 1977). The various supposed targets all have a bearing on when the authors *presume* the play was written; it was not printed until 1598.
16. Rowse, *Shakespeare's Southampton*, pp. 89–90. There is a tradition going back to Bishop Warburton in the eighteenth century that *Holofernes* is based on Florio. E. A. J. Honigmann, *Shakespeare: The 'Lost Years'*, pp. 64–9.
17. Dr Stanley Wells is a notable Doubting Thomas on this question. See his New Penguin edition of the play (Harmondsworth, 1967), pp. 13–14.
18. Harold F. Brooks (ed.) *A Midsummer Night's Dream* (London, 1979) pp. lv–lvii; Honigmann, *Shakespeare: The 'Lost Years'*, pp. 150–3; William B. Hunter, 'The First Performance of *A Midsummer Night's Dream*', *Notes and Queries*, NS. 32 (1985) pp. 45–7.
19. See the letter of James Burbage and other members of Leicester's Men to the Earl in 1572, when the authorities were enforcing the vagrancy laws more strictly. Chambers, *ES*, Vol. II, p. 86.
20. See Josephine W. Bennett, 'Oxford and *Endimion*', *PMLA*, **57** (1942) pp. 354–69; but also G. K. Hunter, *John Lyly* (London, 1962) pp. 187–9.
21. See L. Michel (ed.) *The Tragedy of Philotas* (Northford, Connecticut, 1949).
22. Chambers, *WS*, Vol. II, pp. 320–1.
23. Ibid., pp. 266–7.

Chapter 4

1. Chambers, *ES*, Vol. IV, p. 316.
2. Thomas Heywood may have combined the three roles for the Queen Anne's Company that performed at the Red Bull, though he had probably given up acting by the time he became a shareholder.
3. The character became Old Kno'well in the revised version of the play, but we do not know if that was ever staged, with or without Shakespeare.
4. The sketch is a *copy* of one made by the Dutch tourist, Johannes De Witt, and it begs almost as many questions as it answers. But it is the only contemporary picture of the inside of an Elizabethan playhouse we have and we must make the most of it. See. R. Hosley, 'The Playhouses', in *The Revels History of Drama in English, III, 1576–1613*, pp. 119–235, for a concise discussion of our knowledge of Elizabethan playhouses. The De Witt drawing is reproduced in Plate 11, opposite p. 222.
5. As late as 1614 the Hope theatre was constructed to take both plays and animal-baiting.
6. Based on the version given in Gurr, *The Shakespearean Stage 1574–1642*, pp. 171–2. It is difficult to make sense of some of the entries; there has been some debate about just how literate Henslowe was.
7. Prologue to *Every Man In His Humour*, folio version, 9–11.
8. Characters in *Every Man Out of His Humour* do, nevertheless, sneer at common players with social pretensions: 'They forget they are i'the statute, the rascals; they are blazoned there, there they are tricked, they and their pedigrees; they need no other herald, iwis'. In a 1602 internal squabble in the College of Arms, York Herald complained about the arms granted to 'Shakespeare the Player'; Garter King of Arms defended himself on the strength of John Shakespeare's status.
9. In *Skialetheia*, Satire V, by Everard Guilpin.
10. C. W. Wallace, *The First London Theatre: Materials for a History*, in *Nebraska University Studies*, **xiii** (1913), pp. 278–9.
11. Chambers, *ES*, Vol. IV, pp. 322–3.
12. Ibid., pp. 321–2.
13. Ibid., pp. 324–5.
14. Ibid., p. 298.
15. Ibid., p. 323.
16. Ibid., p. 325.
17. Ibid., pp. 332–3.
18. Ibid., pp. 334–5. See Herbert Berry, *The Boar's Head Playhouse* (Washington, Toronto and London, 1986) particulary pp. 191–7.
19. Gary Taylor, one of the editors of the new *Oxford Shakespeare*, has reviewed the Oldcastle/Falstaff issue in several contexts, most recently in 'William Shakespeare, Richard James and the House of Cobham', *Review of English Studies*, n.s. 38 (1987) pp. 334–54. See also Robert J. Fehrenbach, 'When Lord Cobham and Edmund Tilney "were att odds"', *Shakespeare Studies*, **18** (1986) pp. 87–101.

20. David Wiles has argued that Falstaff was originally created by Will Kempe, who left the company around 1599. That in itself might explain the decision not to continue the role into a fourth play. See David Wiles, *Shakespeare's Clown: Actor and Text in the Elizabethan Playhouse* (Cambridge, 1987) pp. 116–35.

21. Epistle to *Volpone*. Jonson told Drummond that when he and Chapman were imprisoned for *Eastward Ho*, 'The report was, that they should then have their ears cut and noses' (273–4). Jonson was almost certainly being disingenuous about his own practices (see R. Dutton, *Ben Jonson: To the First Folio*, Chapter 6), and it would be a mistake to assume that Shakespeare *never* made provocative topical references in his plays.

22. Actually, the joint-tenancy failed in its purpose quite rapidly, and shares did pass out of the syndicate when Thomas Pope died, before February 1604, and Augustine Phillips died in May 1605. See Chambers, *ES*, Vol. II, p. 417–19.

23. See John Orrell, *The Quest for Shakespeare's Globe*; and Peter Thomson, *Shakespeare's Theatre*.

24. The nearby Swan had not yet reopened after the *Isle of Dogs* affair, and was never a serious rival. See Gurr, *The Shakespearean Stage*, p. 44.

25. Taken from Gurr, *The Shakespearen Stage*, pp. 127–9.

26. The most famous picture of seventeenth century London, Wenzel Hollar's 'Long View of London from the Bankside' (1647), shows the second Globe, which replaced the first after it burned down in 1613 and must have been similar in many respects. That is definitely circular. Unfortunately, Hollar mislabelled it. What he designates as the Globe is actually the Hope; the Globe is what he labels 'beere baything h.'. See *Revels History*, plate 12b, opposite p. 223.

27. See above, p. 24.

28. See R. Dutton, '*Hamlet, An Apology for Actors* and the Sign of the Globe', *Shakespeare Survey*, **41** (Cambridge, 1989).

29. Chambers, *ES*, Vol. IV, p. 331.

Chapter 5

1. Only the anonymous *Famous Victories of Henry the Fifth* (pre-1588) is demonstrably earlier than most datings of Shakespeare's first histories. Peele's *Edward I* is roughly contemporaneous. Marlowe's *Edward II* is now generally conceded to be later than one or more of the *Henry VI* plays, though in turn it probably influenced Shakespeare's *Richard II*.

2. See E. M. W. Tillyard, *Shakespeare's History Plays* (Harmondsworth, 1962) p. 104.

3. Chambers, *WS*, Vol. II, p. 212.

4. Verbal details suggest that he normally referred to the *second* edition, though often we cannot be sure that the first edition of ten years earlier might not have served him just as well.

5. A notable treatment of the first tetralogy as a unit was the John Barton/Peter Hall *The Wars of the Roses*, performed on stage and television in the early 1960s by the Royal Shakespeare Company. See

Michael L. Greenwald, *Directions by Indirections: John Barton of the Royal Shakespeare Company* (London and Toronto, 1985) pp. 39–56.

6. It is reproduced in Chambers, *WS*, Vol. I, Plate XI, facing p. 312. It is credited to Henry Peacham, whose name appears in the margin.
7. See Michael Hattaway, *Elizabethan Popular Theatre*, for accounts of the stage potential of both plays.
8. In the Induction to *Bartholomew Fair*, written up to thirty years later, Jonson mocked those who thought these two 'the best plays, yet'.
9. See 'Machevill's' Prologue to *The Jew of Malta*; Hiram Haydn, *The Counter-Renaissance* (New York, 1953).
10. The mistake only occurs in the 1623 first folio text of the play, and not in any of the six quartos that preceded it. The editors of the folio aparently had access to an early version of the play (Shakespeare's own 'foul papers'?) as well as to the quartos.
11. See above, p. 55.
12. See also Jonson's comment on plays built around identical twins, p. 89.
13. Quoted from Geoffrey Bullough, *Narrative and Dramatic Sources of Shakespeare*, Vol. III (London, 1957–75) p. 300.
14. In *The Letting of Humour's Blood*.
15. See below, re. Haywood's *Henry IV*.
16. The full title of the book says it all: *The Discovery of a Gaping Gulf whereinto England is like to be swallowed by another French marriage, if the Lord forbid not the banns by letting her Majesty see the sin and punishment thereof.* See J. E. Neale, *Queen Elizabeth I* (Harmondsworth, 1960) pp. 245–6.
17. See *The Compact Edition of the Dictionary of National Biography*, Vol. I (Oxford, 1975) p. 245.
18. See Chapter 9 for a definition of this term and the plays I mean.
19. See Anne Barton (Righter), *Shakespeare and the Idea of the Play* (London, 1962).
20. We do not know if the scene was also cut for performance. None of the texts as printed shows evidence of playhouse adjustments to cover omissions, necessary if it had been. After the cut passage the Abbot of Westminster says 'A woeful pageant have we here beheld' (IV.i.321), which is meaningless if the deposition scene was not played. Heminge and Condell certainly had access to an intact copy of the original, perhaps a prompt-copy, when they were working on the 1623 folio. The 1600 quarto of *2 Henry IV* similarly shows signs of cuts that may be due to the censor, with no attempt to mask them for performance. See the Arden edition, A. R. Humphreys (ed.) (London, 1966) pp. lxx–lxxii.
21. See Chapter 9.

Chapter 6

1. Chambers, *WS*, Vol. II, p. 320.

2. Coleridge's phrase, 'willing suspension of disbelief', is invaluable in this context. See *Biographia Literaria*, Chapter XIV.
3. This is even more true of Shakespeare's last plays; see Chapter 9.
4. See K. M. Briggs, *The Anatomy of Puck* (London, 1959); Keith Thomas, *Religion and the Decline of Magic*, (Harmondsworth, 1978) pp. 724–34.
5. The dating of *The Taming of the Shrew* is a vexed question; it was not printed until the 1623 first folio. The key issue is its relationship with the anonymous *The Taming of A Shrew*, printed in 1594 and performed (according to Henslowe) in June of that year by the combined Admiral's and Chamberlain's Men. If *A Shrew* was a *source* of Shakespeare's play, the latter must be post-1594; if, however, *A Shrew* as printed is a corrupt version of Shakespeare's play, *The Shrew* must have been written before that date (and may have been the play performed on 11 June 1594, despite Henslowe's version of the title). Most scholars assume the latter to be the case, but the issue is far from dead.
6. In *A Shrew* (see note 5), Sly is carried off asleep at the end.
7. Only *The Cobbler's Prophecy*, of surviving works, is definitely by him; *The Three Ladies of London* and *The Three Lords and Three Ladies of London*, both printed as 'by R. W.' may well be.
8. Berowne: so the 1598 quarto. Biron in the first folio text.
9. Even allowing for the absence of much in the way of moving scenery or props, it is difficult to understand how the average Elizabethan play could be performed in the 'two hours' Shakespeare suggests, though contemporary evidence supports his claim. Most Shakespeare plays, uncut, take about three hours to perform today; *Hamlet* takes well over four.
10. Ben Jonson's phrase in 'To Penshurst' (*The Forest*, II), a panegyric to the Sidney family seat, praised as an ideal court-in-miniature.
11. By 'play' in this context I mean to include a whole range of lesser theatricals: masques, tableaux, pageants, dumb-shows etc.
12. This is not an exhaustive list, of course. Rosaline in *Love's Labour's Lost* is a prototype of the Shakespearean comic heroine. Beatrice stands in a different relationship to the action of *Much Ado About Nothing* than do the heroines I discuss here. Helena in *All's Well That Ends Well* has something of their spirit; that Isabella in *Measure for Measure* does *not*, contributes to the disturbing comedy of that play.
13. Jonson's moving tribute to the boy actor, Salomon Pavy, in 'Epitaph on S.P., a Child of Q.E. Chapel' (*Epigrams*, 120) is unreliable evidence, since he only performed with other children, not alongside adults.
14. See Leonard Tennenhouse, *Power on Display: The Politics of Shakespeare's Genres* (London, 1986) for a penetrating ideological study of Shakespeare's genres.

Chapter 7

1. Chambers, *WS*, Vol. II, p. 194.
2. See David Bevington, *Tudor Drama and Politics* (Cambridge, Massachu-

setts, 1968), pp. 14–24, for a thorough and sceptical account of the Shakespeare/Essex mythology.
3. Even this is not beyond dispute. The relevant passage is not in the garbled 1600 quarto. It is *possible* (if not, to my mind, likely) that the first folio version reflects a revision of the play c. 1602, when the lines would refer to the much more competent Lord Mountjoy. See Warren D. Smith, 'The *Henry V* Choruses in the First Folio', *JEGP*, **53** (1954) pp. 38–57. The play *was* acted in 1599, Essex allusion or no: Henslowe commissioned *The Life and Death of Sir John Oldcastle* (a riposte to Falstaff) that October and the play draws on incidents from *Henry V*.
4. See p. 24. Platter does not name the Globe or the playwright, but it was certainly on the Bankside, and there is no real reason to doubt that it was Shakespeare's play.
5. See p. 86 re. *Henry VIII*.
6. See Harrison, *The Life and Death of Robert Devereux, Earl of Essex,* pp. 214–15 and note to p. 214, 226–7, 280.
7. Lines 802–28.
8. *Conversations with Drummond*, 11.200–2.
9. David Galloway (ed.) *Norwich, 1540–1642*, Records of Early English Drama (Toronto, 1984) Appendix 3, p. 336. See David Wiles, *Shakespeare's Clown: Actor and Text in the Elizabethan Playhouse* (Cambridge, 1987) for a helpful examination of the theatrical personae adopted by both Kempe and Armin.
10. Quoted in Chambers, *WS*, Vol. II, p. 261. It is possible that Gildon invented this to explain the bawdiness in Iago's dialogue, especially with Desdemona, which offended neo-classical tastes of his time.
11. Feste is his name, but he is usually just called 'Clown', which is how he appears in many texts.
12. See Dutton, *Ben Jonson: To the First Folio*, pp. 24–6.
13. The odd history of the play does not end there, since it caused problems for those compiling the first folio. They started to set it up among the tragedies, after *Romeo and Juliet*, but abandoned the text after three sides were set. It was subsequently printed between the histories and the tragedies, but without pagination and without a mention in the list of contents. There is no way of knowing if these problems were related to the play's possibly unusual origins.
14. See Chambers, *ES*, Vol. IV, p. 319–20.
15. See J. H. Penniman, *The War of the Theatres* (Boston, 1897) and R. A. Small, *The Stage Quarrel betweeen Ben Jonson and the so-called Poetasters* (Breslau, 1899) for detailed and complementary accounts.
16. *Satiromastix* (1602) states on its title page that it was publicly acted by the Chamberlain's Men and privately by the Children of Paul's.
17. See Reavely Gair, *The Children of Paul's*, (Cambridge, 1982) pp.133–8.
18. See above, p. 70 and note 28.
19. See Harold Jenkins (ed.) *Hamlet* (London, 1982) pp. 7–13.
20. Both plays were influenced by *Hamlet* and staged by the King's Men, Marston's *The Malcontent* oddly, since it was first performed by the Blackfriars boys. *The Revenger's Tragedy* is usually credited to Cyril

Tourneur, though many people now think Thomas Middleton was the author.

21. Quoted from Chambers, *ES*, Vol. II, p. 309. Some versions of the 'Elegy' have forged interpolations – a common fate of Shakespeare-related items. But there is no reason to doubt the authenticity of this passage.

22. From *A Short Discourse of the English Stage* attached to Flecknoe's play, *Love's Kingdom* (1664), quoted in Chambers, *ES*, Vol IV, pp. 369–70.

23. Quoted in Chambers, *ES*, Vol. II, p. 205.

24. See S. Schoenbaum, '*Richard II* and the Realities of Power', in *Shakespeare and Others* (Washington and London, 1985) pp. 80–96.

25. Neale, *Queen Elizabeth I*, p. 387.

26. See Chambers, *WS*, Vol. II. p. 323.

27. The textual problems surrounding *Hamlet* are the most complex of any Shakespeare play. There are three early texts: the 1603 ('bad') quarto, a poor, unauthorised memorial reconstruction, though with interesting details which may be genuine (e.g. 'Enter the Ghost in his night gown', when he appears in Gertrude's chamber); the 1604/5 ('good') quarto, an excellent text apparently sanctioned by the Lord Chamberlain's Men; the 1623 folio text, which is also excellent, though different in many particulars from the 'good' quarto. The play was probably revised at least once, probably by Shakespeare himself, though no one has determined when and why.

Chapter 8

1. Their old patron, Lord Hunsdon, died later that year.

2. See Chambers, *ES*, Vol. II, p. 208. Lawrence Fletcher, who heads the list, had performed before James in Scotland, and may have been a royal favourite. There is no evidence that he ever had much to do with the King's Men, though it may have been politic to have him in the company.

3. Chambers, *ES*, Vol. II, p. 308.

4. In 1611–12 they were actually paid for twenty-two performances, but two of these were for joint performances with Queen Anne's Men.

5. Chambers, *ES*, Vol. IV, pp. 168–9.

6. See J. W. Bennett, '*Measure for Measure' as Royal Entertainment* (New York, 1966).

7. See Bullough, *Narrative and Dramatic Sources of Shakespeare*, Vol. VII, pp. 270–1.

8. See G. Taylor and M. Warren (eds) *The Division of the Kingdoms: Shakespeare's Two Versions of 'King Lear'* (Oxford, 1983).

9. The implication that Edgar is the king at the end of the play is strong in both versions of the play, though not beyond dispute in the 1608/19 quarto, where Albany speaks the final lines; in all Shakespeare's other major tragedies the convention is that the senior figure on stage pronounces the final lines.

10. From *An Apologie for Actors* (published 1612, written c. 1608). Cited from extracts in G. E. Bentley (ed.) *The Seventeenth Century Stage: A Collection of Critical Essays* (Chicago, 1968) p. 16.
11. See D. H. Willson, *King James VI & I* (London, 1963) pp. 249–57; J. W. Draper, 'The Occasion of *King Lear*', *Studies in Philology*, **34** (1937) pp. 176–85.
12. See H. N. Paul, *The Royal Play of 'Macbeth'* (New York, 1950); this is the most sustained reading of the play as written for King James.
13. Quoted in Chambers, *ES*, Vol. I, p. 328.
14. See Cleopatra's speech, quoted p. 77.

Chapter 9

1. Heminge and Condell talk in their preface to the first folio of 'magistrates[s] of wit [who] sit on the stage at Blackfriars . . . to arraign plays daily'.
2. This has no bearing on the question of the play's authorship. *Pericles* is the only play not in the 1623 first folio which is now generally thought to be mainly, if not wholly, written by Shakespeare. Critics have long been dissatisfied with the sketchiness of the first two acts (though there is no agreement about who *did* write them, if not Shakespeare) but there is a similar unanimity about the last three acts – with their densely involved verse and echoes of earlier plays – being genuinely Shakespearean. (See note 17 re. *The Two Noble Kinsmen*, which is also not in the first folio.)
3. Unfortunately, Forman's habit was to write down a bare précis of the plots he saw, not an account of the productions. His notes on 'Common Policy' were not very profound either. From *The Winter's Tale*, observing Autolycus, he resolved to 'Beware of trusting feigned beggars or fawning fellows'. See A. L. Rowse, *Simon Forman: Sex and Society in Shakespeare's Age* (London, 1976) pp. 308–11. The quotation is on p. 311.
4. Sir Henry Wotton described *Henry VIII* as 'new' when it was performed at the Globe in June 1613. See below, p. 155.
5. See Chambers, *ES*, Vol. II, p. 425 and note 2.
6. If the tragi-comedies of Beaumont and Fletcher are thought comparable to the late plays of Shakespeare, their staging has a bearing on the debate about the relative statuses of the Globe and the Blackfriars, and their audiences. The earliest printed versions of the two key texts reinforce my contention that there was, at this date, no systematic demarcation between the two theatres on grounds of style or attempts to suit particular audiences. *Philaster* was 'acted at the Globe' (1620) as was *A King and No King* (1619), though subsequent editions of both plays also mention performance at the Blackfriars.
7. *Il Pastor Fido* (*The Faithful Shepherd*) was published in 1590 and again in 1602; in 1601 Guarini also published *Il Compendio della Poesia Tragicomica*, a theoretical defence of his play. R. Dutton, *Modern Tragicomedy and the British Tradition* (Brighton, 1986) discusses Renais-

sance tragi-comedy in general (pp. 17–53), including that of Shakespeare.

8. See A. H. Thorndike, *The Influence of Beaumont and Fletcher on Shakespeare* (Worcester, Massachusetts, 1901) pp. 152–60; James Nosworthy (ed.) *Cymbeline* (London, 1955; reset 1969) pp. xxxvii–xl; A. Gurr (ed.) *Philaster* (London, 1969) pp. xlv–l.

9. See, for example, N. Frye, *A Natural Perspective: The Development of Shakespearean Comedy and Romance* (London, 1964).

10. See Dutton, *Ben Jonson: To the First Folio*, pp. 159–60, 168–71.

11. See R. Dutton (ed.) *Jacobean and Caroline Court Masques*, Vol. I (Nottingham, 1981) p. 126. It is unlikely live bears were used in a Court masque, and I am dubious if one would have been used at the Globe, much less the Blackfriars. Bear-skin costumes seem more likely.

12. See, for example, Frances Yates, *Shakespeare's Last Plays: A New Approach* (London, 1975); David M. Bergeron, *Shakespeare's Romances and the Royal Family* (Lawrence, Kansas, 1986).

13. See F. P. Wilson, 'Elizabethan and Jacobean Drama', in R. J. Kaufmann (ed.) *Elizabethan Drama: Modern Essays in Criticism* (New York, 1961) p. 4. Also J. F. Danby, 'Beaumont and Fletcher: Jacobean Absolutists', in *Elizabethan and Jacobean Poets* (London, 1964).

14. See Frank Kermode's review of the possibilities of his Arden edition of *The Tempest* (reprinted with corrections, London, 1961), pp. xvii–xxiv.

15. 'Shakespeare's Final Period', first published in the *Independent Review*, iii, August 1904, pp. 405–18, but often reprinted.

16. See V.i.48–57 and the Epilogue. The theory was first proposed by Thomas Campbell in his 1838 edition of Shakespeare's *Dramatic Works*.

17. See N. W. Bawcutt (ed.) *The Two Noble Kinsmen* (Harmondsworth, 1977) pp. 48–9, for a review of the debate on the authorship question.

18. See pp. 86–7.

19. Quoted in Chambers, *ES*, Vol. II, pp. 419–20.

20. *Underwoods*, XLIII, 11.129–38.

21. I have already commented on the dedication of the book to the Earls of Pembroke and Montgomery. See p. 128.

Index

Bold type indicates a main entry. Dates attached to Shakespeare's plays refer to their putative first performances (in some cases first performances broadly in the form that has come down to us, possibly revised from an earlier state) and then to significant early editions. Dates attached to other works refer to first publication, which may be some time after composition.